The Nonprofits' Guide to Internet Communications Law

BRUCE R. HOPKINS

T0328393

John Wiley & Sons, Inc.

Library of Congress Cataloging-in-Publication Data:

ISBN 0-471-22278-X

10 9 8 7 6 5 4 3 2 1

Contents

This book is dedicated to my granddaughter, Isabel Marie Ash, for many reasons, not the least of which is that, just days before her third birthday, she, having come across one of my books, announced that she, too, was "going to write a book." It will undoubtedly be published as an e-book.

Foreword

Mommy! We've got a lawyer!"

With her six-year-old eyes dancing, my youngest child came bouncing into the room to share this revelation with me.

"What? What do you mean?"

She began a patient daughter-to-mother explanation. "The man on TV just said, *'If you have a phone, YOU'VE GOT A LAWYER!'* We have a phone! So, we've got a lawyer!!"

"Oh, I see. That's good to know!" I smiled inwardly.

Ah, the power of television advertising.

Well, I'm here to tell you that if you have this book, **you** have a lawyer! His name is Bruce R. Hopkins.

Having this book is like having Bruce Hopkins at your beck and call to advise and educate you in Internet communications law. Well, it's almost the same. It happens to be a lot more economical for you to buy the book!

The Nonprofits' Guide to Internet Communications Law is a reference for the earth's newest frontier. It doesn't surprise me a bit that Bruce Hopkins has been the one to scout out the territory and to bring back a map for the rest of us. Three reasons:

1. Bruce Hopkins is a voracious reader and a prolific writer. To his credit, he has authored 11 books and coauthored four more—so far. We won't even try to count the articles, presentations, and seminars. If there is a law that touches the operations of the nonprofits as they are working to make the world a better place, Bruce will write about it.

2. Complementing his thorough understanding of the law as it pertains to charitable organizations is Bruce's ability to translate that complexity into something understandable, practical, palatable, and, yes, even interesting!

   Ten years ago a group of us attended a seminar—a two-day presentation on nonprofit tax law held at Georgetown University. It was the first time I'd heard Bruce Hopkins instruct. At the conclusion of the seminar, I was not thinking about how smart *he* was. Rather, I was feeling quite encouraged at how easily I had understood the material and quite optimistic about my ability to incorporate my newfound knowledge into my daily work. Only now do I realize how much talent it takes for teachers to have that kind of impact on learners.

3. In 1995, with the help of an informal advisory group made up of some of the philanthropic and nonprofit world's most prestigious and progressive leaders, I founded NonProfit Forum™ Online. It was initially launched on CompuServe® and later debuted on the World Wide Web. (For the youngsters reading this, that was way back when 14.4 bps computer modems were considered to be lightning fast.)

   Bruce was immediately intrigued by the concept of trying to help nonprofit leaders, trustees, and volunteers with dynamic resources and interactive discussion forums in a virtual format that doesn't depend on anyone being in the same place at the same time.

   As soon as we could get a dial tone through to his laptop, Bruce commenced exploration of cyberspace. He was helpful, supportive, and generous with his time, tax law wisdom, and materials to those pioneering members of NonProfit Forum™ Online during its existence—and to other fledgling efforts hosted by the Forum: the Association for Healthcare Philanthropy's *AHP Online* and Master Software Corporation's *MSC Online*, as well as to CharityAuction. com. Those initial ventures—and Bruce's proclivity for being the first to embrace new challenges—led to the volume you are now holding.

As a nonprofit leader, advisor, trustee, or volunteer, you will do well to acquaint yourself with the issues of Internet communications law. Don't wait to get started. Accelerate your learning and protect your organization. To do that, either hire an attorney or get this book.

Got this book?

You've got a lawyer! :)

Sheree Parris Nudd, **FAHP**
Vice President
Washington Adventist Hospital
Takoma Park, Maryland
Designs for Giving
www.designsforgiving.com

Preface

Around the time I started practicing law in 1969, the Internet and e-mail were being invented. Like most of the world, I was not paying attention. To the extent that I was noticing the intertwining of law practice, modes of communication, and revolutionary technology, I was marveling at the emergence of photocopying. In the ensuing years, of course, communications by lawyers and others ceased being confined to use of the U.S. mail and office-based telephones, and exploded into utilization of overnight delivery services, facsimiles, cell phones, handheld devices, and e-mail.

There are, today, lawyers and others who do not communicate by e-mail and/or otherwise do not use a computer. (They are a rapidly diminishing group.) I do not understand how these individuals function in the modern world, and I feel sorry for them because of what they are missing (both exhilaration and frustration). While I am hardly at the forefront of the technological revolution, I am frequently struck by the amount of time I spend each day, enslaved but yet having a love affair with the computer: processing words, searching for information, retrieving documents, and sending messages by e-mail. The computer, over recent years, has transformed the way I and thousands of other lawyers practice law and otherwise go about our daily tasks. More and more, I communicate with my nonprofit clients and others by means of computers, visiting Web sites, and sending e-mail messages (always worried, of course, about confidentiality and client privilege). To my initial astonishment, I have just established a Web site of my own (www.hopkins-nonprofitlaw.com).

In all of this, obviously, lawyers are not alone. Other individuals and organizations are flailing about, trying to understand and keep up with developments in technology. This includes my favorite subject, nonprofit organizations. There are many manifestations of this. As merely one example, as a devoted reader of *The Chronicle of Philanthropy*, I wonder as I peruse each issue, what other subjects it would cover or how much thinner it would be, absent the articles about charities and technology, and the advertisements of technology-based services and products.

As a lawyer, I am less interested in the operations of nonprofit organizations and the enhancements of technology as such, and much more interested in the law environment in which these operations are undertaken. Here, the lawyer faces a unique situation (opportunity, really): There is almost no specific law on which to base a practice! How many chances does a lawyer get in his or her career to practice in a field in which there is no law? It is a rare phenomenon, indeed.

While this will soon change, what lawyers representing nonprofit organizations in the Internet context do today is *extrapolate*. We take existing law, and its underlying rationale and principles, and try to make it fit and work in the Internet setting. Sometimes this process leads to interesting and productive results; on other occasions, the outcome is nonsense.

This book is one nonprofit lawyer's attempt to explore the contemporary interrelationship of law directly affecting tax-exempt organizations and use of the Internet by these organizations. The focus thus is on related and unrelated business activities, administration of charitable giving programs, fundraising, lobbying, political campaign activities, and several other aspects of this law unique to nonprofit entities. There are, of course, many other areas of the law that have a bearing on this subject: constitutional law principles, contracts, and intellectual property issues are examples. They are not treated in the book because (1) there is nothing particularly unique about these aspects of the law for nonprofit organizations and (2) the book would otherwise be about four times its size.

Extrapolation is the underlying theme in these pages. The approach is to briefly recite existing law, summarize the pertinent issues concerning Internet communications by nonprofit organizations (aided in some instances by the extraordinary IRS Announcement 2000-84), then blend the two by musing on what the law pertaining to Internet communications by these organizations may be and will be.

As was illustrated by the final corporate sponsorship regulations, guidance in this area from the Department of the Treasury and the IRS will be trickling out, perhaps almost grudgingly. There will not be any torrent of information on the subject, however, from these or other government agencies, or from Congress. Likely, much of the guidance we will be getting will come from the courts. Ferreting out the law in this area is going to be a long, drawn-out process. Lawyers will salivate over and benefit from these extended explorations and revelations; others will find them tedious and exasperating.

There are two topics addressed throughout the book which warrant highlighting here, because they are of such importance and should be of widespread concern. One is the matter of the potential of attribution of the content of the communication of one entity to another by reason of Web site linkages. The other is the application of the primary purpose test (or, if you prefer, interpretation of the word *substantial*) in fields such as unrelated business and lobbying. The former needs to be curbed; the latter cries out for new definitions of the term, in that traditional measurements by means of time or money do not work in the Internet setting.

There is no greater collection of issues in the realm of the law facing nonprofit organizations than those pertaining to communications by means of the Internet. This phenomenon entails new interpretations of existing law and the development of much new law. As nonprofit organizations increasingly embrace the benefits and wonders of electronic technology, the ramifications in law will continue to mount. Lawyers and others who advise nonprofit organizations are required, if they are to perform effectively, to understand the issues in this area—and be prepared to participate meaningfully in the extrapolation process.

It may not be long before this book is antiquated. This vacuum of law must start to be filled in a substantial manner. As noted, the IRS and Treasury are not prepared to act and Congress does not seem inclined to do so. Cases will be transmuted into applicable court opinions. Guidance and law in this area is inevitable. But, for now, we lawyers and our nonprofit clients are stuck with this matter of extrapolation.

I think, for legal minds, it is going to be a fascinating experience. I, for one, am looking forward to it. This book is intended to help the nonprofit lawyer and others become oriented and focused as the experience begins.

I thank my editor at John Wiley & Sons, Susan McDermott, for her support in the development of this book and Kerstin Nasdeo, assistant managing editor, for her skills in the production of it.

September, 2002
Bruce R. Hopkins

About the Author

Bruce R. Hopkins is a lawyer in Kansas City, Missouri, with the firm of Polsinelli Shalton Welte, P. C., having previously practiced law in Washington, D.C., for 26 years. He specializes in the representation of charitable and other nonprofit organizations. His practice ranges over the entirety of legal matters involving nonprofit organizations, with emphasis on fundraising law issues, charitable giving (including planned giving), the formation of nonprofit organizations, acquisition of recognition of tax-exempt and public charity status, unrelated business planning, application of intermediate sanctions, use of nonprofit and for-profit subsidiaries, and review of annual information returns.

Mr. Hopkins serves as chair of the Committee on Exempt Organizations, Tax Section, American Bar Association; chair, Section of Taxation, National Association of College and University Attorneys; and president, Planned Giving Study Group of Greater Washington, D.C. He was accorded the Assistant Commissioner's (IRS) Award in 1984.

Mr. Hopkins is the series editor of Wiley's Nonprofit Law, Finance, and Management Series. In addition to *The Nonprofits' Guide to Internet Communications Law*, he is the author of *The Tax Law of Charitable Giving, Second Edition*; *The Law of Fundraising, Third Edition*; *The First Legal Answer Book for Fund-Raisers*; *The Second Legal Answer Book for Fund-Raisers*; *The Legal Answer Book for Nonprofit Organizations*; *The Second Legal Answer Book for Nonprofit Organizations*; *The Law of Tax-Exempt Organizations, Seventh Edition*; *Charity, Advocacy, and the Law*; *The Nonprofit Law Dictionary*; *Starting and Managing a Nonprofit Organization*; *A Legal Guide, Third Edition*; and is the co-author, with Jody Blazek, of *Private Foundations*; with D. Benson

Tesdahl, of *Intermediate Sanctions: Curbing Nonprofit Abuse*; and with Thomas K. Hyatt, of *The Law of Tax-Exempt Healthcare Organizations, Second Edition.* He also writes *The Nonprofit Counsel,* a monthly newsletter, published by John Wiley & Sons.

Mr. Hopkins earned his J.D. and L.L.M. degress at the George Washington University and his B.A. at the University of Michigan. He is a member of the bars of the District of Columbia and the state of Missouri.

CHAPTER 1

Introduction to Legal Aspects of Internet Communications by Nonprofit Organizations

The *power of the Internet*—here is a phrase that is now nearly hackneyed, one that has been uttered on countless occasions yet continues indefatigably in daily discourse. The fact that it may be a tiresome cliché does not undermine its inherent truth: The Internet is indeed a medium with clout and increasing dominance, a force of great might. The power of the Internet goes beyond its potency as a means of communication—the Internet is transforming American society and the world.

Some are fascinated by the rich history of the Internet. Some love to grapple with and comprehend the electronic technology itself. Others study and worry about the societal implications of the Internet: its impact on relationships, youth, modes of communication, worsening of the information-overload phenomenon, and the future of reading and print publications. Still others try to understand the import of the mammoth invasion of e-commerce into their personal, professional, and business endeavors.[1]

---

[1] There is much to read on this subject. Some of these books are referenced in the bibliography. The best summary of the history of the Internet that the author has read is in Chapter 1 of Castells, *The Internet Galaxy* (Oxford University Press, 2001) ("Castells"). *The* book on the history of the World Wide Web (since its author invented it) is Berners-Lee, *Weaving the Web* (HarperBusiness 2000) ("Berners-Lee").

As with all things new, large, overwhelming, and change-fomenting, the Internet invasion is benefiting lawyers, including those representing nonprofit organizations. It is and will be creating new law and regulation and is expanding preexisting law. Nonprofit organizations are in the thick of these transformations, because the Internet is such a potent communications tool for them.

Before exploring the various areas of the federal and state law involving use of the Internet directly applicable to tax-exempt organizations,[2] some attention to Internet basics is in order. This is a book about aspects of the law, not about the Internet as such; yet some attention to the latter is necessary to fully appreciate the former. Portions of the next three sections of this chapter are based largely and liberally (with permission, of course) on Michael Johnston's absolutely essential book, *The Nonprofit Guide to the Internet, Second Edition.*[3] Readers who want or need background information on the Internet, its use by nonprofit organizations, and/or elements of computing jargon may want to spend some time with that book before becoming too immersed in this one.[4]

§ 1.1 SOME BASICS ABOUT THE INTERNET

(a) Introduction to the Internet

Johnston observed that the first step in learning how to use any new technology is to obtain a basic understanding of how it works.[5] The Internet is

---

[2] There is, of course, considerable law concerning Internet communications applicable to nearly all organizations and thus to nonprofit organizations; this law is outside the scope of this book. Summaries of this other law appear in Ferrera et al., *Cyberlaw: Your Rights in Cyberspace* (Thomson Learning, 2001); Smedinghoff (ed.), *Online Law: The SPA's Legal Guide to Doing Business on the Internet* (Addison-Wesley, 1996).

[3] This book was published by John Wiley & Sons in 1999.

[4] Another helpful technical overview of the Internet appears in Livingston, "Tax-Exempt Organizations and the Internet: Tax and Other Legal Issues," *31 Exempt Org. Tax Rev.* (No. 3) (March 2001) ("Livingston"), at 419–420.

[5] There is wisdom in this observation, although there are those who use technology without much concern with or interest in how it works. One may drive a car or use a cell phone, for example, without regard or care as to what makes these things function.

a cooperative networking effort that spans the globe. It is a network of millions of computers around the world that communicate with each other using the same telecommunications links (satellites, broadcast towers, and cables) that carry telephone conversations and television channels.

A person, company, or country does not own the Internet. Yet the computers networked on the Internet communicate in a consistent, organized manner. Information can travel through the Internet only because the computers at the signposts along the way all speak the same language and pass the information on to the next stop in the journey. This passage of information is the fundamental structure of the Internet and the key to its continued operation.

All of this hardware and organization is hidden from the Internet user's view in the same way that television viewers see nothing of the transmission towers, production studios, and orbiting satellite transceivers that bring them the shows they are watching. The experience of using the Internet, however, is much more human centered than is television.

In human terms, the Internet can be seen as a loosely structured global community that meets in cyberspace—an artificial environment that exists only within the bounds of the Internet. In cyberspace, individuals, companies, governmental bodies, and nonprofit (or nongovernmental) organizations meet with each other to exchange information, opinions, and entertainment. Cyberspace can seem like a vast and confusing territory, but it has its own kind of organization, a kind of geography.

The principal terms to know in connection with nonprofit organization operations (as well as others) on the Internet are in the glossary at the back of this book.

(b) Internet as Seen by the Supreme Court

This being a book about law, it is appropriate to summarize a description of the Internet that was written by the Supreme Court.[6]

The Internet is an international network of interconnected computers. It is the outgrowth of what began in 1969 as a military program called "ARPANET," which was designed to enable computers operated by the military, defense contractors, and universities conducting defense-related

---

[6] *Reno v. American Civil Liberties Union,* 521 U.S. 844 (1997).

research to communicate with one another by redundant channels, even if some portions of the network were damaged in a war.[7] While the ARPANET no longer exists, it provided an example for the development of a number of civilian networks that, eventually linking with each other, now enable tens of millions of people to communicate with one another and to access vast amounts of information from around the world. The Internet is a unique and wholly new medium of worldwide human communication.

The Internet has experienced extraordinary growth. The number of "host" computers—those that store information and relay communications—increased from about 300 in 1981 to approximately 9,400,000 by the time of trial in the case considered by the Supreme Court, which was in 1996. Roughly 60 percent of these hosts are located in the United States. About 40 million people were using the Internet at the time of this trial, a number that is expected to mushroom to 200 million by 1999. (The current number of users is thought to be about 500 million.[8])

Individuals can obtain access to the Internet from many different sources, generally hosts themselves or entities with a host affiliation. Most colleges and universities provide access for their students and faculty; many corporations provide their employees with access through an office network; many communities and local libraries provide free access; and an increasing number of storefront "computer coffee shops" provide

---

[7] ARPANET was a computer network established by the Advanced Research Projects Agency (ARPA), which was formed by the U.S. Department of Defense in 1958. Other milestones, in terms of dates, occurred in 1971 (invention of e-mail), 1976 (word processor invented), 1978 (invention of successful commercial word processor), 1981 (introduction of personal computer), and 1991 (World Wide Web invented) (Curtis and Quick, *how to get your e-Book published* (Writer's Digest Books 2002) ("Curtis and Quick"), at 16).

[8] Another way to look at this phenomenon is to contemplate the fact that, according to the National Safety Council, as many as 315 million computers have or will become obsolete from 1997 to 2004 (Markoff, "Technology's Toxic Trash Is Sent to Poor Nations," *The New York Times*, Feb. 25, 2002, at C1).

access for a small hourly fee. Several major national "online services," such as America Online, CompuServe, the Microsoft Network, and Prodigy, offer access to their own extensive proprietary networks as well as a link to the much larger resources of the Internet. These commercial online services had almost 12 million individual subscribers at the time of the trial.

Anyone with access to the Internet may take advantage of a wide variety of communication and information retrieval methods. These methods are constantly evolving and are difficult to categorize precisely. But, as presently constituted, those most relevant to this case are electronic mail ("e-mail"), automatic mailing list services ("mail exploders," sometimes referred to as "listservs"), "newsgroups," "chat rooms," and the "World Wide Web." All of these methods can be used to transmit text; most can transmit sound, pictures, and moving video images. Taken together, these tools constitute a unique medium—known to its users as "cyberspace"—located in no particular geographic location but available to anyone, anywhere in the world, with access to the Internet.

E-mail enables an individual to send an electronic message—generally akin to a note or letter—to another individual or to a group of addresses. The message is generally stored electronically, sometimes waiting for the recipient to check his or her "mailbox" and sometimes making its receipt known through some type of prompt. A mail exploder is a sort of e-mail group. Subscribers can send messages to a common e-mail address, which then forwards the message to the group's other subscribers. Newsgroups also serve groups of regular participants, but these postings may be read by others as well. There are thousands of such groups, each serving to foster an exchange of information or opinion on a particular topic running the gamut from, say, the music of Wagner, to Balkan politics, to AIDS prevention, to the Chicago Bulls. About 100,000 new messages are posted every day. In most newsgroups, postings are automatically purged at regular intervals. In addition to posting a message that can be read later, two or more individuals wishing to communicate more immediately can enter a chat room to engage in real-time dialog—in other words, by typing messages to one another that appear almost immediately on the others' computer screens. The lower court found that at any given time, "tens of thousands of users are engaging in conversations on a huge range of subjects."[9] It is "no exaggeration to conclude that the content on the Internet is as diverse as human thought."[10]

The best-known category of communication over the Internet is the World Wide Web, which allows users to search for and retrieve information stored in remote computers as well as, in some cases, to communicate back to designated sites. In concrete terms, the Web consists of a vast number of documents stored in different computers all over the world. Some of these documents are simply files containing information. More elaborate documents, however, commonly known as Web "pages," are also prevalent. Each has its own address. Web pages frequently contain information and sometimes allow the viewer to communicate with the page's (or "site's") author. They generally also contain "links" to other documents created by that site's author or to other (generally) related sites. Typically, the links are either blue or underlined text—sometimes images.

Navigating the Web is relatively straightforward. A user may either type the address of a known page or enter one or more keywords into a commercial "search engine" in an effort to locate sites on a subject of interest. A particular Web page may contain the information sought by the "surfer," or, through its links, it may be an avenue to other documents located anywhere on the Internet. Users generally explore a given Web page, or move to another, by clicking a computer "mouse" on one of the page's icons or links. Access to most Web pages is freely available, but some pages allow access only to those who have purchased the right from a commercial provider. The Web is thus comparable, from the readers' viewpoint, to both a vast library including millions of readily available and indexed publications and a sprawling mall offering goods and services.

From the publishers' point of view, it constitutes a vast platform from which to address and hear from a worldwide audience of millions of readers, viewers, researchers, and buyers. Any person or organization with a computer connected to the Internet can "publish" information. Publishers include government agencies, educational institutions, commercial entities, advocacy groups, and individuals. Publishers may either make their

---

[9] 929 F. Supp. 824, 835 (E.D. Pa. 1996).

[10] *Id.* at 842.

material available to the entire pool of Internet users or confine access to a selected group, such as those willing to pay for the privilege. "No single organization controls any membership in the Web, nor is there any centralized point from which individual Web sites or services can be blocked from the Web."[11]

(c) Internet as Seen by Others

The Center for Democracy and Technology has written about the Internet, summarizing its architecture and economics.[12] These "unique characteristics" of the Internet were identified:

- The architecture of the Internet is *decentralized* and distributed. It is a network of networks consciously designed to function without gatekeepers.

- The Internet is *global,* providing immediate access to information from around the world.

- The Internet is *abundant,* in that it can accommodate a virtually unlimited number of speakers.

- The Internet is *inexpensive,* so that an individual can send a mass mailing by e-mail to hundreds of thousands of individuals with little expense and can communicate by means of Web pages for free.

- The Internet is *interactive,* allowing responsive communications from one to one, from one to many, and from many to one.

---

[11] *Id.* at 838. In its opinion striking down the Children's Internet Protection Act of 2001, a law requiring libraries to filter the Internet for materials harmful to minors, on free speech grounds, a federal court wrote that the Web is "extremely dynamic, with an estimated 1.5 million new pages added every day and the contents of existing Web pages changing very rapidly" (*American Library Association* v. *United States* (E. D. Pa., No. 01-1303, June 1, 2002)).

[12] Grossman, Mulligan, and Dempsey, "Square Pegs & Round Holes: Applying Campaign Finance Law to the Internet/Risks to Free Expression & Democratic Values," *Digital Issues* (No. 4) (Oct. 1999).

- The Internet is *user-controlled,* so that individuals enjoy an unequaled ability to direct and control the information that they come in contact with.[13]

There are countless other descriptions of the Internet. Here is a sample: It is a "network whose many incarnations—an obscure academic playpen, information superhighway, vast marketplace, sci-fi–inspired matrix—have seen it through more than three decades of ceaseless evolution."[14] It is a "global network of computer networks made user-friendly by the world wide web, an application running on top of the Internet."[15] It is a "general communications infrastructure that links computers together, on top of which the Web rides."[16] The Internet is "nothing more than millions of computers connected with each other, mostly by telephone wires or larger cables"; the "Net is not the Web, though the Web depends on the Net in order to exist and function."[17]

§ 1.2 Main Applications of the Internet

There are four main Internet applications: electronic mail, the World Wide Web as an information source, operation of newsgroups, and chat rooms.

(a) Electronic Mail

One of the most common of the Internet applications is electronic mail (e-mail). E-mail messages can be sent from one computer to another anywhere in the world, usually within minutes. If a user is not at his or her computer, the message is stored and can be read at any time. It is so fast

---

[13] This and other information published by The Center for Democracy and Technology is available at www.cdt.org.

[14] Hafner, "The Internet's Invisible Hand," *The New York Times,* Jan. 10, 2002, at D1.

[15] Castells at 10.

[16] Berners-Lee at 6.

[17] Curtis and Quick at 80.

and convenient that users refer to mail sent via the U.S. postal system or similar system (terrestrial mail) as *snail mail*.

E-mail addresses provide a key to understanding the internal geography of the Internet in the same way that an address written on an envelope reflects the real-world geography of place names, streets, and countries. All e-mail addresses have a common basic structure. They follow the two-part pattern of someone@somewhere (with the @ sign being read as *at*). The first part—someone—usually refers to an individual and is commonly some combination of that person's first initial and up to seven characters of his or her last name. The somewhere that follows the @ symbol describes where on the Internet that person's e-mail account is. This part of the address is known as the *domain name*.

Most individuals who subscribe to a commercial Internet service will have an e-mail address that is composed of their user identification and the domain name of the Internet service provider (e.g., jsmith@aol.com). Organizations looking to give individual e-mail addresses to their staff members may want to create their own domain name, then assign their staff members e-mail addresses using that domain name (e.g., jsmith@asae .org).

The last portion of the domain name (for U.S. entities) identifies the type of organization. Most nonprofit organizations are referenced as .org. Educational institutions, however, are identified as .edu. Commercial organizations are referenced as .com. Governmental entities are referenced as .gov.

Even though no single organization runs the Internet, there is a system for registering domain names. Most countries have their own domain registration body, which assigns and organizes the names in their geographic region.

(b) World Wide Web in General

The Web has become the premier feature of the Internet. It offers vast amounts of information in easily accessible text and graphics format. For this reason, it is appealing to almost any user, regardless of purpose.

The Web is viewed through a browser. As noted, a browser is software that allows the user to gain access to the Web. Information on the Web is organized in collections of pages. Each page has its own unique address—its URL (uniform resource locator). In order to access an item of information, its location must be known.

The addressing system for the Web is similar to a street address. Each address has a URL. The URL tells the computer what type of protocol is being used, where the site is located, and what type of site it is. For example, the address http://www.whitehouse.gov brings the user to the Web site for the White House. A Web address is made up of several parts. The first part tells the computer what type of protocol to use to access the site. It is similar to a long-distance access code for the telephone. Many Web site addresses, such as the one for the White House, begin with *http* (Hypertext Transfer Protocol). The *www*, of course, stands for World Wide Web. The name of the site is *whitehouse*. The suffix *.gov* is the domain name for a government site.

The Web has thousands of sites that consist of a home page and additional pages in which the text may contain embedded hyperlinks to other sites. A hyperlink (or just plain link) is easily distinguishable from other text on the page because it appears in a different color and format, such as blue, underlined text. When a user points to a link and clicks on it with a mouse, the computer is instructed to go to the address embedded within that link and retrieve the document that is housed there. This new page of information may in itself have more links to other pages, so one can easily navigate—browse—from page to page by clicking on links. This activity, as even most newbies know, is commonly called *surfing the Web* or *surfing the Net*.

(c) Newsgroups

Users can read and post messages on bulletin boards (or newsgroups). The cyberspace bulletin board area is one of the oldest parts of the Internet. When individuals started sending messages across the early networks that gave rise to the Internet, they began to group the messages according to subject. As more subjects were added, the list of newsgroups expanded.

Before the emergence of the World Wide Web, the newsgroups area was the focus of public activity and discussion. These days much of the attention has shifted to the Web, but the newsgroups remain useful places for nonprofit organizations to seek out their online constituents.

(d) Internet Chat

Most interactions between individuals on the Internet do not happen live. E-mails take a few moments at best to travel through the Internet to their destination. World Wide Web pages often are made once, then posted online for months at a time without any updates. Newsgroup postings may be days or weeks old by the time someone reads them.

Chat is the only area of the Internet that is specifically designed to allow real-time, live interaction between individuals online. Many thousands of individuals use chat today, but the level of interaction is still somewhat frustrating because chat only works reliably with typed text. No universally accepted voice or video chat program that would let individuals communicate across the Internet with more than keystrokes currently exists.

§ 1.3 UNDERSTANDING THE INTERNET— QUESTIONS AND ANSWERS

An understanding of the early development of the Internet will make some of its quirks more comprehensible—maybe even endearing.

(a) Why Does the Internet Appear Disorganized?

With all the commotion over the Internet, it may seem puzzling that information on the Internet is not neatly organized. This disorganization, however, is linked to the Internet's origin in the military think tanks of the Cold War.

The Internet was born as a solution to one of the major strategic military dilemmas of the nuclear age: how to ensure that communication could continue during and after a nuclear war, when whole cities may be destroyed? The solution that emerged was an interconnected web of nodes that could each function independently from the rest of the network but that could receive and forward information as needed. Each packet of information would travel the network like a giant game of hot potato, so that if one node computer disappeared from the network, the information packet could bypass it and still reach its destination.

This same design strategy that allows each part of the Internet to function as an independent whole makes the Internet virtually impossible to organize or quantify.

(b) Who Can Use the Internet?

For most of the first 20 years of the Internet's existence, it was used primarily by nonprofit organizations, namely, educational and scientific institutions. The only way to gain access to the Internet was as a government agency or through a university or research facility.

This situation changed in 1990 when the Federal Networking Council modified its membership policy from only organizations with sponsorship by a U.S. government agency to anyone who wanted membership. This policy change opened the door to commercialization of the Internet and resulted in its exponential growth, particularly in the United States. Commercial Internet service providers also came into existence in 1990.

Today anyone can have access to the Internet. The Internet's reach is global, but there are still some blank spots on the map. Many developing countries have Internet access only in their capital cities and even then at prices that put access far out of the reach of ordinary citizens.

(c) How Does the World Wide Web Fit into the Internet?

The researchers at CERN (Conseil Europeen pour la Recherche Nucleaire) in Geneva, Switzerland, developed a means for physicists to actively collaborate with other physicists around the world in real time. They established a simple hypertext system in which one document contained live and active links to other documents. This system grew into the Hypertext Transfer Protocol that enables the Web to function. CERN's programmers also developed the first prototype Web browser.

In just five years, the World Wide Web grew to become the most popular part of the Internet, with many hundreds of thousands of Web sites and a staggering growth rate. This area is where all the online action is and where future advances are most likely to appear first.

(d) How Can Nonprofits Compete with For-Profits on the Internet?

As noted, nonprofit organizations—specifically, universities and research institutions—were a substantial part of the very foundation that shaped the Internet. They were the first users of the Internet and were the first to grasp its potential as a multidimensional communications vehicle. The commercial potential of the Internet has sparked its current rapid growth, but nonprofit organizations led the charge to push for use of the Internet as a global communications medium.

In 1994 commercialization of the Internet got into full swing, years after the nonprofit community had been using the Internet for information retrieval and exchange. Nonprofit organizations and related entities hold the second largest number of domains, second only to commercial domains. The Internet is friendly territory to nonprofits. There is no inherent value in one Internet address or another. Content, not money, determines the value of a Web site.

(e) Does Anyone Monitor the Quality and Accuracy of Information on the Internet?

No overseer or gatekeeper monitors information on the Internet. Also, without a doubt, the sheer volume of material available on the Internet is staggering.

At this time, users have to judge the quality and accuracy of Internet materials themselves, based in part on the source. The more credible the source, the more reliable is the information. Obviously, the inherent content of the materials is a factor in determining their accuracy. Moreover, there is no authority to go to with complaints about content.

(f) What Are the Security Concerns on the Internet?

Security concerns have been around since the earliest days of the Internet. The greatest threat to Internet users has been the possibility of infection by a computer virus. A computer *virus* is a piece of software programming code that adds itself to an existing computer program. The type of damage a virus can cause ranges from the alteration of data, to the display of messages, to crashing the computer.

In the past, it was not possible to get a virus from surfing the Internet. Viewing Web pages alone was not considered a risky activity because Web browsers only displayed information and did not actually run programs. A virus could be contracted only by running a program on the user's local computer that came from an infected disk or some other local source.

Today there is more concern about viruses because the Web has become more advanced. The newest, most sophisticated Web pages are more like programs in themselves, and there is some danger that a virus could infect a computer just because the virus was viewed by a Web browser. The Internet industry is working to eliminate these sorts of dangers, yet new ones seem to be discovered every week. Antivirus software should be installed on every computer that is connected to the Internet. Some antivirus software currently on the market monitors a user's activity on the Internet and watches for any potential virus dangers.

§ 1.4 REASONS A NONPROFIT ORGANIZATION SHOULD GO ONLINE

Many nonprofit organizations, because of limited budgets and growing demands for their services, have to be careful when contemplating entry into a new medium, such as the Internet. Before most nonprofit organizations move into new areas or means of service, outreach, fundraising, and the like, they need to prove to staff, volunteers, and board members that the new initiative is a good investment of time and money—in the short term and the long term.

There are four important reasons why a nonprofit organization should go online.

(a) Improvement in Communications

The Internet allows a nonprofit organization to communicate more effectively, both internally and externally.

(i) Improving Internal Communications. Because of the size of the cyberspace community, the Internet is often trumpeted as a way for nonprofit organizations to increase the base of individuals who know of, find services from, or support the organization. The Internet, however, can also be used effectively to improve communications within a non-profit organization.

Creating an e-mail coordinator opens mind-boggling opportunities for nonprofit organizations. Nonprofit managers who are thinking of using the Internet, either initially or more intensively within their organization, should realize that the nonprofit workplace often is following the way of the private sector, with staff demanding greater flexibility and telecommuting. The Internet provides an excellent chance for nonprofit staff to work in a more flexible environment. Further, more volunteers, donors, and staff will be working together in a virtual environment in the future. By making appropriate use of the Web, mailing lists, and chat areas, organizations can strengthen their work. Although e-mailing within an organization is often rather impersonal, it is also a quick, efficient, and sometimes clearer way to communicate at any time of day or night.[18]

(ii) Improving External Communications. The Internet provides incredible opportunities to communicate externally as well. The work of the organization can be spread across the world—at very little cost.

The Internet community consists of tens of millions of users. The financial cost to reach an organization's potential audience via the Internet is far lower than is the case for traditional media, such as print publications, radio, or television. The Internet is a remarkably flexible and diverse outreach vehicle that can expand a nonprofit organization's ability to communicate.

Today, information about an organization can be obtained directly from its Web site at any time. Users who may never have heard of an organization before can directly interact with it at their own convenience. Nonprofit organizations that use the Internet will find that it is a cost-effective place to reach new publics: prospective clients, supporters, volunteers, and staff.

---

[18] E-mail communications, however, unlike the merely spoken word, can be saved in hard copy and retrieved long after they are sent, with consequences not always pleasant to the message-sender, as illustrated by the various investigations into e-mail messaging in the Clinton White House and Enron.

A wide range of nonprofit organizations may have new programs and projects that can grow and thrive through the low-cost external communication ability of the Internet. Similarly, nonprofit organizations may have old programs and projects that need fresh ideas and new blood. The Internet may be able to infuse old programs with enthusiasm and support. Some nonprofit organizations may have volunteer-run programs that the Internet can bolster.

(b) Improved Access to Information

The Internet contains a vast resource library of information that is relevant to nonprofit organizations. This library can help staff and volunteers perform their day-to-day work more effectively and provide them an opportunity for professional growth.

Without a doubt, information is the currency of the nonprofit sector. The Internet is full of information—on Web sites, in newsgroups, in chat areas, and on mailing lists. (There may even be too much information or at least a lot of misinformation.) The challenge for a nonprofit organization (and any other Internet user) is to find the needed information online quickly and inexpensively. Every nonprofit organization needs leadership to help in adapting to this medium. Each organization requires staff who will use, research, and help others discover how the Internet will help them do their jobs more effectively and therefore better serve their client base.

(c) Professional Development

The Internet is a wonderful place for nonprofit professionals to share, learn, and acquire information to become better nonprofit staff and managers. Staff and volunteers can find professional development opportunities principally in three places: (1) professional association Web sites and related online resources, (2) mailing lists or e-mail subscription lists of colleagues and peers, and (3) newsgroups, again consisting of colleagues and peers.

Many nonprofit managers rely on a range of professional associations to help them share information, understand those in similar positions, and learn from mentors in their field. These associations provide services online. Also, these Web sites provide detailed information on educational opportunities, such as conference and course listings, and perhaps the ability to register online.

Being online provides an organization with access to information from a broad constituency. Once online, staff and volunteers can find a wide range of resources that are not restricted by geography and are most often free. Every decision maker in a nonprofit organization would do well to prepare a list of possible resources for staff and volunteers and show them accurately, explicitly, and clearly how they can gather information on the Internet to do their jobs better.

Sometimes nonprofit organization managers need advice from outside the organization to support their work. Nonprofit budgets are often stretched to the limit; outside consultants may be too expensive. The Internet, however, can be a cost-effective way to find advice from outside the organization that can augment a nonprofit manager's stand on a particular issue.

(d) Taking Action

The Internet is an important medium in which innovative fundraising and advocacy activities can be explored.

(i) Cyberfundraising. The Internet holds great potential for fundraising by nonprofit organizations because it offers contact with tens of millions of affluent users, young and old. Nonprofit organizations should begin testing online fundraising so they do not get left behind, inasmuch as other organizations are increasing fundraising efforts by means of the Internet. Yet the pressure of being forced to master a new fundraising medium, when an organization may still be working on the ins and outs of direct mail, telephone, and/or television fundraising, is an additional stress. Now, with the frenzied press coverage of the Internet, more organizations are being asked by staff, volunteers, and board members about the fundraising potential of this electronic medium.

There are three questions that nonprofit organization managers, staff, and volunteers should be asking about the Internet:

1. Should the organization get online?

2. What are other groups up to with the Internet?

3. Will the organization be successful in using the Internet for fundraising purposes?

The answers are, respectively, yes, a lot, and with time. There is no doubt that almost every nonprofit organization should get online. There are just too many people on the Internet now and in the future to ignore. Many nonprofit organizations are already using this medium to reach a wider audience to accomplish their mission and mandate, including ways to raise money. Every nonprofit organization should make the small investment necessary to have the Internet as a part of its media mix.

The World Wide Web is the fastest-growing part of the Internet. The Web is where nonprofit organizations are going to raise money. On the Web, pages of hypertext can be browsed, almost like flipping through the pages of a magazine, replete with pictures, graphics, and even sound and video clips. Individuals and organizations can publish their own home pages by storing them on a computer that is connected to the Internet and letting interested individuals come to and browse the site. The Web is where organizations are publishing for a wider audience as well as for their constituencies. The majority of new Internet users are using the Web to find information, browse, research, chat, and make contributions to charitable organizations.

Because other fundraising media are becoming more competitive and cluttered with solicitations, fundraising professionals are looking to gain a competitive edge. Nonprofit organizations are using cyberspace to gain that edge—whether by raising money through direct donations, pledges, merchandise sales, auctions, lotteries, corporate sponsorship, or foundation grants. Every fundraising opportunity in the real (off-line) world is also available online. Nonprofit organizations should be exploring all avenues of opportunity; the Internet certainly is one of them.

(ii) Cyberadvocacy. Many nonprofit organization managers and volunteers need to get their supporters to act, as opposed to making contributions. Studies have shown that the level of involvement of donors (i.e., actions taken on behalf of the organization, such as signing petitions, demonstrating, or sending letters to government officials) is the most crucial factor that affects their decisions to give. When donors decide to become involved in activities that are associated with a nonprofit organization, they are showing their interest in the purpose and activities of the organization. By acting, donors can identify with the interests of the nonprofit entity.

The challenge for many nonprofit organizations is to find cost-effective involvement devices that can be immediately acted on by a motivated supporter. The Internet can provide a wide range of methods of getting a nonprofit organization's supporters more involved—and thus more likely to make a contribution.

A nonprofit organization often needs to persuade the public, government, and/or other institutions to take action on its behalf. The organization may want to alter or create legislation on an issue of deep concern to it and its constituency. Lobbying, demonstrating, petitioning, and other strategies do not change significantly when conducted by means of the Internet, but a nonprofit organization that understands the best methods for using a Web site might supplement its other advocacy activities by Internet use. (This approach is likely to interrelate with fundraising.) Multiple faxes and e-mail writing are highly interactive and effective strategies that can make advocacy integral to a Web site.

§ 1.5   OTHER ASPECTS OF NONPROFIT ORGANIZATIONS' USE OF THE INTERNET

Other aspects of nonprofit organization's use of the Internet are outside the scope of this work. As described by Michael Johnston,[19] these are:

- Assessing existing and prospective computer equipment and systems
- Arranging an Internet connection
- Membership recruitment and the like via the Internet
- Creating a Web site

---

[19] Johnston, *The Nonprofit Guide to the Internet, Second Edition* (John Wiley & Sons, 1999) ("Johnston").

- Conducting research on the Internet
- Modes of fundraising on the Internet

§ 1.6 NONPROFIT ORGANIZATIONS AND THE INTERNET: ORIGINS AND CULTURE

Nonprofit organizations were not only present at the creation of the Internet, they participated directly in the establishment of this communications medium. The principal players at the outset were universities and research institutions. This fact has import, in and of itself, but it goes beyond history to inform the very nature of the Internet. This is because the "criteria of excellence, peer review, and open communication of research work originated with these institutions."[20]

Thus, from the larger perspective, the "Internet culture is the culture of the creators of the Internet."[21] There is a "direct link between these cultural expressions [academics and science] and the technological development" of the Internet, with the "key connection" being the "openness and free modification of Internet software, and particularly of the source code of software."[22] Within this culture, "merit results from contribution to the advancement of a technological system that provides a common good for the community of discovers."[23] Thus, the culture of the Internet is "rooted in the scholarly tradition of the shared pursuit of science, of reputation by academic excellence, of peer review, and of openness in all research findings, with due credit to the authors of each discovery."[24] It does not get much more nonprofit (charitable, educational, and scientific) than that.

There are, of course, other forces that have shaped and are shaping the Internet. Here is a fine summary of them: "The culture of the Internet is a culture made up of a technocratic belief in the progress of humans through technology, enacted by communities of hackers [computer technologists,

---

[20] Castells at 38.

[21] *Id.* at 36.

[22] *Id.* at 38.

[23] *Id.* at 39.

[24] *Id.* at 40.

not those who illegally penetrate computer systems] thriving on free and open technological creativity, embedded in virtual networks aimed at reinventing society, and materialized by money-driven entrepreneurs into the workings of the new economy."[25]

Nonprofit organizations have played other roles in the advancement of technology by means of the Internet. There are too many examples of this to note them all, but here are some examples. In 1984 the Free Software Foundation was launched to promote the free use of software on the Internet (based on the principle of "copyleft" rather than "copyright").[26] The Electronic Frontier Foundation was created in 1990 to "fight government control" of the Internet.[27] CERN, the "Geneva-based, European high-energy physics research center," released the Web browser software over the Internet in 1991.[28] The Direct Action Network "provided the training and organizational skills for many protestors" against the World Trade Organization in Seattle in 1999.[29] A major phenomenon today are "[s]ocial movements in defense of freedom on the Internet, such as the coalition formed around the Electronic Privacy Information Center."[30]

To the extent there is any governance of the Internet, it is accomplished by means of nonprofit organizations. Leaders in the Internet community in the late 1970s established an advisory group of networking experts, the Internet Configuration Control Board, which "encouraged the participation of the overall Internet community in improving the protocols."[31] Later came the Internet Activities Board, which subsequently became the organizations named the Internet Engineering Task Force and the Internet Research Task Force.[32] To move the Internet beyond the direct control of the U.S. government, a nonprofit organization by the

---

[25] *Id.* at 61.

[26] *Id.* at 14.

[27] *Id.* at 51.

[28] *Id.* at 15.

[29] *Id.* at 141.

[30] *Id.* at 184.

[31] *Id.* at 29.

[32] *Id.* at 29–30.

name of the Internet Society was given oversight over these two "task forces."[33]

The Internet Corporation for Assigned Names and Numbers came into being in 1998, as a nonprofit entity that "assumes the management of IP [Internet protocol] address space allocation, protocol parameter assignment, domain name system management, and root server system management."[34] The World Wide Web Consortium "presides over the protocols and development" of the Web.[35]

§ 1.7 INTERNET AND PROGRAM ADVANCEMENT

The principal use of the Internet by nonprofit organizations is for advancement of their program activities. For the most part—and this is certainly true for charitable organizations[36]—these activities will be other than lobbying and political campaign efforts and certainly will be other than unrelated business endeavors.

The core of all of this is *communication* to and by nonprofit organizations.[37] A visit to the Web site of just about every nonprofit organization that maintains one verifies this. This is what is likely to be found:

- A summary of the organization's purposes
- The text of the organization's articles of incorporation, other articles of organization, and/or bylaws
- A description of the organization's activities
- Basic information about the organization, such as its mailing and e-mail address and telephone and fax numbers
- A calendar of events

---

[33] *Id.* at 30.

[34] *Id.* at 31.

[35] *Id.* at 33.

[36] That is, organizations that are tax-exempt pursuant to Internal Revenue Code of 1986, as amended, section ("IRC §") 501(a) by reason of description in IRC § 501(c)(3).

[37] See *supra* § 2.

- Interactive features, where an individual can send an e-mail message, purchase publications and other items, register for an event, and the like
- An archive of documents
- A members-only section, including a chat room and registry
- Picture(s) of facilities, individuals engaged in program activities, and/or staff
- Map(s) providing direction to and/or around its grounds and facilities
- A code of ethics
- Advocacy statements
- Solicitation of contributions
- A listing of the organization's staff members, with titles and perhaps telephone number and e-mail addresses
- One or more links to other Web sites
- Posting of the organization's application for recognition of tax exemption
- Posting of the organization's most recent annual information returns

This and other material constitutes an unprecedented volume of information that is available for nearly anyone in the world to review at any time. This medium—the Internet—means, too, that nearly anyone can communicate with the organization at any time. As Michael Johnston wrote: "Being on-line establishes a 24-hours-a-day, 365-days-a-year location where anyone can access information about an organization directly from their [its] Web site. Users who may never have heard of an organization before can directly interact with the nonprofit at their own convenience."[38]

This electronic technology can also be used in the *conduct* of a nonprofit organization's program or programs. Obviously, these operations include word processing, number-crunching, e-mailing, constituency communications, and Internet-based research. This use of the Internet, however, goes beyond these functions, although this application of technology is not (yet) widespread.

---

[38] Johnston at 15.

An emerging use of the Internet by nonprofit organizations in the program context is the Web site-based seminar or other educational or instructional experience. Versions differ, but one uses PowerPoint slides that appear on the screen of a user, who has logged in with a personal code. The audio portion of the experience flows by telephone (although that is certain to change). It was inevitable that these conferences, seminars, and the like have come to be termed *webinars*.

A report, published in early 2001, stated that a "few" nonprofit organizations "have found that by exploiting the Internet and other information technologies they can slash expenses, extend the reach of their programs, and transform the way they work." But, this report continued, "many others have been frustrated as they wrestle with increasingly complex hardware and software, hampered by a lack of technical expertise, unable to raise funds to get the equipment and training they need, or perhaps merely skeptical about the need to change."[39] It may be anticipated that the number of the organizations in the first group will increase, and the number in the second group will decline.

Here are some examples that sustain that view:

- Charitable organizations are using the Internet to advance their programs.[40]

- Charitable organizations are soliciting contributions online, of course[41] but, as part of that process, are engaging in forms of electronic communication such as the sending of newsletters.[42]

- Charitable organizations are starting to use e-mail to acknowledge contributions, particularly those that are made online.[43]

---

[39] Greene, "Astride the Digital Divide," XIII *Chronicle of Philanthropy* (No. 6) 1 (Jan. 11, 2001).

[40] E.g., Greene, "Technology Helps Small Environmental Group Get Big Results," XIII *Chronicle of Philanthropy* (No. 6) 10 (Jan. 11, 2001).

[41] Hall, "A Brave New World of Giving," XII *Chronicle of Philanthropy* (No. 17) 1 (June 15, 2000), which includes a sampler of charitable giving sites (at 34).

[42] Lewis, "You've Got a Charity Solicitation," XIII *Chronicle of Philanthropy* (No. 4) 25 (Nov. 30, 2000).

[43] Schwinn, "How Charities Give Thanks," XIV *Chronicle of Philanthropy* (No. 4) 21 (Nov. 29, 2001).

- Nonprofit organizations are using the Internet for advocacy purposes.[44]
- "More than 80 percent of executives at human-service organizations say that information technology has changed their organizations' daily operations over the past five years, with 87 percent calling information technology either important or essential."[45]
- This technology is being used to augment worship services, such as by providing digitally enhanced music and interactive sermons.[46]
- Associations are using this technology to provide new and improved services to their members.[47]
- Nonprofit organizations are being created to help other nonprofit organizations utilize Internet technology.[48]

To place all this in perspective, it should be noted, as one commentator nicely did, that "[t]here is nothing about Web technology per se that suggests that posting a Web site jeopardizes compliance with the requirements of section 501(c)(3)."[49] That section of the Internal Revenue Code is the basis for tax exemption for charitable, educational, religious, and like entities. This comment also extends to other categories of tax-exempt organizations because Web sites are "simply another means of communication with the public."[50]

---

[44] Wallace, "Charities Use Internet to Educate Voters," XIII *Chronicle of Philanthropy* (No. 1) 36 (Oct. 19, 2000).

[45] Partial summary of Independent Sector's "Wired, Willing and Ready: Nonprofit Human Service Organizations' Adoption of Information Technology" (2001) at XIV *Chronicle of Philanthropy* (No. 6) 51 (Jan. 10, 2002).

[46] Biersdorfer, "When Worship Gets Wired," *The New York Times*, May 16, 2002, at E1.

[47] E.g., Schweitzer, "Virtual Values," 54 *Association Management* (No. 3) 32 (Mar. 2002).

[48] E.g., Schwinn, "New Fund Exposes Charities to the Outer Limits of Technology," XIII *Chronicle of Philanthropy* (No. 6) 8 (Jan. 11, 2001).

[49] Livingston at 420.

[50] *Id.* Some may question use of the word *simply* in this context, but otherwise the observation certainly is accurate. As this commentator went on to state, however, "[t]ax questions tend to arise as a charity considers the specific content it wants to place on the Web site" (*id.*). Hence Chapters 2 through 7.

§ 1.8 THREE OVERARCHING ISSUES

Three overarching issues, from a law standpoint, permeate the intertwining of the use of the Internet by nonprofit organizations and the law that regulates their operations. Two are of immense importance: the costs associated with functions by means of the Internet and the inherent qualities to be assigned to hyperlinks. The third issue is the matter of record keeping—maintenance of prior versions of Web sites.

(a) Cost of Internet Operations

There is so much that can be said about the Internet, and most of it is positive. Whether it is the history of the Internet, its vastness, the gargantuan amount of information to be found there or created on it, the potential it provides for learning, or, in Michael Johnston's portrayal, the "fun and wacky" nature of it, the Internet is marvelous. There is, nonetheless, another facet of the matter—the fact that the cost of operations on the Internet is so low.

Johnston repeatedly stressed this point. He wrote that the "work of the [nonprofit] organization can be spread across the world—with very little cost."[51] "To reach this potential audience [of Internet users], the costs are much lower than for traditional media like television, radio, or print."[52] Advocacy activities by nonprofit organizations on the Internet "can be taken effectively and cheaply on any nonprofit's Web site."[53] Seen from the perspective of publishing, "if you have a computer and a connection to the Internet, you can create and publish works available to hundreds of millions of people and do so at a cost of pennies."[54]

---

[51] *Id.* at 14.

[52] *Id.*

[53] *Id.* at 29.

[54] Curtis and Quick at 20. The point was expressed from another perspective: "If Gutenberg's invention of movable type dropped the total costs of print by 99 percent over handwritten parchments folios, these digital 'presses' lowered the cost of publishing by 999 percent over the printed and bound books that Gutenberg made possible" (*id.* at 257).

Traditionally, from a federal tax law perspective, the activities of a non-profit organization are assessed and quantified in terms of the amount of money expended in the conduct of them.[55] (Sometimes the amount of time involved also is a factor.[56]) This is the case, irrespective of whether the issue is ongoing eligibility for tax-exempt status pursuant to application of the primary purpose rule, ascertaining the amount of lobbying or political activity, or measuring the extent of unrelated business activity. The conduct of the activity usually has been stated in terms of staff expense and the cost of communication by modes such as travel, U.S. mail, radio, television, and various forms of print media.

This approach does not work very well, or not at all, in the context of activities conducted by means of the Internet. Important lobbying, fundraising, political campaign, and unrelated business undertakings can be transacted at a fraction of the expense that would have been incurred were traditional means of communication used.[57] A lobbying message on a Web page of a well-known nonprofit organization, for example, may have cost a few dollars to create and post yet have enormous influence over a legislative process. On what basis is an organization, or the Internal Revenue Service[58] or a court, going to quantify these undertakings?

---

[55] In general, to be tax-exempt, an organization must devote a substantial or primary amount of its efforts in the furtherance of exempt purposes and the conduct of exempt activities. This is known as the *primary purpose test*, which is the most developed in the charitable (IRC § 501(c)(3)) setting. Often, the primary purpose test is applied by assessing the amount of funding devoted to programs.

[56] In the context of charitable (IRC § 501(c)(3)) organizations, the IRS occasionally applies the *commensurate test* to determine whether an organization is entitled to be tax-exempt. This test, which assesses entitlement to exemption in terms of the amount of an organization's resources that are devoted to program, can take into account the amount of time expended, particularly if that amount is greater than the amount of expenditures for program activities.

[57] Cost-effectiveness may not always be an overriding factor. In a cartoon, a fundraiser says to a colleague: "Soliciting donations via e-mail is efficient, but I miss making people feel guilty face to face" (XIII *Chronicle of Philanthropy* (No. 3) 39 (Nov. 16, 2000).

[58] The Internal Revenue Service is referenced throughout as the "IRS."

There are only three options here. One is to disregard Internet communications of this nature for purposes of applying the federal law of tax-exempt organization. While having the virtue of simplicity, that is a highly unlikely and improbable outcome. The second approach is to apply some sort of safe-harbor test. The third alternative is an ephemeral (and thus dangerous) facts-and-circumstances test, which would take into account, among other elements, the nebulous factor of *influence*.

How this aspect of the law and Internet communications is going to be resolved is unknown at this point.[59] But the matter nags and permeates all aspects of the subject, as is reflected in subsequent chapters.

(b) Essence of Hyperlinks

One definition of a *hyperlink*—or *link*—is that it is a "connection between two hypertext documents," by means of which users can "travel freely in any direction throughout an HTML [see above[60]] document series or Web site."[61] Another, fuller, explanation of a link[62] noted that it can be incorporated into an e-mail message or a Web site; it can appear as a displayed address for another site or as a graphic image. "Clicking on the link," as this explanation pointed out, "causes the routine built into the link to run, issuing a request to see the Web site whose address is built into the link." A key point: "The link does not function until the user clicks on it." Having said that, however, an issue is the amount of consideration that should be given to the effort required to execute the click.

This explanation also noted that a link "can carry the user directly to the new site, with no way to return to the original site other than to use the 'back' function of the Web browser." Alternatively, the "link can function as a 'framing link,' causing a new copy of the Web browser to start

---

[59] An outcome that is not really a legal issue is how the cost savings are to be channeled. In a cartoon, a fundraiser is addressing a group of donors, using a projector, saying: "Here again what you see from this next bar chart is that your donation bought me new presentation software, a color printer, and way too much free time" (XII *Chronicle of Philanthropy* (No. 22) 32 (Sep. 7, 2000).

[60] See *supra* § 1.

[61] Johnston at 229.

[62] Livingston at 420.

running on top of the existing copy, leaving the existing copy of the Web browser and the original site still visible in the background." Moreover, "[s]ites can also have a frame of their own," so that "[c]licking on a link may leave the original site's frame in place but change the content that appears inside the frame to be that of a new site."

The Web site of a nonprofit organization can contain—and often does—one or more links to other Web sites. These other sites may be those maintained by other nonprofit organizations, government agencies, or for-profit organizations. In situations where a nonprofit organization's link is to that of another nonprofit entity, that other entity may have the same tax-exempt status as the linking organization, a different exempt status, or perhaps no exempt status at all.

The law is a long way from sorting out the inherent qualities of these links. What does the presence of a link mean? The most serious aspect of this is the prospect of *attribution* of the Web site content, or a particular message on it, of a linked organization to a tax-exempt organization, principally for federal tax law purposes. In an announcement, issued by the IRS in 2000 requesting comments on a series of questions posed by the agency concerning Internet communications by tax-exempt organizations,[63] for example, the IRS asked whether the provision of a link by a charitable organization to the Web site of another organization that engages in lobbying or political campaign activity constitutes lobbying or political campaign activity by the charitable organization.

As to this matter of a link's inherent quality, it was observed that links "do not create an identity between the sites on either side of the link." That is, they "are nothing more than a communications tool and are completely independent of the content they bridge."[64] This observation is not fully accurate; it is an overstatement, like saying that a road connecting City A and City B is just a road, that it does not create an "identity" between the two cities, which, of course, these pathways often do. This characterization of links accords too much sterility to them. Links do not simply materialize. They are put in place by human beings and are placed where they are for a reason.

---

[63] Ann. 2000-84, 2000-2 C.B. 385 ("Announcement").

[64] Livingston at 426.

To this observer's credit, it was also stated that the IRS "should look only to what the charity intends when it affirmatively establishes a connection, as demonstrated by the context created for the link."[65] While this observation is somewhat overstated also, it is much closer to what should be the standard. Intent clearly is far more important than the mere fact of the existence of a link. Thus, for example, if a charitable organization controls another entity, there is a link between the two organizations, and there is a political campaign message on the Web site of the other entity, the charitable organization may have some difficulty arguing that it is not engaged in political campaign activity because it did not intend to be associated with the message.[66]

This observer advanced another argument, this one based on the thought that links "function entirely at the user's discretion."[67] The example is given of an individual reading educational material on the Web site of a charitable organization, who thereafter uses a link in that material to move to educational material on a Web site created by a noncharitable entity and then links to a third site that contains a political campaign message. The thought presumably is that the charitable organization created the first link but not the second, so that the political message should not be attributed to it. The observation was that the charitable organization "did not connect that series of events even though it invited the reader to take the first step."[68] To the extent that that is all the argument connotes, the conclusion is correct. But there is danger in assigning too much neutrality in links; the argument can border on disingenuity. If, in this example, the charity knew that the second link would be created, once it initiated the first link, the outcome would be different. In these circumstances, it will not do to blandly assert that the political message should not be attributable to the charity because the user exercised "discretion" in getting to it. If the charity builds it, the charity has responsibility when they come. Again, the matter boils down to intent, not some inherent characteristic of a hyperlink or user discretion.

---

[65] *Id.*

[66] See Chapter 6.

[67] Livingston at 426.

[68] *Id.*

Another factor to be taken into account is *identity of interests*. In determining whether the content of an organization's Web site should be attributed to a tax-exempt organization because of a hyperlink connecting the two entities, the IRS should explore whether there is an identity of interest between them. In a private letter ruling discussed in the context of the political activities rules,[69] the IRS emphasized that certain political action committees were sponsored by unions, which, on labor issues, may have political interests differing from those of a related charity. This fact was relied on in the IRS's conclusion that there was no identity of interest between the charity and the political action committees, so that the charity's tax-exempt status was not endangered.

As to the law on identity of interests, the IRS relied on a Supreme Court decision, holding that partnerships formed to develop apartment complexes were the owners of the complexes for federal tax purposes, even though each partnership caused a corporation to hold legal title to the property for the purpose of securing financing, inasmuch as the relationship between the parties was that of agent and principal, with the partnerships as the principals.[70]

Thus, if there is no identity of interest between two organizations with linked sites, that fact should go a long way—perhaps give rise to a presumption—in showing that the content of the Web site of an organization is not to be attributable to another organization. (At the same time, just because there is an identity of interest, that should not mean that attribution of views because of a link is automatic.)

As to law development, one outcome might be that a link alone is the ground for attributing a statement posted by an organization to another organization that is linked. Automatic attribution of this nature is awesome to contemplate. (One commentator found the prospect "breathtaking."[71]) Surely this is not where the law is taking us. That is, as long as the link itself is all that is involved in the analysis, the answer to this question must be no. This is because a link from one organization to another does

---

[69] See § 6.5(b)(ii).

[70] *Commissioner v. Bollinger*, 485 U.S. 340 (1988).

[71] Livingston at 426.

not—or at least should not—generally, by itself, cause any activity of the linked organization to be attributed to the linking organization.

Another factor in this regard is the content of the linked message. In many instances, a link will be in advancement of a program, as charitable, educational, and like organizations link to similar organizations. Matters will become more complex, however, when nonprofit organizations with differing tax-exempt statuses link. For example, a trade association is not likely to endanger its tax-exempt status by linking to its related foundation—but the foundation may have an exemption problem if it is perceived as linking to the association, because of message content (such as lobbying) on the association's Web site. Not surprisingly, this aspect of linkages will be even more problematic when a tax-exempt organization maintains a link with a for-profit company. The federal tax law issues here are manifold: They principally involve the unrelated business rules,[72] the private inurement doctrine,[73] the private benefit doctrine,[74] and the intermediate sanctions rules.[75]

Some clues as to the emerging law on these points are in the tax regulations, pertaining to the tax treatment of corporate sponsorships, issued by the IRS in early 2002.[76] In that body of law, the sponsorship revenue is not taxable as unrelated business income as long as the recipient tax-exempt organization merely *acknowledges* the support, by referencing only the corporation's name, logo, product lines, and similar items. Services in the nature of *advertising* may cause the sponsorship payments to be taxable. The question thus arises in this context as to whether the exempt organization receiving the payment goes beyond the bounds of gift acknowledgment by providing a link to the Web site of the sponsor, thereby raising the prospects of taxation of the payment.

By means of two examples in these regulations, the IRS has taken the position that the mere presence of a link by a tax-exempt organization to the site of a corporate sponsor does not defeat characterization of the

---

[72] See Chapter 2.

[73] See § 7.4.

[74] See § 7.5.

[75] See § 7.6.

[76] See § 2.2(b).

payment as a nontaxable sponsorship. In one of these examples, a music shop is a sponsor of a concert series presented by an exempt organization that has as its function the operation of a symphony orchestra. Although the exempt organization posts the shop's Internet address on its site and the address links the exempt organization's Web site to the shop's site, the organization does not promote the shop or advertise its merchandise. This payment, in its entirety is a qualified sponsorship payment, which means that it is not taxable as unrelated business income.[77]

In the other example, however, a health-based charity has a link to its corporate sponsor, which is a pharmaceutical company that funds an educational initiative of the charity. The company manufactures a drug that is used in treating the medical condition that is the focus of the charity's programs. On the company's Web site, there is a statement that the charity "endorses the use of our drug" and "suggests that you ask your doctor for a prescription if you have this medical condition." The charity reviewed the endorsement (which is advertising) before it was posted and gave the company permission for the endorsement to appear. This payment may be taxable as unrelated business income.[78]

These examples show how a message on another entity's Web site can be attributed to a tax-exempt organization for tax purposes. The analysis clearly took into account not only the content of the message but also the intent of the parties in posting it. Had the exempt organization posted the communication on its site, it would have been advertising there. Posting it on the sponsor's site, coupled with the link, led to the same result. Thus, nonprofit organizations seem to be headed toward the vagaries of another facts-and-circumstances test, where factors such as intent (both that of the organizations and users), the content of the message, which organization created and/or initiated the link, why it was created, who clicked on it, and why will be in play.

Lack of attribution of this type, however, does not mean that a link does not have inherent value or benefit. Should a link be regarded as an inanimate thing, passively reposing on a Web page, of no utility until an individual clicks on it? "Many argue," wrote the IRS as part of a discussion of

---

[77] Income Tax Regulations ("Reg.") § 1.513-4(f), Example 11.

[78] *Id.*, Example 12.

links and the exclusion from taxation for certain corporate sponsorships, where the exempt organization's Web site is linked to the sponsor's site, "that the payment should retain its character as a mere acknowledgment since the website visitor must take an affirmative action to reach the donor's website." The IRS seems to be of the view that a link retains the "passive character" associated with corporate sponsorship while a moving banner is "more likely to be considered" advertising.

This is a generous position to be sure, dictated in large part by the widespread nature of the practice and the fact that the IRS would be awash in controversy should the presence of a link be decreed to destroy the tax shield otherwise accorded a corporate sponsorship. At the same time, the provision of a link can be a valuable service or benefit. It certainly goes beyond the mere utilization of a corporation's name or logo. Moreover, casting a link as passive because reaching the supporter's Web site requires something as mighty as an affirmative action—that is, the strenuous activity of a click with a mouse—borders on the ludicrous.

As with the matter of costs associated with Internet operations, how this aspect of the law and Internet communications is going to be resolved is unknown at this point. Thus, also, the matter nags and permeates all aspects of the subject, as is reflected in subsequent chapters.

(c) Web Site Record Keeping

In the Announcement, the IRS observed that, "[u]nlike other publications of an exempt organization, a website may be modified on a daily basis." The IRS then posed this remarkable question: "To what extent and by what means should an exempt organization maintain the information from prior versions of the organization's website?"

It would be impractical for a tax-exempt organization to be required to maintain the information posted on every prior version of its Web site, whether in search of unrelated business activity, lobbying, political campaign activity, and the like. Such a requirement alone could be a deterrent to Web-based activities to begin with. One commentator asserted that this archive retention mandate would be "incredibly burdensome."[79]

---

[79] Livingston at 436. See *supra* note 11.

As with all other aspects of Internet use by nonprofit organizations, the federal tax law does not directly address the point. Yet the IRS probably has the discretion to impose the requirement if it wished. Every person liable for a tax must "keep such records, render such statements, make such returns, and comply with such rules and regulations as the Secretary [IRS] may from time to time prescribe." Moreover, "[w]henever in the judgment of the Secretary it is necessary, he may require any person, by notice served upon such person or by regulations, to make such returns, render such statements, or keep such records, as the Secretary deems sufficient to show whether or not such person is liable for tax. . . ."[80]

While it may seem that the law does not get much broader than that, it does.[81] The tax regulations provide that a person subject to tax or required to file a "return of information with respect to income" must keep "such permanent books of account or records, including inventories, as are sufficient to establish the amount of gross income, deductions, credits, or other matters required to be shown by such person in any return of such tax or information."[82] Indeed, in addition to such *permanent* books and records, tax-exempt organizations must "keep such permanent books of account or records, including inventories, as are sufficient to show specifically the items of gross income, receipts and disbursements."[83] Moreover, exempt organizations "shall also keep such books and records as are required to substantiate the information required" to prepare and file annual information returns.[84]

Thus, unless restrained by a court as inflicting an unreasonable requirement, the IRS could dictate these Internet archives. It is to be hoped, however, that such an outcome does not transpire.

---

[80] IRC § 6001.

[81] There are taxes in these contexts. The unrelated business rules (Chapter 2) entail taxes (IRC § 511), as do the lobbying rules (Chapter 5) (IRC §§ 4911, 4912), the political activities rules (Chapter 6) (IRC § 4955), the intermediate sanctions rules (§ 7.6) (IRC § 4958), and the private foundations rules (§ 7.7) (IRC chapter 42).

[82] Reg. § 1.6001-1(a).

[83] Reg. § 1.6001-1(c).

[84] *Id.* Also Reg. §§ 1.6033-2, 3.

§ 1.9 CONTEMPORARY STATE
OF THE "LAW"

Another aspect of use of the Internet by nonprofit organizations and the law applicable to them that is amply pervasive throughout the book is that there is little real *law* on the points. For whatever reasons, the IRS has not come close to keeping pace with the explosive use of the Internet by nonprofit organizations; (with the exception of the two examples in the corporate sponsorship regulations) there is no regulation, ruling, notice, announcement, or other IRS writ providing any substantive guidance in the area. The same is true regarding other federal and state government agencies as well as the courts. This state of affairs obviously will change radically; it is merely a matter of when.

The IRS has not been wholly silent on these matters, however. It has addressed the subject of Internet use by tax-exempt organizations and the tax law on five occasions:

1. In 2000 the IRS issued its dramatic Announcement in which it requested comments on a series of questions it posed concerning Internet communications by tax-exempt organizations.

2. In the preamble accompanying the proposed regulations on the taxation of corporate sponsorships,[85] which also appeared in 2000, the IRS requested comments on such sponsorships in the Internet context.[86]

3. In its tax-exempt organizations continuing professional education technical instruction program textbook for the government's fiscal year 2002, issued in the fall of 1999, the IRS included an article titled "Tax-Exempt Organizations and Worldwide Web Fundraising and Advertising on the Internet."[87]

4. In its tax-exempt organizations continuing professional education technical instruction program textbook for the government's fiscal year 1999, issued in the fall of 1998, the IRS included an article

---

[85] See § 2.2(b).

[86] 65 Fed. Reg. (No. 41) 11013, 11015 (March 1, 2000).

[87] This article is referenced throughout as "IRS FY 2000 CPE Text on Exempt Organizations and Internet Use."

titled "Internet Service Providers Exemption Issues Under IRC 501(c)(3) and 501(c)(12)."[88]

5. On April 24, 2002, the IRS issued, in final form, the regulations to accompany the corporate sponsorship rules, which includes the two examples referred to above.

Of these issuances, only the last one is a formal statement of law; nonetheless, together they provide some helpful clues and hints, which will be referenced and explored in subsequent chapters. The IRS basically believes that existing—or "traditional"—law principles can be used to divine the law as to nonprofit organizations' use of the Internet.

This viewpoint basically is accurate; that is largely how the law generally evolves. The coming months and years will be bringing much extrapolation from existing law concerning off-line activities of tax-exempt organizations for the purpose of creating law in the Internet setting. This process is already underway, by the IRS and commentators.

Thus, in the first private letter ruling in this area, the IRS pondered the question as to whether a nonprofit organization that functioned as an Internet service provider, serving the general public, could qualify as a tax-exempt organization on the grounds that it was advancing charitable and educational purposes. The answer to this question was, obviously, no; that is a commercial, non-exempt undertaking—and the IRS so ruled.[89] To get there, however, the IRS analogized these activities to those of a nonprofit lawyer referral service, which was ruled to be a non-exempt activity.[90]

One of the momentous issues of the day involving nonprofit organizations' use of the Internet is whether links will cause the speech and activities of others to be attributed to the linking organization.[91] In the area of political activities, for example, the IRS has asked, in the Announcement, whether a link on a charitable organization's Web site to another organization that engages in political campaign activity results in automatic

---

[88] This article is referenced throughout as "IRS FY 1999 CPE Text on Internet Service Providers."

[89] IRS Technical Advice Memorandum ("Tech. Adv. Mem.") 200203069. See § 7.9.

[90] Rev. Rul. 80-287, 1980-2 C.B. 185.

[91] E.g., see *supra* § 8(b).

political intervention by the charitable organization.[92] The answer to this and comparable questions, presumably (or at least hopefully), is no. Support for that answer can be found in a private letter ruling, where the IRS concluded (in a bit of a stretch) that a charitable organization can administer a payroll deduction plan pursuant to a collective bargaining agreement to collect and remit its employees' voluntary contributions earmarked for political action committees established by the employees' unions.[93] The IRS placed great reliance on the concept that there was no "identity of interests" between the charitable organization and the political action committee. This support is also found in the above-noted examples in the corporate sponsorship regulations. It is to be anticipated that the IRS and/or the courts will extrapolate from that principle in discerning the legal import of the hyperlinks of nonprofit organizations.

As has been noted, however, "[s]ome of these [traditional] rules are likely to transition easily into cyberspace," while the "application of other rules may be cumbersome and inappropriate to cyberspace activities."[94]

This means, however, that lawyers today must, when advising nonprofit organizations in this area, extrapolate from existing law rationales and principles. It is not the preferred state for lawyers to be in, although admittedly it provides them with stimulation of the intellect.

The IRS was quite salient when it observed, in 1999, that the "use of the Internet to accomplish a particular task does not change the way the tax laws apply to that task." This means that "[a]dvertising is still advertising and fundraising is still fundraising."[95]

This indisputable principle serves as a lodestar for purposes of the analyses contained in the following chapters.

---

[92] See § 6.5(b)(ii).

[93] IRS Private Letter Ruling ("Priv. Ltr. Rul.") 200151060.

[94] Reaves and Bennett, "UBIT.COM? Can the Old Laws Apply in the New Cyber Frontier," 27 *Exempt Org. Tax Rev.* (No. 2) 251 (Feb. 2000) ("Reaves and Bennett").

[95] IRS FY 2000 CPE Text on Exempt Organizations and Internet Use, at 64. On that occasion, however, the IRS also noted that the "nature of the Internet does change the way in which these tasks are accomplished." (*id.*)

CHAPTER 2

Business Activities

One of the most significant components of the law of tax-exempt organizations is the body of law that defines, and taxes the net income from, exempt organizations' unrelated trade or business activities. This body of law is being significantly enhanced and increased because of business activity by tax-exempt organizations by means of the Internet.

Tax-exempt organizations are permitted to engage in some activities that are not related to their exempt purposes. This type of undertaking is termed an *unrelated business.* Nearly all of what exempt organizations otherwise do is considered *related business* activity. Tax-exempt organizations are engaging in both related and unrelated business activities by means of the Internet—and this practice is expanding rapidly.[1]

The law as to the conduct of unrelated business does not change or is not applied differently simply because the business is undertaken by means of the Internet. The IRS observed, in 1999, that the "use of the Internet to accomplish a particular task does not change the way the tax laws apply to that task." This means that "[a]dvertising is still advertising and fundraising is still fundraising."[2] The IRS might have also written that "unrelated business activity is still unrelated business activity." Nonetheless, the operation of unrelated business activities over the Internet is raising several federal tax law issues.

---

[1] See § 1.6.

[2] IRS FY 2000 CPE Text on Exempt Organizations and Internet Use, at 64. On that occasion, the IRS also noted that the "nature of the Internet does change the way in which these tasks are accomplished" (*id.*)

The unrelated business rules contain many modifications of and exceptions to this body of law. These modifications and exceptions contribute to the complexity (and enrichment) of these rules. Not surprisingly, the application of these modifications and exceptions with respect to business efforts on the Internet is also raising a number of federal tax law issues.

§ 2.1 INTRODUCTION

(a) Scope of Law

Taxation of the unrelated business income of tax-exempt organizations, a feature of the federal tax law introduced in 1950, is predicated on the concept that this approach is a more effective and workable sanction for enforcement of this aspect of the law of exempt organizations than denial or revocation of tax-exempt status because of unrelated business activity. This aspect of the law rests on two simple concepts: Activities that are unrelated to an exempt organization's purposes are to be segregated from related business activities and the net income from unrelated business activities is taxed essentially in the same manner as the net income earned by for-profit organizations. That is, the unrelated business income tax applies only to income generated by active business activities that are unrelated to an exempt organization's tax-exempt purposes.

The primary objective of the unrelated business rules is to eliminate a source of unfair competition with for-profit businesses, by placing the unrelated business activities of tax-exempt organizations on the same tax basis as the nonexempt business endeavors with which they compete.[3] The House Ways and Means Committee report that accompanied the Revenue Act of 1950 observed that the "problem at which the tax on unrelated business income is directed here is primarily that of unfair competition," in that tax-exempt organizations can "use their profits tax-free to expand operations, while their competitors can expand only with the

---

[3] Reg. § 1.513-1(b).

profits remaining after taxes."[4] The Senate Finance Committee reaffirmed this position nearly three decades later when it noted that one "major purpose" of the unrelated business rules "is to make certain that an exempt organization does not commercially exploit its exempt status for the purpose of unfairly competing with taxpaying organizations."[5]

This rationale for the unrelated business rules has begun to be subjected to revisionist theories, namely, the view that other objectives are equally important. Thus, one federal appellate court observed that, "although Congress enacted the . . . [unrelated business income rules] to eliminate a perceived form of unfair competition, that aim existed as a corollary to the larger goals of producing revenue and achieving equity in the tax system." [6] Another appellate court, electing more reticence, stated that "while the equalization of competition between taxable and tax-exempt entities was a major goal of the unrelated business income tax, it was by no means the statute's sole objective."[7] At a minimum, however, elimination of this type of competition clearly was Congress's principal aim; the tax regulations proclaim that it was the Federal legislature's "primary objective."[8]

Generally, unrelated business activities must be confined to something less than a substantial portion of a tax-exempt organization's overall activities.[9] This is a manifestation of the *primary purpose test*.[10] It is common to measure substantiality and insubstantiality in terms of percentages of

---

[4] H. Rep. No. 2319, 81st Cong., 2d Sess. 36–37 (1950). Also S. Rep. No. 2375, 81st Cong., 2d Sess. 28–29 (1950).

[5] S. Rep. No. 94-938, 94th Cong., 2d Sess. 601 (1976).

[6] *Louisiana Credit Union League* v. *United States*, 693 F.2d 525, 540 (5th Cir. 1982).

[7] *American Medical Association* v. *United States*, 887 F.2d 760, 772 (7th Cir. 1989).

[8] Reg. § 1.513-1(b).

[9] Rev. Rul. 66-221, 1966-2 C.B. 220.

[10] To be tax-exempt, the *primary* purpose of an organization must be furtherance of appropriate tax-exempt purposes; sometimes the word *substantial* is used. See § 1.8(a), text accompanied by note 55.

expenditures or time.[11] Thus, generally, if a substantial portion of an exempt organization's income is from unrelated sources, the organization cannot qualify for tax exemption. For example, a court barred an organization from achieving tax-exempt status where the organization received about one-third of its revenue from an unrelated business.[12]

Yet there are countervailing principles. The IRS also applies the *commensurate test*, which compares the extent of an organization's resources to its program efforts. Pursuant to this test, an organization may derive a substantial portion of its revenue in the form of unrelated business income yet be tax-exempt because it also expends a significant amount of its time on exempt functions. Thus, in one instance, although a charitable organization derived 98 percent of its income from an unrelated business, it remained tax-exempt because 41 percent of the organization's activities, as measured in terms of expenditure of time, constituted exempt programs.[13] Utilizing another approach, the IRS permitted an organization to remain exempt, even though two-thirds of its operations were unrelated businesses, inasmuch as the purpose for the conduct of these businesses was achievement of charitable purposes.[14] On that occasion, the IRS said that one way in which a business may be in furtherance of exempt purposes "is to raise money for the exempt purposes of the organization, notwithstanding that the actual trade or business activity may be taxable." The

---

[11] One court wrote, however, that "[w]hether an activity is substantial is a facts-and-circumstances inquiry not always dependent upon time or expenditure percentages" (*The Nationalist Movement v. Commissioner*, 102 T.C. 558, 589 (1994), *aff'd*, 37 F.3d 216 (5th Cir. 1994). As the IRS framed the matter, there is no "quantitative limitation" on the amount of unrelated business in which a tax-exempt organization may engage (Tech. Adv. Mem. 200021056). These concepts are taking on great importance in the Internet context (see § 1.7(a)).

[12] *Orange County Agricultural Society, Inc. v. Commissioner*, 893 F.2d 647 (2d Cir. 1990).

[13] Tech. Adv. Mem. 9711003.

[14] Tech. Adv. Mem. 200021056.

agency reiterated that the "proper focus is upon the purpose of [the organization's] activities and not upon the taxability of its activities."[15]

An organization may qualify as a tax-exempt entity, although it operates a trade or business as a substantial part of its activities, where the operation of the business is in furtherance of the organization's exempt purposes. In determining the nature of a primary purpose, all of the circumstances must be considered, including the size and extent of the trade or business and of the activities that are in furtherance of one or more exempt purposes.[16] For example, an organization that purchased and sold at retail products manufactured by blind individuals was held by a court to qualify as an exempt charitable organization because its activities resulted in employment for the blind, notwithstanding its receipt of net profits and its distribution of some of these profits to qualified workers.[17]

The portion of a tax-exempt organization's gross income that is subject to the tax on unrelated business income[18] is generally includible in the computation of unrelated business taxable income when three factors are present: the income is from a *trade or business*,[19] the business is *regularly carried on* by the exempt organization,[20] and the conduct of the business is not *substantially related* to the performance by the organization of its exempt functions.[21] In addition, there are certain types of income and certain types of activities that are exempt from unrelated business income taxation.[22]

---

[15] The fact that a business generates net income for exempt activities is alone insufficient to cause the business to be regarded as a related one (see the text accompanied by *infra* note 109).

[16] Reg. § 1.501(c)(3)-1(e)(1).

[17] *Industrial Aid for the Blind* v. *Commissioner*, 73 T.C. 96 (1979).

[18] See *infra* § 3(d).

[19] See *infra* § (b).

[20] See *infra* § (c).

[21] See *infra* § (d). In general, Reg. § 1.513-1(a).

[22] See *infra* § 3.

In recent years, considerable attention has been accorded the phenomenon of tax-exempt organizations that are considered to be operating in a commercial manner or unfairly competing with for-profit organizations.[23] Some of the activities that come under review as being ostensibly commercial or competitive are those that are *related*, rather than *unrelated*, businesses.[24]

(b) Definition of *Business*

As noted, some or all of the gross income of a tax-exempt organization may be includible in the computation of unrelated business income where it is income from a *trade or business*.

(i) General Principles. The statutory definition of the term *business*, used for unrelated business purposes, states that it includes "any activity which is carried on for the production of income from the sale of goods or the performance of services."[25] This definition is sweeping and encompasses nearly every activity that a tax-exempt organization may undertake. Indeed, the federal tax law views an exempt organization as a cluster of businesses, with each discrete activity susceptible to evaluation independently from the others.[26]

The definition of the term *business*, however, also embraces an activity that otherwise possesses the characteristics of a business as that term is defined by the federal income tax law in the business expense deduction setting.[27] This definition, then, is even more expansive than the statutory

---

[23] E.g., *At Cost Services, Inc.* v. *Commissioner*, 80 T.C.M. 573 (2000).

[24] E.g., Priv. Ltr. Rul. 200051049 (operation of fitness centers, that compete with for-profit health clubs, by exempt hospitals and universities).

[25] IRC § 513(c).

[26] See the discussion of the *fragmentation rule* (*infra* § (v)).

[27] Reg. § 1.513-1(b). The business expense deduction is the subject of IRC § 162.

one, being informed by the considerable body of law as to the meaning of the word *business* that has accreted in the federal tax law generally.

There is a third element to consider in this regard, stemming from the view that, to be a business, an income-producing activity of a tax-exempt organization must have the general characteristics of a trade or business. Some courts of appeals have recognized that an exempt organization must carry out extensive business activities over a substantial period of time to be considered engaged in a trade or business.[28] In one case, a court held that the proceeds derived by an exempt organization from gambling operations were not taxable as unrelated business income, inasmuch as the organization's functions in this regard were considered insufficiently "extensive" to warrant treatment as a business.[29] This aspect of the analysis, however, is close to a separate test altogether, which is whether the business activities are regularly carried on.[30]

Where an activity carried on for profit constitutes an unrelated business, no part of the business may be excluded from classification as a business merely because it does not result in profit.[31]

Traditionally, the government has almost always prevailed on the argument that an activity of a tax-exempt organization constitutes a trade or business. In recent years, however, courts have been more willing to conclude that an exempt organization's financial undertaking does not rise to the level of a business.[32]

(ii) Requirement of Profit Motive. The most important element in the federal tax law as to whether an activity is a trade or business, for purposes of the business expense deduction, is the presence of a *profit motive*.

---

[28] E.g., *Professional Insurance Agents* v. *Commissioner,* 726 F.2d 1097 (6th Cir. 1984).

[29] *Vigilant Hose Company of Emmitsburg* v. *United States,* 2001-2 U.S.T.C. ¶ 50,458 (D. Md. 2001).

[30] See *infra* § (c).

[31] IRC § 513(c).

[32] E.g., *Laborer's International Union of North America* v. *Commissioner,* 82 T.C.M. 158 (2001).

The courts have exported the profit objective standard into this aspect of the law of tax-exempt organizations.

The Supreme Court held that the principal test in this regard is that the "taxpayer's primary purpose for engaging in the activity must be for income or profit."[33] In the exempt organizations context, the Court said that the inquiry should be whether the activity "was entered into with the dominant hope and intent of realizing a profit."[34] An appellate court stated that the "existence of a genuine profit motive is the most important criterion for . . . a trade or business."[35]

Various federal courts of appeal have applied the profit motive element to ascertain whether an activity of a tax-exempt organization is a business for purposes of the unrelated business rules. For example, one appellate court employed an *objective profit motivation test* to ascertain whether an activity is a business. This court wrote that "there is no better objective measure of an organization's motive for conducting an activity than the ends it achieves."[36] Subsequently, this court held that an activity of an exempt organization was a business because it "received considerable financial benefits" from performance of the activity, which was found to be "persuasive evidence" of a business endeavor.[37] On this latter occasion, the court defined as a business the situation where a "non-profit entity performs comprehensive and essential business services in return for a fixed fee."[38] Thereafter, this appellate court wrote simply that, for an activity of a

---

[33] *Commissioner* v. *Groetzinger*, 480 U.S. 23, 35 (1987).

[34] *United States* v. *American Bar Endowment*, 477 U.S. 105, 110, note 1 (1986).

[35] *Professional Insurance Agents* v. *Commissioner, supra* note 28, at 1102.

[36] *Carolinas Farm & Power Equipment Dealers Association, Inc.* v. *United States*, 699 F.2d 167, 170 (4th Cir. 1983).

[37] *Steamship Trade Association of Baltimore, Inc.* v. *Commissioner*, 757 F.2d 1494, 1497 (4th Cir. 1985).

[38] *Id.* This latter statement is, however, a gross mischaracterization of the law. There is no requirement, for an activity to be a business, that the endeavor be *comprehensive*, and there certainly is no requirement that the activity be *essential*. Also, the mode of payment is not relevant; whether the payment is by fixed fee, commission, or some other standard has no bearing on whether the income-producing activity is a business.

tax-exempt organization to be a business, it must be conducted with a "profit objective."[39] Other courts of appeals have adopted this profit motive test.[40]

A court concluded, in the case of a tax-exempt labor union that collects per capita taxes from unions affiliated with it, that, other than the services the union provides its members and affiliated unions in furtherance of its exempt purposes, the union "provides no goods or services for a profit and therefore cannot be in a trade or business."[41]

The IRS applies the profit motive test. In one example, a tax-exempt healthcare provider sold a building to another provider organization; it was used to operate a skilled nursing and personal care home. The selling entity provided food service to the patients for about seven months, at a net loss; the IRS characterized the food service operation as merely an "accommodation" to the purchasing entity.[42] Finding the activity to not be conducted in a manner characteristic of a commercial enterprise—that is, an operation motivated by profit—the IRS looked to these factors: There was no evidence, such as a business plan, that a food service business was being started; the organization did not take any steps to expand the food service to other unrelated organizations; the organization did not actively solicit additional clientele for a meal (or food catering) business; the organization did not take any steps to increase the per-meal charge, which was substantially below cost; and the service relationship between the organizations was not evidenced by a contract.

A tax-exempt organization may have more than one activity that it considers a business. An activity of this nature may generate net income or it may generate a net loss. When calculating net taxable unrelated business income, an exempt organization may offset the loss from one business against the gain from another business in determining taxable income. If

---

[39] *West Virginia State Medical Association* v. *Commissioner*, 882 F.2d 123, 125 (4th Cir. 1989), *cert. den.*, 493 U.S. 1044 (1990).

[40] E.g., *Louisiana Credit Union League* v. *United States, supra* note 6; *American Academy of Family Physicians* v. *United States*, 91 F.3d 1155 (8th Cir. 1996).

[41] *Laborer's International Union of North America* v. *Commissioner, supra* note 32, at 160.

[42] Tech. Adv. Mem. 9719002.

the loss activity, however, consistently (year in and year out) produces losses, the IRS may take the position that the activity is not a business, because of absence of a profit motive, and disallow the loss deduction. Occasional losses, however, should not lead to this result.

(iii) Factor of Competition. The presence or absence of competition—fair or unfair—is not among the criteria, in statute or regulation, applied in assessing whether an activity of a tax-exempt organization is an unrelated business. This is the case notwithstanding the fact that concern about competition between exempt and for-profit organizations is the principal reason for and underpinning of the unrelated business rules.[43]

Thus, an activity of a tax-exempt organization may be wholly noncompetitive with an activity of a for-profit organization and nonetheless be considered an unrelated business. For example, in an opinion finding that the operation of a bingo game by an exempt organization was an unrelated business, a court wrote that the "tax on unrelated business income is not limited to income earned by a trade or business that operates in competition with taxpaying entities."[44]

Yet in a case concerning a tax-exempt labor union that collected per capita taxes from unions affiliated with it, a court concluded that the imposition of these taxes, which enabled the union to perform its exempt functions, "simply is not conducting a trade or business," in part because the union was not providing any services in competition with taxable entities.[45]

(iv) Commerciality. Where there is competition, a court may conclude that the activity of a tax-exempt organization is being conducted in a commercial manner and thus is an unrelated business. Thus, the operation of a television station by an exempt university was held to be an unrelated

---

[43] See the text accompanied by *supra* notes 2-4.

[44] *Clarence LaBelle Post No. 217 v. United States*, 580 F.2d 270, 272 (8th Cir. 1978).

[45] *Laborer's International Union of North America v. Commissioner, supra* note 32, at 160.

business because it was operated in a commercial manner; the station was an affiliate of a national television broadcasting company.[46]

(v) Fragmentation Rule. The IRS has the authority to tax net income from an activity, as unrelated business taxable income, where the activity is an integral part of a cluster of activities that is in furtherance of a tax-exempt purpose. To ferret out unrelated business, the IRS regards a tax-exempt organization as a bundle of activities and evaluates each of the activities in isolation to determine if one or more of them constitutes a trade or business. This assessment process is known as *fragmentation*.

The *fragmentation rule* states that an "activity does not lose identity as trade or business merely because it is carried on within a larger aggregate of similar activities or within a larger complex of other endeavors which may, or may not, be related to the exempt purposes of the organization."[47] Thus, as noted, the IRS is empowered to fragment the operations of a tax-exempt organization, operated as an integrated whole, into its component parts in search of one or more unrelated businesses.

The fragmentation rule was fashioned to tax the net income derived by a tax-exempt organization from the soliciting, selling, and publishing of commercial advertising, even where the advertising is published in a publi-cation of an exempt organization that contains editorial matter related to the exempt purposes of the organization.[48] That is, the advertising func-tions constitute an unrelated business even though the overall set of pub-lishing activities amounts to one or more related businesses; the advertising is an integral part of the larger publication activity.[49]

There are no stated limits as to the level of detail the IRS may pursue in application of the fragmentation rule. A university may find the agency's agents probing its campus bookstore operations, evaluating goods for sale on nearly an item-by-item basis. An association may watch as the

---

[46] *Iowa State University of Science and Technology* v. *United States*, 500 F.2d 508 (Ct. Cl. 1974).

[47] IRC § 513(c); Reg. § 1.513-1(b).

[48] IRC § 513(c).

[49] Reg. § 1.512(a)-1(f).

IRS slices up its various services to members into numerous businesses. A charitable organization may be surprised to see the IRS carve its fundraising program into a range of business activities.

A tax-exempt blood bank that sold blood plasma to commercial laboratories was found by the IRS to not be engaging in unrelated business when it sold by-product plasma and salvage plasma, because these plasmas were produced in the conduct of related businesses, but was ruled to be engaged in unrelated business when it sold plasmapheresed plasma and plasma it purchased from other blood banks.[50] An exempt organization, the primary purpose of which was to retain and stimulate commerce in the downtown area of a city where parking facilities were inadequate, was ruled to be engaged in related businesses when it operated a fringe parking lot and shuttle service to the downtown shops and an unrelated business by conducting a park-and-shop plan.[51]

The use of a university's golf course by its students and employees was ruled to not be unrelated businesses, while use of the course by alumni of the university and major donors to it were found to be unrelated businesses.[52] The fragmentation rule was applied to differentiate between related and unrelated travel tours conducted by an educational and religious organization.[53] A charitable organization was held to be a dealer in certain parcels of real property and thus engaged in unrelated business with respect to those properties, even though the principal impetus for the acquisition and sale of real property by the organization was achievement of exempt purposes.[54] A tax-exempt monastery, the members of which made and sold caskets, was ruled to be engaged in a related business as long as the caskets were used in funeral services conducted by churches that are part of the religious denomination supporting the monastery but was held to be conducting an unrelated business where the caskets were used in services conducted by other churches.[55] An organization established to benefit deserving women, in part

---

[50] Rev. Rul. 78-145, 1978-1 C.B. 169.

[51] Rev. Rul. 79-31, 1979-1 C.B. 206.

[52] Tech. Adv. Mem. 9645004.

[53] Tech. Adv. Mem. 9702004.

[54] Priv. Ltr. Rul. 200119061.

[55] Priv. Ltr. Rul. 200033049.

by enabling them to sell foodstuffs and handicrafts, was held to operate a consignment shop as a related business but a retail gift shop and a small restaurant were found to be unrelated businesses.[56]

(vi) Nonbusiness Activities. Not every activity of a tax-exempt organization that generates a financial return is a trade or business for purposes of the unrelated business rules. As the Supreme Court observed, the "narrow category of trade or business" is a "concept which falls far short of reaching every income or profit making activity."[57] Specifically in the exempt organizations context, an appellate court wrote that "there are instances where some activities by some exempt organizations to earn income in a noncommercial manner will not amount to the conduct of a trade or business."[58]

The most obvious of the types of nonbusiness activities is the management by a tax-exempt organization of its own investment properties. Under the general rules, as stated in the business expense deduction rules, defining *business activity*, the management of an investment portfolio composed wholly of the manager's own securities does not constitute the carrying on of a trade or business. The Supreme Court held that the mere derivation of income from securities and keeping of records is not the operation of a business.[59] On that occasion, the Court sustained the government's position that "mere personal investment activities never constitute carrying on a trade or business."[60] Subsequently, the Court stated that "investing is not a trade or business."[61] Likewise, a court of appeals observed that the "mere management of investments . . . is insufficient to constitute the carrying on of a trade or business."[62]

---

[56] Tech. Adv. Mem. 200021056.

[57] *Whipple v. Commissioner*, 373 U.S. 193, 197, 201 (1963).

[58] *Steamship Trade Association of Baltimore, Inc. v. Commissioner, supra* note 37, at 1497.

[59] *Higgins v. Commissioner*, 312 U.S. 212 (1941).

[60] *Id.* at 215.

[61] *Whipple v. Commissioner, supra* note 57, at 202.

[62] *Continental Trading, Inc. v. Commissioner*, 265 F.2d 40, 43 (9th Cir. 1959), *cert. den.*, 361 U.S. 827 (1959).

This principle of law is applicable in the tax-exempt organizations context. For example, the IRS ruled that the receipt of income by an exempt employees' trust from installment notes purchased from the employer-settlor was not income from the operation of a business, noting that the trust "merely keeps the records and receives the periodic payments of principal and interest collected for it by the employer."[63] Likewise, the agency held that a reversion of funds from a qualified plan to a charitable organization did not "possess the characteristics" required for an activity to qualify as a business.[64] For a time, there was controversy over whether the practice, engaged in by some tax-exempt organizations, of lending securities to brokerage houses for compensation was an unrelated business; the IRS ultimately arrived at the view that securities lending is a form of "ordinary or routine investment activities" and thus is not a business.[65] A court held that certain investment activities conducted by a charitable organization were not businesses.[66]

Other, similar activities do not rise to the level of a business. In one instance, an association of physicians was held to be not taxable on certain payments it received annually by reason of its sponsorship of group insurance plans that were available to its members and their employees, with the court writing that the payments "were neither brokerage fees nor other compensation for commercial services, but were the way the parties decided to acknowledge the . . . [association's] eventual claim to the excess reserves while . . . [the insurance company involved] was still holding and using the reserves."[67] In another case, an exempt dental society that sponsored a payment plan to finance dental care was held to not be taxable on refunds for income taxes and interest on amounts paid as excess reserve funds from a bank and as collections on defaulted notes.[68] A comparable position was taken by a court in concluding that an exempt organization

---

[63] Rev. Rul. 69-574, 1969-2 C.B. 130, 131.

[64] Priv. Ltr. Rul. 200131034.

[65] Rev. Rul. 78-88, 1978-1 C.B. 163. Also IRC § 512(a)(5).

[66] *The Marion Foundation v. Commissioner,* 19 T.C.M. 99 (1960).

[67] *American Academy of Family Physicians v. United States, supra* note 40, at 1159.

[68] *San Antonio District Dental Society v. United States,* 340 F. Supp. 11 (W.D. Tex. 1972).

did not engage in an unrelated business by making health insurance available to its members, in that the organization did not control the financial result of the insurance activities.[69]

As noted, activities can escape classification as businesses by not being conducted with a profit motive,[70] by not being competitive with for-profit activity,[71] by not being commercial in nature,[72] and/or by not being sufficiently extensive and not possessing the general characteristics of a trade or business.[73]

Still another illustration of a transaction involving a tax-exempt organization that is not a business undertaking is the occasional sale of an item of property. For example, the IRS held that a sale of property by an exempt entity was not under circumstances where the property was held primarily for sale to customers in the ordinary course of business.[74] This aspect of the law, however, is closely analogous to the *regularly carried on* test.[75]

(c) Definition of *Regularly Carried On*

As noted, the gross income of a tax-exempt organization may be includible in the computation of its unrelated business income where the trade or business that produced the income is *regularly carried on* by the organization.

(i) General Principles. In determining whether a trade or business from which an amount of income is derived by a tax-exempt organization is *regularly carried on*,[76] regard must be paid to the frequency and continuity

---

[69] *Carolinas Farm & Power Equipment Dealers Association, Inc.* v. *United States*, 541 F. Supp. 86 (E.D.N. Car. 1982), aff'd, supra note 36. Cf. IRC § 501(m).

[70] See *supra* § (ii).

[71] See *supra* § (iii).

[72] See *supra* § (iv).

[73] See *supra* § (iii).

[74] Priv. Ltr. Rul. 9316032. By contrast, the subdivision, development, and sale of real estate parcels by an exempt organization was held by the IRS to be a business carried on in a manner similar to the activities of for-profit residential land development companies (Tech. Adv. Mem. 200047049).

[75] See *infra* § (c).

[76] IRC § 512.

with which the activities productive of the income are conducted and the manner in which they are pursued. This requirement is applied in light of the purpose of the unrelated business income rules, which is to place exempt organization business activities on the same tax basis as the nonexempt business endeavors with which they compete.[77] Thus, specific business activities of an exempt organization will ordinarily be deemed to be regularly carried on if they manifest a frequency and continuity, and are pursued in a manner generally similar to comparable commercial activities of nonexempt organizations.[78]

As an illustration, a tax-exempt organization that annually published a yearbook was ruled by the IRS to be operating an unrelated business because it was "engaging in an extensive campaign of advertising solicitation" for the book and thus to be "conducting competitive and promotional efforts typical of commercial endeavors."[79] By contrast, an exempt organization that was formed to deliver diagnostic and medical healthcare, and that developed a series of computer programs concerning management and administrative matters, such as patient admissions and billings, payroll, purchases, inventory, and medical records, sold some or all of the programs to another exempt organization comprising three teaching hospitals affiliated with a university; the income derived by the sale was held to be from a "one-time only operation" and thus not taxable as unrelated business income.[80] Likewise, the transfer of investment assets from a public charity to its supporting organization was ruled to be exempt from unrelated business taxation under this rule.[81] As noted, infrequent sales of real estate are not businesses that are regularly carried on.[82]

(ii) Determining Regularity. Where income-producing activities are of a kind normally conducted by nonexempt commercial organizations on a year-round basis, the conduct of the activities by a tax-exempt organization over a period of only a few weeks does not constitute the regular car-

---

[77] See *supra* § (a).

[78] Reg. § 1.513-1(c)(1).

[79] Rev. Rul. 73-424, 1973-2 C.B. 190, 191.

[80] Priv. Ltr. Rul. 7905129.

[81] Priv. Ltr. Rul. 9425030.

[82] See the text accompanied by notes 74-75.

rying on of a business.[83] For example, the operation of a sandwich stand by a hospital auxiliary organization for two weeks at a state fair is not the regular conduct of a business.[84] The conduct of year-round business activities for one day a week, such as the operation of a commercial parking lot once a week, constitutes the regular carrying on of a business.[85]

If income-producing activities are of a kind normally undertaken by nonexempt commercial organizations only on a seasonal basis, the conduct of the activities by a tax-exempt organization during a significant portion of the season ordinarily constitutes the regular conduct of a business.[86] For example, the operation of a horse racing track for several weeks in a year is the regular conduct of a business where it is usual to carry on the business only during that particular season.[87] Similarly, where a distribution of greeting cards celebrating a holiday was deemed by the IRS to be an unrelated business, the agency measured regularity in terms of that holiday's season.[88]

In determining whether intermittently conducted activities are regularly carried on, the manner of conduct of the activities must, as noted, be compared with the manner in which commercial activities are normally pursued by nonexempt organizations.[89] In general, tax-exempt organization business activities that are engaged in merely discontinuously or periodically are not considered regularly carried on if they are conducted without the competitive and promotional efforts typical of commercial endeavors.[90] As an illustration, the publication of advertising in programs for sports events, or music or drama performances, is not ordinarily deemed to be the regular carrying on of a business.[91] Conversely, where the nonqualifying sales are not merely casual but are systematically and

---

[83] Reg. § 1.513-1(c)(2)(i).

[84] *Id.*

[85] S. Rep. No. 2375, *supra* note 4, at 106–107.

[86] Reg. § 1.513-1(c)(2)(i).

[87] *Id.*

[88] Priv. Ltr. Rul. 8203134.

[89] Reg. § 1.513-1(c)(1), (2)(ii).

[90] Reg. § 1.513-1(c)(2)(ii).

[91] *Id.*

consistently promoted and carried on by the organization, they meet the requirement of regularity.[92]

In determining whether a business is regularly carried on, the functions of a service provider with which a tax-exempt organization has contracted may be attributed to the exempt organization for these purposes. This is likely to be the case where the contract denominates the service provider as an agent of the exempt organization, in that the functions of an agent are deemed to be those of the principal for law analysis purposes. In such a circumstance, the activities of the service provider, undertaken for the exempt organization, are attributed to the organization for purposes of determining regularity.[93]

Noncompetition under a covenant not to compete, characterized as a "one-time agreement not to engage in certain activities," is not a taxable business inasmuch as the "activity" is not "continuous and regular."[94]

(iii) Fundraising and Similar Activities. Fundraising activities, by charitable and other tax-exempt organizations, can amount to unrelated business activities. This is particularly the case with special events, which meet the tax law definition of a *business*.[95] Inasmuch as these activities rarely are inherently exempt functions, the rules as to *regularity* are often the only basis on which the income from these activities is not taxable as unrelated business income.

Certain intermittent income-producing activities occur so infrequently that neither their recurrence nor the manner of their conduct will cause them to be regarded as businesses that are regularly carried on.[96] Thus,

---

[92] *Id.* A leasing arrangement that was "one-time, completely fortuitous" was held to constitute a business, albeit one that was not regularly carried on (*Museum of Flight Foundation v. United States*, 99-1 U.S.T.C. ¶ 50,311 (W.D. Wash. 1999)), whereas a lease of extended duration was found to entail a business that was regularly carried on (*Cooper Tire & Rubber Company Employees' Retirement Fund v. Commissioner*, 306 F.2d 20 (6th Cir. 1962)).

[93] *National Collegiate Athletic Association v. Commissioner*, 92 T.C. 456 (1989), *aff'd*, 914 F.2d 1417 (10th Cir. 1990).

[94] *Ohio Farm Bureau Federation, Inc. v. Commissioner*, 106 T.C. 222, 234 (1996).

[95] See *supra* § (b), *infra* § 2(c).

[96] Reg. § 1.513-1(c)(2)(iii).

fundraising activities lasting only a short time are not ordinarily treated as being regularly carried on if they recur only occasionally or sporadically.[97] Furthermore, activities are not regarded as regularly carried on merely because they are conducted on an annual basis.[98]

It is for this reason that many special event fundraising activities, such as dances, dinners, theater outings, auctions, sports tournaments, car washes, and bake sales, do not give rise to unrelated business income.[99] In one instance, a court concluded that a vaudeville show conducted one weekend per year was an intermittent fundraising activity and thus not regularly carried on.[100] The IRS ruled that activities such as an annual charity ball and an annual golf tournament were not taxable activities because they were not regularly carried on.[101]

(iv) Preparatory Time. An issue of considerable controversy is whether the time expended by a tax-exempt organization in preparing for a business undertaking should be taken into account in assessing the presence of business activity that is regularly carried on. The IRS asserts that preparatory time should be considered, even where the event itself occupied only a few days each year.[102] This preparatory time argument, however, has been rejected on the occasions it was considered by a court.[103] In the principal case, a federal court of appeals held that the preparatory time argument is inconsistent with the tax regulations, which are silent on the point. The court referenced the example in the regulations concerning operation of the sandwich stand at a state fair,[104] denigrating the thought

---

[97] *Id.*

[98] *Id.*

[99] E.g., *Orange County Builders Association, Inc.* v. *United States,* 65-2 U.S.T.C. ¶ 9679 (S.D. Cal. 1965).

[100] *Suffolk County Patrolmen's Benevolent Association, Inc.* v. *Commissioner,* 77 T.C. 1314 (1981).

[101] Priv. Ltr. Rul. 200128059.

[102] E.g., Tech. Adv. Mem. 9147007; Priv. Ltr. Rul. 9137002.

[103] E.g., *Suffolk County Patrolmen's Benevolent Association, Inc.* v. *Commissioner, supra* note 100.

[104] See the text accompanied by note 84.

that preparatory time should be taken into account: "The regulations do not mention the time spent in planning the activity, building the stand, or purchasing the alfalfa sprouts for the sandwiches."[105]

Nonetheless, the IRS is in disagreement with these court holdings, has issued technical advice memoranda and private letter rulings that are contrary to these cases, and continues to maintain this stance as its litigation position.[106] One of these instances concerned a tax-exempt labor organization that sponsored a concert series open to the public occupying two weekends each year, one in the spring and one in the fall. The preparation and ticket solicitation for each of the concerts usually occupied up to six months. Taking into account the preparatory time involved, the IRS concluded that the concerts were unrelated business activities that were regularly carried on.[107]

(d) Definition of *Substantially Related*

As noted, the gross income of a tax-exempt organization may be includible in the computation of unrelated business income where it is income from a trade or business that is regularly carried on and that is not *substantially related* to the exempt purposes of the organization.[108] (The fact that an exempt organization needs or uses the funds for an exempt purpose does not make the underlying activity a related business.[109]) Thus, it is necessary—indeed, the majority of the cases turn on this element—to examine the relationship between the business activity in question and the accomplishment of the exempt purposes of the organization.[110]

(i) General Principles. A trade or business is *related* to tax-exempt purposes of an organization only where the conduct of the business activity

---

[105] *National Collegiate Athletic Association* v. *Commissioner, supra* note 93, at 1423.

[106] Action on Decision No. 1991-015.

[107] Tech. Adv. Mem. 9712001. The IRS acquiesced in the *Suffolk County Patrolmen's Association* case (*supra* note 100) (Action on Decision 1984-1249); that acquiescence had no bearing in the *National Collegiate Athletic Association* case, the IRS said, inasmuch as the preparatory time in the former case was "much shorter."

[108] IRC § 513(a); Reg. § 1.513-1(a).

[109] IRC § 513(a).

[110] Reg. § 1.513-1(d)(1).

has a causal relationship to the achievement of an exempt purpose. It is *substantially related* only if the causal relationship is a substantial one.[111] Thus, for the conduct of a business from which a particular amount of gross income is derived to be substantially related to tax-exempt purposes, the production or distribution of the goods or the performance of the services from which the gross income is derived must contribute importantly to the accomplishment of these purposes.[112] Where the production or distribution of the goods or the performance of services does not contribute importantly to the accomplishment of the exempt purposes of an organization, the income from the sale of the goods or the performance of the services is not income from the conduct of related business.[113] A court wrote that resolution of the substantial relationship test requires an "examination of the relationship between the business activities which generate the particular income in question . . . and the accomplishment of the organization's exempt purposes."[114]

Certainly, gross income derived from charges for the performance of a tax-exempt function does not constitute gross income from the conduct of an unrelated business.[115] Thus, income is not taxable when it is generated by functions such as performance by students enrolled in a school for training children in the performing arts, the conduct of refresher courses to improve the trade skills of members of a union, and the presentation of a trade show for exhibiting industry products by a trade association to stimulate demand for the products.[116]

Whether activities productive of gross income contribute importantly to the accomplishment of an organization's exempt purpose depends in each case on the facts and circumstances involved.[117] A court observed that each of these instances requires a case-by-case identification of the exempt purpose involved and an analysis of how the activity contributed

---

[111] Reg. § 1.513-1(d)(2).

[112] *Id.*

[113] *Id.*

[114] *Louisiana Credit Union League* v. *United States, supra* note 6, at 534.

[115] Reg. § 1.513-1(d)(4)(i).

[116] *Id.*

[117] Reg. § 1.513-1(d)(2).

to the advancement of that purpose.[118] By reason of court opinions and IRS rulings over the years, there is a plethora of determinations as to whether particular activities are related businesses or unrelated businesses.

(ii) Size and Extent Test. In determining whether an activity contributes importantly to the accomplishment of a tax-exempt purpose, the *size and extent* of the activity must be considered in relation to the nature and extent of the exempt function that it purportedly serves.[119] Thus, where income is realized by a tax-exempt organization from an activity that is generally related to the performance of its exempt functions, but the activity is conducted on a scale that is larger than reasonably necessary for performance of the functions, the gross income attributable to the portion of the activity that is in excess of the needs associated with exempt functions constitutes gross income from the conduct of an unrelated business.[120] This type of income is not derived from the production or distribution of goods or the performance of services that contribute importantly to the accomplishment of any exempt purpose of the organization.[121]

For example, one of the activities of a trade association, which had a membership of businesses in a state, was to supply companies (members and nonmembers) with job injury histories on prospective employees. Despite the association's contention that this service contributed to the accomplishment of exempt purposes, the IRS ruled that the operation was an unrelated business, in that the activity went "well beyond" any mere development and promotion of efficient business practices.[122] The IRS adopted a similar posture in ruling that a retail grocery store operation, formed to sell food in a poverty area at below-market prices and to provide job training for unemployed residents in the area, could not qualify for tax exemption because the operation was conducted on a "much larger scale than reasonably necessary" for the training program.[123] Likewise, the

---

[118] *Hi-Plains Hospital v. United States*, 670 F.2d 528 (5th Cir. 1982).

[119] Reg. § 1.513-1(d)(3).

[120] *Id.*

[121] *Id.*

[122] Rev. Rul. 73-386, 1973-2 C.B. 191, 192.

[123] Rev. Rul. 73-127, 1973-1 C.B. 221, 222.

IRS ruled that the provision of private duty nurses to unrelated tax-exempt organization, by an exempt healthcare organization that provided temporary nurses and private duty nurses to patients of related organizations as related businesses was an activity performed on a scale "much larger" than necessary for the achievement of exempt functions.[124]

By contrast, a tax-exempt organization formed to provide a therapeutic program for emotionally disturbed adolescents was the subject of a ruling from the IRS that a retail grocery store operation, almost fully staffed by adolescents to secure their emotional rehabilitation, was not an unrelated business because it was operated on a scale no larger than reasonably necessary for its training and rehabilitation program.[125] A like finding was made in relation to the manufacture and marketing of toys, which was the means by which an exempt organization accomplished its charitable purpose of training unemployed and underemployed individuals.[126]

(iii) Same–State Rule. Ordinarily, gross income from the sale of products that result from the performance of tax-exempt functions does not constitute gross income from the conduct of an unrelated business if the product is sold in substantially the *same state* it is in upon completion of the exempt functions.[127] Thus, in the case of a charitable organization engaged in a program of rehabilitation of disabled individuals, income from the sale of items made by them as part of their rehabilitation training is not gross income from the conduct of an unrelated business. The income in this instance is from the sale of products, the production of which contributes importantly to the accomplishment of the organization's exempt purposes, namely, rehabilitation of the disabled.[128] Conversely, if a product resulting from an exempt function is utilized or exploited in further business endeavors beyond that reasonably appropriate or necessary for disposition in the state it is in upon completion of

---

[124] Priv. Ltr. Rul. 9535023.

[125] Rev. Rul. 76-94, 1976-1 C.B. 171.

[126] Rev. Rul. 73-128, 1973-1 C.B. 222.

[127] Reg. § 1.513-1(d)(4)(ii).

[128] *Id.*

exempt functions, the gross income derived from these endeavors would be from the conduct of unrelated business.[129]

As an illustration, in the case of an experimental dairy herd maintained for scientific purposes by an exempt organization, income from the sale of milk and cream produced in the ordinary course of operation of the project is not gross income from the conduct of unrelated business. If, however, the organization utilized the milk and cream in the manufacture of food items, such as ice cream and pastries, the gross income from the sale of these products would be from the conduct of unrelated business—unless the manufacturing activities themselves contributed importantly to the accomplishment of an exempt purpose of the organization.[130] Similarly, a charitable organization that operated a salmon hatchery as an exempt function was ruled to be able to sell a portion of its harvested salmon stock in an unprocessed condition to fish processors without taxation. By contrast, when it converted the fish into salmon nuggets (fish that was seasoned, formed into nugget shape, and breaded), the sale of the fish in that state was an unrelated business.[131]

(iv) Dual-Use Rule. An asset or facility of a tax-exempt organization that is necessary to the conduct of exempt functions may also be utilized for commercial purposes. In these *dual use* instances, the mere fact of the use of the asset or facility in an exempt function does not, by itself, make the income from the commercial endeavor gross income from a related business. The test is whether the activities productive of the income in question contribute importantly to the accomplishment of exempt purposes.[132]

For example, a tax-exempt museum may have an auditorium that is designed and equipped for showing educational films in connection with its program of public education in the arts and sciences. The theater is a principal feature of the museum and is in continuous operation during the hours the museum is open to the public. If the museum were to operate the theater as a motion picture theater for public entertainment during the evening hours when the museum is otherwise closed, gross income

---

[129] *Id.*

[130] *Id.*

[131] Priv. Ltr. Rul. 9320042.

[132] Reg. § 1.513-1(d)(4)(iii).

from that operation would be gross income from an unrelated business.[133] Similarly, a mailing service operated by a tax-exempt organization was ruled to be an unrelated business even though the mailing equipment was also used for exempt purposes.[134]

Another illustration is the athletic facilities of a tax-exempt college or university, which, while used primarily for educational purposes, may also be made available for members of the faculty, other employees of the institution, and members of the general public. Income derived from the use of the facilities by those who are not students or employees of the institution is likely to be unrelated business income.[135] For example, the IRS ruled that the operation of a ski facility by an exempt school for the general public was the conduct of an unrelated business, while use of the facility by the students of the school for recreational purposes and in its physical education program were ruled to be related activities.[136] Likewise, a college that made its facilities and personnel available to an individual not associated with the institution for the conduct of a summer tennis camp was ruled to be engaged in an unrelated business.[137]

(v) Exploitation Rule. Activities carried on by a tax-exempt organization in the performance of exempt functions may generate goodwill or other intangibles that are capable of being exploited in commercial endeavors. Where an exempt organization exploits this type of intangible in commercial activities, the mere fact that the resultant income depended in part on an exempt function of the organization does not make it gross income from a related business. In these cases, unless the activities contribute importantly to the accomplishment of an exempt purpose, the income that they produce is gross income from the conduct of an unrelated business.[138]

Thus, the rules with respect to taxation of advertising revenue received by tax-exempt organizations treat advertising in publications as a form of

---

[133] *Id.*

[134] Rev. Rul. 68-550, 1968-2 C.B. 249.

[135] E.g., Tech. Adv. Mem. 9645004 (concerning dual use of a university's golf course).

[136] Rev. Rul. 78-98, 1978-1 C.B. 167.

[137] Rev. Rul. 76-402, 1976-2 C.B. 177.

[138] Reg. § 1.513-1(d)(4)(iv).

exploitation of exempt activity, namely, the charitable, educational, scientific, and/or religious content of the publications.[139] As another illustration of the *exploitation rule*, where access to athletic facilities of an educational institution by students is covered by a general student fee, outside use may trigger the exploitation rule; if separate charges for use of the facilities are imposed on students, faculty, and outsiders, any unrelated income is a product of the dual-use rule.[140]

§ 2.2 GENERAL RULES

The unrelated business income rules apply to nearly all tax-exempt organizations—with emphasis these days on healthcare entities, colleges and universities, museums, social welfare organizations, and associations—and entail a wide range of activities. Those of particular pertinence to use of the Internet are discussed next.

(a) Advertising

Generally, the net income derived by a tax-exempt organization from the sale of advertising is taxable as unrelated business income.[141]

(i) Definition of Advertising. Despite the extensive body of tax regulations and case law concerning when and how advertising revenue is taxed, there is little law as to what constitutes *advertising*. Essentially, to advertise is to give public notice of something, usually a product or service; in nearly all cases, the emphasis in on the desirable qualities of the item advertised, as an inducement to purchase, patronize, visit, and the like. Synonyms include notify, declare, and inform. The corporate sponsorship rules[142] are helpful on this point.

The regulations that accompany these rules provide that *advertising* means "any message or other programming material which is broadcast or otherwise transmitted, published, displayed or distributed, and which promotes or

---

[139] See *infra* § 2(a).

[140] E.g., Priv. Ltr. Rul. 7823062.

[141] IRC § 513(c).

[142] See *infra* § (b).

markets any trade or business, or any service, facility or product."[143] Advertising includes messages containing qualitative or comparative language, price information or other indications of savings or value, an endorsement, or an inducement to purchase, sell, or use any company, service, facility, or product.[144]

In one instance, a court concluded that the publication of "business listings," consisting of "slogans, logos, trademarks, and other information which is similar, if not identical in content, composition and message to the listings found in other professional journals, newspapers, and the 'yellow pages' of telephone directories," was advertising.[145] On another occasion, displays and listings in a yearbook published by a tax-exempt organization were found to be advertising—and an unrelated business.[146]

Web site advertising is relatively easy to identify; it may be in the form of text, graphic images, or both. There may be a "banner" that appears on one or more Web pages. An advertisement on a Web site of a nonprofit organization may include a link to the Web site of the advertising entity.

(ii) General Principles. Under the rules defining what is a *trade or business*,[147] income from the sale of advertising in publications of tax-exempt organizations (including publications that are related to the exempt purpose of the organization) generally constitutes unrelated business income, taxable to the extent it exceeds the expenses directly related to the advertising. If the editorial aspect of the publication is carried on at a loss, however, the editorial loss may be offset against the advertising income from the publication. Thus, there will not be any taxable unrelated business income because of advertising where the publication as a whole is published at a loss.

These rules are not intended to encompass the publication of a magazine with little or no advertising, which is distributed free or at a nominal

---

[143] Reg. § 1.513-4(c)(2)(iv).

[144] IRC § 513(i)(2)(A); Reg. § 1.513-4(c)(2)(iv).

[145] *Fraternal Order of Police, Illinois State Troopers Lodge No. 41* v. *Commissioner*, 87 T.C. 747, 754 (1986), *aff'd*, 833 F.2d 717 (7th Cir. 1987).

[146] *State Police Association of Massachusetts* v. *Commissioner*, 97-2 U.S.T.C. ¶ 50,627 (1st Cir. 1997).

[147] IRC § 513(c). See *supra* § 1(b).

charge not intended to cover costs. This type of publication would likely be published basically as a source of public information and not for the production of income. For a publication to be considered an activity carried on for the production of income, it must be contemplated that the revenues from advertising in the publication or the revenues from sale of the publication, or both, will result in net income (although not necessarily in a particular year). Nonetheless, for the tax on unrelated business income to apply, the advertising activity must constitute a trade or business that is regularly carried on.

As an example, an association of law enforcement officials published a monthly journal containing conventional advertising, featuring the products or services of commercial enterprises. The IRS ruled that the regular sale of space in the journal for the advertising was carried on for the production of income and constituted a business, which was not substantially related to the organization's tax-exempt functions.[148] The "controlling factor in this case," wrote the IRS, was that the "activities giving rise to the income in question constitute the sale and performance of a valuable service on the part of the publisher, and the purchase of that service on the part of the other party to the transaction."[149]

In a similar situation, the IRS ruled that income derived by a tax-exempt membership organization from the sale of advertising in its annual yearbook was unrelated business income.[150] Preparation of the editorial materials in the yearbook was largely done by the staff of the organization, which also distributed it. An independent commercial firm was used, however, to conduct an intensive advertising solicitation campaign in the organization's name, and the firm was paid a percentage of the gross advertising receipts for selling the advertising, collecting from advertisers, and printing the yearbook. The IRS stated that, by "engaging in an extensive campaign of advertising solicitation, the organization is conducting competitive and promotional efforts typical of commercial endeavors."[151]

---

[148] Rev. Rul. 74-38, 1974-1 C.B. 44, *clarified by* Rev. Rul. 76-93, 1976-1 C.B. 170.

[149] *Id.,* Rev. Rul. 74-38, at 45.

[150] Rev. Rul. 73-424, *supra* note 79.

[151] *Id.* at 191.

(iii) Related Advertising. Advertising income is almost always regarded as unrelated business income, although on rare occasions, advertising activity is considered an exempt function.[152] The Supreme Court held that the standard is whether the conduct of the tax-exempt organization in selling and publishing the advertising is demonstrative of a related function rather than a determination as to whether the advertising is inherently educational.[153] The case concerned a tax-exempt medical organization that sold advertising in its scholarly journal; the organization believed that the purpose of the advertising was to educate physicians as to the latest products, pharmaceuticals, procedures, and the like. The advertising appeared only in bunches, at the beginning and end of the publications, was screened and controlled as to content, and was indexed by advertiser. Only advertisements directly relevant to the field of medicine involved were published.

Reversing the appellate court, the Supreme Court wrote that, in ascertaining relatedness in this context, it is not sufficient to cluster the advertising in the front and back of the exempt organization's publications. Other facts that mitigated against relatedness, in the view of the Court, were that all advertising was paid, the advertising was for established products or services, advertising was repeated month to month, or the advertising concerned matters having "no conceivable relationship" to the exempt purpose of the organization.[154] The test, said the Court, is whether the organization uses the advertising to "provide its readers a comprehensive or systematic presentation of any aspect of the goods or services publicized."[155] The Court wrote that an exempt organization can "control its publication of advertisements in such a way as to reflect an intention to contribute importantly to its . . . [exempt] functions."[156] This can be done, said the Court, by "coordinating the content of the advertisements with

---

[152] E.g., Priv. Ltr. Rul. 7948113 (holding that the proceeds from the sale of advertising in the program published in promotion of a postseason all-star college football game were not unrelated business income).

[153] *United States v. American College of Physicians*, 475 U.S. 834 (1986).

[154] *Id.* at 849.

[155] *Id.*

[156] *Id.*

the editorial content of the issue, or by publishing only advertisements reflecting new developments."[157] Therefore, even though the government prevailed in this case, the law recognizes—under admittedly strict conditions—the concept of related advertisements.[158]

The foregoing may be contrasted with the situation involving a charitable organization that raised funds for a tax-exempt symphony orchestra. As part of this effort, the organization annually published a concert book that was distributed at the orchestra's annual charity ball. The IRS ruled that the solicitation and sale of advertising by volunteers of the organization was not an unrelated taxable activity because the activity was not regularly carried on[159] and because it was conducted as an integral part of the process of fundraising for charity.[160] Yet the same type of organization that engaged in the sale of advertising over a four-month period by its paid employees, for publication in concert programs distributed free at symphony performances over an eight-month period, was found by the IRS to be carrying on an unrelated business.[161] These activities, wrote the agency, do not "substantially differ from the comparable commercial activities of nonexempt organizations."[162]

Similarly, a business league that sold a membership directory, but only to its members, was held to not be engaged in an unrelated business. The directory was considered to contribute importantly to the achievement of

---

[157] *Id.* at 849–850.

[158] Subsequently, a court concluded that the advertising of a tax-exempt trade association was taxable because it was not substantially related to the organization's exempt purposes and there was no "systematic effort" made to "advertise products that relate to the editorial content of the magazine, and no effort [was] . . . made . . . to limit the advertisements to new products" (*Florida Trucking Association, Inc.* v. *Commissioner*, 87 T.C. 1039 (1986)). A court found that an exempt organization's advertising generally did not contribute importantly to the carrying out of its exempt purposes, although it found that the subject matter of some of the advertising was related to the exempt purposes (*Minnesota Holstein-Friesian Breeders Association* v. *Commissioner*, 64 T.C.M. 1319 (1992)).

[159] See *supra* § 1(c).

[160] Rev. Rul. 75-201, 1975-1 C.B. 164.

[161] Rev. Rul. 75-200, 1975-1 C.B. 163.

[162] *Id.* at 164.

the organization's exempt purposes by facilitating communication among the membership and by encouraging the exchange of ideas and expertise, resulting in greater awareness of collective and individual activities of the membership.[163] The principal aspect governing the outcome of this matter, however, was the fact that the sale of the directory, undertaken in a noncommercial manner, did not confer any private benefit on the organization's members.

(iv) Advertising in Periodicals. Amounts realized by a tax-exempt organization from the sale of advertising in a periodical constitute gross income from an unrelated business involving the exploitation of an exempt activity. Where the circulation and readership of an exempt organization periodical are utilized in connection with the sale of advertising in the periodical, expenses, depreciation, and similar items of deductions attributable to the production and distribution of the editorial or readership content of the periodical qualify as items of deductions directly connected with the unrelated advertising activity.[164]

The total income attributable to a periodical of a tax-exempt organization is the sum of its circulation income and (if any) gross advertising income.[165] *Circulation income* is the income attributable to the production, distribution, or circulation of a periodical (other than gross advertising income), including amounts realized from the sale of the readership content of the periodical.[166] *Gross advertising income* is the amount derived from the unrelated advertising activities of an exempt organization periodical.[167]

The costs attributable to a tax-exempt organization's periodical are characterized as readership costs and direct advertising costs.[168] A reasonable allocation may be made as between cost items attributable to both an exempt organization periodical and to its other activities (such as salaries, occupancy costs, and depreciation). *Readership costs* are the cost items directly connected with the production and distribution of the readership

---

[163] Rev. Rul. 79-370, 1979-2 C.B. 238.

[164] Reg. § 1.512(a)-1(f)(1).

[165] Reg. § 1.512(a)-1(f)(3)(i).

[166] Reg. § 1.512(a)-1(f)(3)(iii).

[167] Reg. § 1.512(a)-1(f)(3)(ii).

[168] Reg. § 1.512(a)-1(f)(6)(i).

content of the periodical, other than the items properly allocable to direct advertising costs.[169] *Direct advertising costs* include items that are directly connected with the sale and publication of advertising (such as agency commissions and other selling costs, artwork, and copy preparation), the portion of mechanical and distribution costs attributable to advertising lineage, and any other element of readership costs properly allocable to the advertising activity.[170]

As noted, a tax-exempt organization is not taxable on its advertising income where its direct advertising costs equal such (gross) income. Even if gross advertising income exceeds direct advertising costs, costs attributable to the readership content of the periodical qualify as costs that are deductible in computing (unrelated) income from the advertising activity, to the extent that the costs exceed the income attributable to the readership content. There are limitations on this rule, however, including the conditions that its application may not be used to realize a loss from the advertising activity nor to give rise to a cost deductible in computing taxable income attributable to any other unrelated activity. If the circulation income of the periodical exceeds its readership costs, any unrelated business taxable income attributable to the periodical is the excess of gross advertising income over direct advertising costs.[171]

Another set of rules requires an allocation of membership dues to circulation income where the right to receive the periodical is associated with membership status in the tax-exempt organization for which dues, fees, or other charges are received.[172]

A tax-exempt organization may publish more than one periodical for the production of income. A periodical is published for the production of income if the organization generally receives gross advertising income from the periodical equal to at least 25 percent of its readership costs and the publication activity is engaged in for profit. In this case, the organization may treat the gross income from all (but not just some) of the periodicals and the deductible items directly connected with the periodicals

---

[169] Reg. § 1.512(a)-1(f)(6)(iii).

[170] Reg. § 1.512(a)-1(f)(6)(ii).

[171] Reg. § 1.512(a)-1(f)(2)(ii), (d)(2).

[172] Reg. § 1.512(a)-1(f)(4).

on a consolidated basis in determining the amount of unrelated business taxable income derived from the sale of advertising.[173]

(b) Corporate Sponsorships

It has become common for charitable organizations to be supported by large transfers of money from for-profit companies. The charities, of course, wish to regard this support as tax-deductible contributions. At the same time, these companies want to be publicly thanked (if not praised) for this support. The issue often arises as to whether this public recognition is merely an *acknowledgment* of the transfer (in which case the status of the payments as contributions is not disturbed) or is sufficiently effusive to amount to *advertising* (in which case the transfer may be taxable as unrelated business income[174]). Statutory rules—embodying the concept of the qualified sponsorship payment—have been enacted in an effort to draw this distinction. Qualified sponsorship payments received by tax-exempt organizations (including state colleges and universities) are exempt from unrelated business income taxation. That is, the activity of soliciting and receiving these payments is not an unrelated business.[175]

The concept of the qualified sponsorship payment is a safe-harbor rule. Thus, if a payment is not *qualified*, it may still escape unrelated business income taxation if it is eligible for another exception from the unrelated business rules.[176]

A *qualified sponsorship payment* is a payment made by a person engaged in a trade or business (usually a for-profit one) to a tax-exempt organization, with respect to which there is no arrangement or expectation that the person will receive a substantial return benefit.[177] In determining whether a payment is a qualified sponsorship payment, it is irrelevant whether the sponsored activity is related or unrelated to the recipient organization's exempt purpose. It is also irrelevant whether the sponsored

---

[173] Reg. § 1.512(a)-1(f)(7).

[174] See *supra* § (a).

[175] IRC § 513(i); Reg. § 1.513-4(a).

[176] See *infra* § 3.

[177] IRC § 513(i)(2)(A); Reg. § 1.513-4(c)(1).

activity is temporary or permanent. *Payment* means the payment of money, transfer of property, or performance of services.[178]

A *substantial return benefit* is any benefit other than certain uses or acknowledgments or certain disregarded benefits.[179] A substantial return benefit does not include the use or acknowledgment of the name or logo (or product lines) of the person's business in connection with the activities of the exempt organization. A use or acknowledgment may include certain exclusive sponsorship arrangements; logos and slogans that do not contain qualitative or comparative descriptions of the person's products, services, facilities, or company; a list of the person's locations, telephone numbers, or Internet address; value-neutral descriptions, including displays or visual depictions, of the person's product line or services; and the person's brand or trade names and product or service listings.[180]

A use or acknowledgment does not include advertising. The term *advertising* means any message or other programming material, which is broadcast or otherwise transmitted, published, displayed, or distributed, and which promotes or markets any trade or business, or any service, facility, or product. Advertising includes messages containing qualitative or comparative language, price information or other indications of savings or value, an endorsement, or an inducement to purchase, sell, or use any company, service, facility, or product. A single message that contains both advertising and an acknowledgment is advertising.[181]

Benefits are disregarded if the aggregate fair market value of all of the benefits provided to the person, or persons designated by the payor, in connection with the payment during the organization's tax year is not more than 2 percent of the amount of the payment. If the aggregate fair market value of the benefits exceeds 2 percent of the amount of the payment, then generally the entire fair market value of the benefits, not merely the excess amount, is a substantial return benefit.[182]

---

[178] Reg. § 1.513-4(c)(1).

[179] Reg. § 1.513-4(c)(2)(i).

[180] Reg. § 1.513-4(c)(2)(iv).

[181] Reg. § 1.513-4(c)(2)(v).

[182] Reg. § 1.513-4(c)(2)(ii).

In one of the few examples of application of this law prior to development of the qualified corporate sponsorship rules, the IRS considered a situation where a pet food company was a major sponsor of an annually televised show conducted as the predominant activity of a tax-exempt organization operated to increase interest in a type of pet animal. In return for a cash payment, the exempt organization provided certain benefits to the company, including exhibition of its logo on a mailing to potential exhibitors, identification on the exhibitor's benches, and identification on the armbands worn by exhibitors in the ring. This package of benefits was ruled to be in the "nature of acknowledgments rather than advertising"; the exempt organization was cast as having "agreed to do nothing for [the company] that reaches the level of providing advertising services for it."[183]

A qualified sponsorship payment does not include any payment where the amount of the payment is contingent on the level of attendance at one or more events, broadcast ratings, or other factors indicating the degree of public exposure to one or more events.[184] The fact that a sponsorship payment is contingent on an event or activity actually being conducted, in and of itself, however, does not cause the payment to fail to qualify.

This safe-harbor rule does not apply to income derived from the sale of advertising or acknowledgments in a periodical of a tax-exempt organization. A *periodical* is regularly scheduled and printed material published by or on behalf of the payee (sponsored) organization that is not related to and primarily distributed in connection with a specific event conducted by the payee organization.[185] For this purpose, *printed material* includes material that is published electronically.[186] Thus, the exception does not apply to payments that lead to acknowledgments in a monthly journal but does apply if a sponsor received an acknowledgment in a program or brochure distributed at a sponsored event. The term *qualified sponsorship*

---

[183] Tech. Adv. Mem. 9805001.

[184] IRC § 513(i)(2)(B)(i); Reg. § 1.513-4(e)(2).

[185] IRC § 513(i)(2)(B)(ii)(I); Reg. § 1.513-4(b).

[186] Reg. § 1.513-4(b).

payment also does not include a payment made in connection with a qualified convention or trade show activity.[187]

To the extent that a portion of a payment would (if made as a separate payment) be a qualified sponsorship payment, that portion of the payment is treated as a separate payment.[188] That is, a single payment may be considered partially qualified and partially not qualified; this allocation is based on value. For example, if a sponsorship payment made to a tax-exempt organization entitles the sponsor to product advertising, as well as use or acknowledgment of the sponsor's name or logo by the organization, the unrelated business income tax does not apply to the amount of the payment that exceeds the fair market value of the product advertising provided to the sponsor.

The provision of facilities, services, or other privileges by an exempt organization to a sponsor or the sponsor's designees (such as complimentary tickets, pro-am playing spots in golf tournaments, or receptions for major donors) in connection with a sponsorship payment does not affect the determination as to whether the payment is a qualified one. Instead, the provision of the goods or services is evaluated as a separate transaction in determining whether the organization has unrelated business income from the event. In general, if the services or facilities do not constitute a substantial return benefit (or if the provision of the services or facilities is a related business activity), the payments attributable to them are not subject to the tax on unrelated business income.

Likewise, a sponsor's receipt of a license to use an intangible asset (such as a trademark, logo, or designation) of the tax-exempt organization is treated as separate from the qualified sponsorship transaction in determining whether the organization has unrelated business income.

This statutory exemption from taxation for qualified sponsorship payments is in addition to other exceptions from the unrelated business tax. These exceptions include the one for activities substantially all the work

---

[187] IRC § 513(i)(2)(B)(ii)(II); Reg. § 1.513-4(b). This type of activity is the subject of *infra* § (d).

[188] IRC § 513(i)(3); Reg. § 1.513-4(d)(1).

for which is performed by volunteers[189] and for activities not regularly carried on.[190]

(c) Fundraising Activities

Fundraising practices of charitable organizations and the unrelated business rules have long had a precarious relationship. For this purpose, the term *fundraising* means the solicitation of contributions and grants, usually by charitable organizations. Fundraising activities are usually distinct from program activities. These activities are often *businesses.*[191]

(i) Fundraising as Unrelated Business. The type of fundraising undertaking that is most likely to be considered a business is the *special event.* These events include functions such as auctions, dinners, sports tournaments, dances, theater events, fairs, car washes, and bake sales.[192] Sometimes a court applies the statutory definition of the term *business*[193] in concluding that the event is an unrelated business; on other occasions a court will utilize other criteria—such as competition or commerciality—to find that the event is or is not an unrelated business.

Conventional fundraising—namely, the solicitation and collection of contributions and grants—technically is a business (or, perhaps, two or more businesses). Yet neither the IRS nor a court has characterized the practices as business—let alone unrelated business.

A case concerned a tax-exempt school that solicited charitable contributions by means of mailing of packages of greeting cards as inducements

---

[189] See *infra* § 3(b)(i).

[190] See *supra* § 1(c).

[191] See *supra* § 1(b).

[192] The IRS, in the instructions that accompany the annual information return filed by most tax-exempt organizations (Form 990; see § 7.1), states: "These activities only incidentally accomplish an exempt purpose. Their sole or primary purpose is to raise funds that are other than contributions to finance the organization's exempt activities."

[193] See *supra* §1(b).

to prospective donors. The IRS asserted that the school was really involved in the unrelated business of selling greeting cards. The tax regulations, however, provide that an "activity does not possess the characteristics of a trade or business . . . when an organization sends out low cost articles incidental to the solicitation of charitable contributions."[194] The government asserted that this rule was inapplicable in this case because the funds involved were not "gifts," but the court disagreed, writing that to read the law in that narrow manner would "completely emasculate the exception."[195] The court held that the case turned on the fact that the unrelated business rules were designed to prevent tax-exempt organizations from unfairly competing with for-profit entities[196] and that the school's fundraising program did not give it an "unfair competitive advantage over taxpaying greeting card companies."

Greeting cards and similar items, when used in conjunction with the solicitation of charitable contributions, are termed *premiums*. This fundraising practice has spawned considerable litigation and IRS ruling activity. An unrelated business may be present where the value of the premium approximates the amount of the "gift." Also, if the premiums are mailed with the gift solicitation, the result probably is charitable giving; if the premiums are made available following the "gifts," there may be commercial activity. Thus, one court wrote, in a case involving a greeting card program of a national veterans' organization, that "when premiums are advertised and offered only in exchange for prior contributions in stated amounts," the activity is commercial, but if the organization "had mailed the premiums with its solicitations and had informed the recipients that the premiums could be retained without any obligation arising to make a contribution," the activity is not a business because it is not a competitive practice.[197] Another court ruled that the revenue derived by a veterans' organization from the distribution of cards to its members constituted unrelated business income, concluding that

---

[194] Reg. § 1.513-1(b).

[195] *The Hope School* v. *United States*, 612 F.2d 298, 302 (7th Cir. 1980).

[196] See *supra* § 1(a).

[197] *Disabled American Veterans* v. *United States*, 650 F.2d 1178, 1187, 1186 (Ct. Cl. 1981).

the organization was acting with a profit motive and that the card program was the "sale of goods."[198] IRS rulings reflect this approach as well.[199] Yet another court held, without referencing the other two cases, that the revenue generated by a veterans' organization from the dissemination of greeting cards was not income from an unrelated business but rather contributions resulting from a fundraising program.[200]

One of the earliest examples of a fundraising event cast as a business was an IRS ruling, issued in 1979, holding that a religious organization that conducted, as its principal fundraising activity, bingo games and related concessions three nights each week was engaged in an unrelated business.[201] The IRS concluded that the games "constitute a trade or business with the general public, the conduct of which is not substantially related to the exercise or the performance by the organization of the purpose for which it was organized other than the use it makes of the profits derived from the games."[202]

A court ruled that the conduct by a charitable organization of weekly and monthly lotteries was activity regularly carried on and thus was a taxable business because the gambling activities were not substantially related to the organization's charitable purposes.[203]

Another court case concerned the tax status of a membership organization for citizens' band radio operators, which used insurance, travel, and discount plans to attract new members.[204] The organization contended

---

[198] *Veterans of Foreign Wars, Department of Michigan* v. *Commissioner*, 89 T.C. 7, 38 (1987).

[199] E.g., Priv. Ltr. Ruls. 8203134, 8232011.

[200] *The American Legion Department of New York* v. *United States*, 93-2 U.S.T.C. ¶ 50,417 (N.D.N.Y. 1993).

[201] Priv. Ltr. Rul. 7946001.

[202] This organization was unable to utilize the exemption from unrelated income taxation accorded to bingo games (IRC § 513(f)) because, under the law of the state in which it was organized, the games constituted, at that time, an illegal lottery.

[203] *United States* v. *Auxiliary to the Knights of St. Peter Claver, Charities of the Ladies Court No. 97*, 92-1 U.S.T.C. ¶ 50,176 (S.D. Ind. 1992).

[204] *U.S. CB Radio Association, No. 1, Inc.* v. *Commissioner*, 42 T.C.M. 1441 (1981).

that it was only doing what many tax-exempt organizations do to raise contributions, analogizing these activities to fundraising events. The court rejected this argument, defining a *fundraising event* as a "single occurrence that may occur on limited occasions during a given year and its purpose is to further the exempt activities of the organization."[205] These events were contrasted with activities that are "continuous or continual activities which are certainly more pervasive a part of the organization than a sporadic event and [that are] . . . an end in themselves."[206]

A nonprofit school consulted with a tax-shelter investments firm in search of fundraising methods, with the result being a program in which individuals would purchase various real properties from the school, which the school would simultaneously purchase from third parties; both the sellers and the buyers were clients of the investments firm. There were about 22 of these transactions during the years at issue, from which the school received income reflecting the difference between the sales prices and the purchase prices. Finding the "simultaneous purchase and sale of real estate . . . not substantially related to the exercise or performance of [the school's] . . . exempt function," a court held that the net income from the transactions was unrelated income.[207]

At issue before a court was whether income received by a charitable organization as the result of assignments to it of dividends paid in connection with insurance coverage purchased by members of a related professional association at group rates is taxable as unrelated business income. The trial court wrote that, where the tax-exempt organization involved in an unrelated business case is a charitable one, the court "must distinguish between those activities that constitute a trade or business and those that are merely fundraising."[208] The court said that this distinction is not always readily apparent, in that charitable activities are "sometimes so similar to commercial transactions that it becomes very difficult to determine whether the organization is raising money 'from the sale of goods or the

---

[205] *Id.* at 1444.

[206] *Id.*

[207] *Parklane Residential School, Inc.* v. *Commissioner*, 45 T.C.M. 988, 992 (1983).

[208] *American Bar Endowment* v. *United States*, 84-1 U.S.T.C. ¶ 9204 (Ct. Cl. 1984).

performance of services' [the statutory definition of a *business*[209]] or whether the goods or services are provided merely as an incident to a fund-raising activity." Nonetheless, the court held that the test is whether the activity in question is "operated in a competitive, commercial manner," which is a "question of fact and turns upon the circumstances of each case." "At bottom," the court wrote, the "inquiry is whether the actions of the participants conform with normal assumptions about how people behave in a commercial context" and "[i]f they do not, it may be because the participants are engaged in a charitable fundraising activity."

In this case, the court stressed the following elements: (1) the activity involved was a pioneering idea at its inception, (2) it was originally devised as a fundraising effort and was subsequently so presented, (3) the "staggering amount of money" and the "astounding profitability" that was generated by the activity, (4) the degree of the organization's candor toward its members and the public concerning the operation and revenue of the program, and (5) the fact that the activity was operated with the consent and approval of the organization's membership. Concerning the third element, substantial profits and consistently high profit margins are usually cited as reasons for determining that the activity involved is a business. In this case, however, the amounts of money involved were so great that they could not be rationalized in conventional business analysis terms; the only explanation that was suitable to the court was that the "staggering amount" of money was the result of successful charitable fundraising.

Notwithstanding this rational analysis, the Supreme Court overturned the opinion.[210] The Court found of consequence the facts that the organization negotiated premium rates with insurers, selected the insurers that provided the coverage, solicited the membership of the association, collected the premiums, transmitted the premiums to the insurer, maintained files on each policyholder, answered members' questions concerning insurance policies, and screened claims for benefits. In deciding that this bundle of activities amounted to an unrelated business, the Court observed that the charitable organization "prices its insurance to remain competitive with the rest of the market," that the Court "can easily view

---

[209] See *supra* § 1(b).

[210] *United States v. American Bar Endowment*, 447 U.S. 105 (1986).

this case as a standard example of monopoly pricing," and that the case "presents an example of precisely the sort of unfair competition that Congress intended to prevent."[211]

The Court in this case concluded that the "only valid argument in the charitable organization's favor, therefore, is that the insurance program is billed as a fund-raising effort."[212] But the Court summarily rejected this contention—in language that highlights why most fundraising efforts are unrelated businesses—writing that that "fact, standing alone, cannot be determinative, or any exempt organization could engage in a tax-free business by 'giving away' its product in return for a 'contribution' equal to the market value of the product."[213]

(ii) Application of Exceptions. Thus, many fundraising endeavors of charitable and other tax-exempt organizations are businesses and are not related practices. Yet they often escape taxation because of one or more exceptions.

The exception that is most frequently utilized to shelter fundraising activities from taxation is the one for business activities that are not regularly carried on.[214] The typical special event, for example, is usually not regularly carried on, although on occasion the inclusion of preparatory time will convert the activity into a taxable unrelated business.[215] The IRS ruled, for example, that the net proceeds resulting from the annual conduct by a charitable organization of a ball and golf tournament were not taxable because the events were not regularly carried on.[216]

In one case, a court concluded that the annual fundraising activity of a tax-exempt charitable organization, consisting of the presentation and sponsoring of a professional vaudeville show, conducted one weekend per year, was a business that was not regularly carried on. The court concluded: "The fact that an organization seeks to insure the success of its

---

[211] *Id.* at 112–114.

[212] *Id.* at 115.

[213] *Id.* Revisions in this program led the IRS to conclude that it was no longer an unrelated business (Priv. Ltr. Rul. 8725056).

[214] See *supra* § 1(c).

[215] See *supra* § 1(c)(iv).

[216] Priv. Ltr. Rul. 200128059.

fundraising venture by beginning to plan and prepare for it earlier should not adversely affect the tax treatment of the income derived by the venture."[217]

Conventional fundraising—the solicitation and collection of gifts and grants—however, is usually regularly carried on, yet there have not been any assertions that these activities are taxable, even though they are businesses and are not related to exempt purposes.

Other exceptions may be available in the fundraising setting. For example, a business, albeit regularly carried on, in which substantially all of the work is performed for the organization by volunteers is not taxable.[218] The same is the case for the sale of merchandise substantially all of which has been received by the organization as gifts.[219] Activities carried on primarily for the convenience of the organization's members, students, patients, officers, or employees are not taxable.[220] The receipts from certain gambling activities (bingo games) are exempted from unrelated business income taxation.[221]

(iii) Tax Planning Advice. It is common for charitable organizations that engage in fundraising efforts to provide financial and tax planning information to prospective donors. This may entail modest amounts of information, such as direction as to valuation of property or the extent of the charitable deduction. In other settings, by contrast, the financial and tax information can be substantial and complex. This is particularly the case with respect to planned giving, where charities are directly involved in charitable gift planning and preparation of documents, such as charitable remainder trusts, other trust arrangements, and wills.

A fundamental precept of the federal tax law concerning charitable organizations is that they may not, without jeopardizing their tax-exempt

---

[217] *Suffolk County Patrolmen's Beneficiary Association, Inc. v. Commissioner, supra* note 100, at 1324.

[218] See *infra* § 3(b)(i).

[219] See *infra* § 3(b)(iii). Although this exception was created for thrift shops, it can be available for charitable auctions, irrespective of the number of them in a year.

[220] See *infra* § 3(b)(ii).

[221] IRC § 513(f).

status, be operated in a manner that causes persons to derive a private benefit from their operations.[222] Occasionally these elements conflict, in that the provision of tax planning information and services by charitable organizations to prospective contributors is considered the provision of impermissible private benefit. While it would seem nearly inconceivable to seriously contend that, when a charitable organization works with a prospective donor to effect a sizable gift that will generate significant tax and other advantages for the donor, by reason of a charitable contribution deduction and other benefits, the organization is imperiling its tax exemption because it is conferring a private benefit, this is the import of three court opinions.

One case concerned the tax-exempt status of an organization that engaged in financial counseling by providing tax planning services, including charitable giving considerations, to wealthy individuals referred to it by subscribing religious organizations. The counseling given by the organization consisted of advice on how a contributor may increase current or planned gifts to these religious organizations, including the development of a financial plan that, among other objectives, resulted in a reduction in federal income and estate taxes. The position of the IRS was that this organization could not qualify for federal income tax exemption because it served the private interests of individuals by enabling them to reduce their tax burden. The organization's position was that it was engaging in activities that exempt charitable organizations may generally undertake without loss of their tax exemption. A court agreed with the government, holding that the organization's "sole financial planning activity, albeit an exempt purpose furthering . . . [exempt] fundraising efforts, has a nonexempt purpose of offering advice to individuals on tax matters that reduces an individual's personal and estate tax liabilities."[223] The court dryly stated that "[w]e do not find within the scope of the word charity that the financial planning for wealthy individuals described in this case is a charitable purpose."[224]

---

[222] See § 7.5.

[223] *Christian Stewardship Assistance, Inc.* v. *Commissioner*, 70 T.C. 1037, 1041 (1978).

[224] *Id.* at 1043.

In this opinion, the court singled out the planned giving techniques for portrayal as methods that gave rise to unwarranted private benefit by this organization. The example was given of the creation of a charitable remainder trust, where the donor receives "considerable lifetime advantages," such as the flow of income for life, reduced capital gain taxes in instances involving appreciated property, and lower probate costs.[225] (The court could have recited other benefits, such as the charitable contribution deduction, the calculation of the deduction based on the full fair market value of property, and the benefits of [free to the donor] professional money and property management.) These were cast as "real and substantial benefits" that inure to the contributors as the consequence of the organization's activities, with these benefits "substantial enough to deny exemption."[226]

In another case, this court held that a religious organization could not be tax-exempt because it engaged in a substantial nonexempt purpose, which was the counseling of individuals on the purported tax benefits accruing to those who become ministers of the organization.[227] The court decided that the organization was akin to a "commercial tax service, albeit within a narrower field (i.e., tax benefits to ministers and churches) and a narrower class of customers (i.e., . . . [the organization's] ministers)," and thus that it served private purposes.[228] The many detailed discussions by the organization in its literature of ways to maximize tax benefits led the court to observe that although the organization "may well advocate belief

---

[225] *Id.* at 1044.

[226] *Id.* This was, indeed, a preposterous conclusion for the court to reach, at least without noting that charitable organizations engage in these practices all the time. (The problem in this case, apparently, was that the financial and tax planning functions were in a separate organization.) Congress provided the benefits to donors who make contributions by means of charitable remainder trusts (IRC § 664). It is absurd to suggest that, when charities make their supporters aware of, and donors elect to avail themselves of, these benefits, the donee charitable organization should in turn lose its tax exemption. Indeed, the court subsequently somewhat circumscribed the reach of this conclusion (see the text accompanying *infra* note 231).

[227] *The Ecclesiastical Order of The Ism of Am, Inc.* v. *Commissioner*, 80 T.C. 833 (1983), *aff'd*, 740 F.2d 967 (6th Cir. 1984), *cert. den.*, 471 U.S. 1015 (1985).

[228] *Id.*, 80 T.C. at 839.

in the God of Am [the deity worshipped by the members of the organization], it also advocates belief in the God of Tax Avoidance."[229] In words that have considerable implications for fundraising for charitable purposes generally, the court wrote that a "substantial nonexempt purpose does not become an exempt purpose simply because it promotes the organization in some way."[230] The court apparently grasped the larger portent of its opinion and attempted to narrow its scope by noting that "[w]e are not holding today that any group which discusses the tax consequences of donations to and/or expenditures of its organization is in danger of losing or not acquiring tax-exempt status."[231] That, of course, was the essence of its holding in the prior case.

The court thereafter held that an organization, the membership of which was "religious missions," was not entitled to tax-exempt status as a religious organization because it engaged in the substantial nonexempt purpose of providing financial and tax advice.[232] The court was heavily influenced by a rush of cases before it concerning, in the words of the court, "efforts of taxpayers to hide behind the cover of purported tax-exempt religious organizations for significant tax avoidance purposes."[233] As the court saw the facts of this case, each member mission was the result of individuals attempting to create churches involving only their families so as to convert after-tax personal and family expenses into deductible charitable contributions. The central organization provided sample incorporation papers, tax seminars, and other forms of tax advice and assistance to those creating the missions. Consequently, the court was persuaded that the "pattern of tax avoidance activities which appears to be present at the membership level, combined with . . . [the organization's] admitted role as a tax advisor to its members" justified the conclusion that the organization was ineligible for tax exemption.[234]

---

[229] *Id.* at 840.

[230] *Id.* at 841.

[231] *Id.* at 842. This decision was affirmed (740 F.2d 967 (6th Cir. 1984), *cert. den.*, 471 U.S. 1015 (1985)).

[232] *National Association of American Churches* v. *Commissioner*, 82 T.C. 18 (1984).

[233] *Id.* at 29–30.

[234] *Id.* at 32.

These three court opinions can be read as meaning (1) the courts are not going to blithely extend tax-exempt status to phony churches and other religious organizations, and (2) where an organization's only function is the provision of financial and tax planning services, it cannot constitute a tax-exempt charitable organization, even where its only "customers" are other charitable, educational, and religious entities. At the same time, particularly when read out of context, some of the court's pronouncements on this point make little sense and are hardly synchronous with real-world fundraising practices. In light of this expansive application of the private benefit doctrine, the court's disclaimer in the second of these cases[235] looms large.

(d) Trade Shows

There are special rules, in the unrelated business context, with respect to the conduct of certain trade show activities by certain tax-exempt organizations. This body of law[236] is available for tax-exempt charitable, social welfare, labor, agricultural, and horticultural organizations, and business leagues[237] that regularly conduct, as a substantial tax-exempt purpose, shows that stimulate interest in and demand for the products of a particular industry or segment of an industry or that educate persons in attendance regarding new developments or products or services related to the tax-exempt activities of the organization.

Under these rules, the term *unrelated business* does not include qualified *convention and trade show activities* of an eligible organization.[238] This phrase is defined to mean "any activity of a kind traditionally conducted at conventions, annual meetings, or trade shows, including but not limited to, any activity one of the purposes of which is to attract persons in an industry generally (without regard to membership in the sponsoring organization) as well as members of the public to the show for the purpose of

---

[235] See the text accompanied by *supra* note 231.

[236] IRC § 513(d)(1), (3).

[237] These are, collectively, organizations that are tax-exempt by reason of IRC § 501(a) and are described in IRC § 501(c)(3)–(6).

[238] IRC § 513(d)(1).

displaying industry products or services, or to educate persons engaged in the industry in the development of new products and services or new rules and regulations affecting the industry."[239]

A *qualified* convention and trade show activity is an activity that is:

- Carried out by an eligible organization;
- Conducted in conjunction with an international, national, state, regional, or local convention, annual meeting, or show;
- Sponsored by an eligible organization that has as one of its purposes in sponsoring the activity the promotion and stimulation of interest in and demand for the products and services of the industry involved in general or the education of persons in attendance regarding new developments or products and services related to the tax-exempt activities of the organization;
- Designed to achieve this purpose through the character of the exhibits and the extent of the industry products displayed.[240]

The income that is excluded from taxation by these rules is derived from the rental of display space to exhibitors. This is the case even though the exhibitors who rent the space are permitted to sell or solicit orders, as long as the show is a qualified trade show or a qualified convention and trade show.[241] This exclusion is also available with respect to a supplier's exhibit that is conducted by an eligible organization in conjunction with a qualified convention or trade show.[242] A *supplier's exhibit* is one in which the exhibitor displays goods or services that are supplied to, rather than by, the members of the qualifying organization in the conduct of the members' own trade or business.[243] This exclusion is not available, however, to a stand-alone suppliers' exhibit that is not a qualified convention show.[244] Nonetheless, income from a suppliers' show is not taxable where

---

[239] IRC § 513(d)(3)(A); Reg. § 1.513-3(c)(4).

[240] IRC § 513(d)(3)(B).

[241] Reg. § 1.513-3(d)(1).

[242] Reg. § 1.513-3(c), Example (2).

[243] Reg. § 1.513-3(d)(2).

[244] Reg. § 1.513-3(e), Example (4).

the displays are educational in nature and are displays at which soliciting and selling are prohibited.[245]

(e) Provision of Services

Until recently, the IRS regarded the provision of services by one tax-exempt organization to another exempt organization as an unrelated business. This is because it is not inherently an exempt function for one exempt entity to provide services to another one, even where both organizations have the same category of tax-exempt status. For example, the IRS ruled that the provision of administrative services by a tax-exempt association to an exempt voluntary employees' beneficiary association (VEBA), where the VEBA provided a health and welfare benefit plan for the association's members' employees, was an unrelated business.[246] Likewise, the provision of management services by a tax-exempt association to a charitable organization was determined by the IRS to be an unrelated business.[247] Indeed, the provision of management services by a nonprofit organization to unaffiliated charitable organizations led to the revocation of the organization's tax exemption as a charitable entity.[248]

In some instances, however, it can be a related business for a tax-exempt organization to provide services to one or more other exempt entities. As an illustration, a business association with an aggressive litigation strategy placed the litigation function in a separate exempt organization because of a substantial risk of counterclaims and other retaliatory actions against the association and its members; the IRS concluded that the provision by the association of management and administrative services to the other exempt organization was in furtherance of the association's exempt purposes.[249] Likewise, the IRS ruled that a national charitable organization engaged in related business activities when it provided certain coordination services for its chapters in connection with a new program it was

---

[245] Rev. Rul. 75-516, 1975-2 C.B. 220.

[246] Tech. Adv. Mem. 9550001.

[247] Tech. Adv. Mem. 9811001.

[248] Tech. Adv. Mem. 9822004.

[249] Tech. Adv. Mem. 9608003.

implementing.[250] Additionally, a tax-exempt organization that was an arm of an association of public school boards, which administered the association's cash/risk management funds, was ruled by the IRS to be engaged in an exempt function (namely, the charitable activity of lessening the burdens of government).[251]

Likewise, the provision of professional, managerial, and administrative services among a group of interrelated healthcare organizations, directly or by means of a partnership, was ruled to be a bundle of related businesses.[252] Similarly, the lease and management of a computer system to a partnership by a supporting organization with respect to a university's medical center, which system was used for billing, collection, and record keeping of the partners, was found to be a related business because the partners were physicians comprising the faculty of the university's medical school and teaching hospital.[253] Further, the IRS ruled that a graduate educational institution was engaged in a related business when it provided "central services" to a group of affiliated colleges (such as campus security, a central steam plant, accounting services, and a risk and property insurance program).[254] Other rulings are issued by the IRS from time to time on this point.[255]

The law in this area started, in the late 1990s, to dramatically change when the IRS began consideration of the tax consequences of creation of a health care delivery system by means of a contractual arrangement known as a *joint operating agreement* (JOA). This type of system is comprised of a number of tax-exempt organizations, including entities such as healthcare providers and supporting organizations; some of these organizations are compensated for the provision of management and administrative services to entities within the system. Under traditional analysis, these services would be unrelated businesses (thereby negating the effective use of JOAs). To avert this outcome, the IRS began issuing rulings that this

---

[250] Priv. Ltr. Rul. 9641011.

[251] Tech. Adv. Mem. 9711002.

[252] Priv. Ltr. Rul. 9839039.

[253] Tech. Adv. Mem. 9847002.

[254] Priv. Ltr. Rul. 9849027.

[255] E.g., Priv. Ltr. Rul. 199910060.

type of financial entanglement was to be treated as "merely a matter of accounting,"[256] which means disregarded for tax purposes (and thus that the services are not unrelated business).[257]

This matter-of-accounting rationale is largely applicable where the tax-exempt organizations in the arrangement are in a parent-subsidiary relationship. In its JOA rulings, however, the IRS has also extended application of the rationale to affiliations that are analogous to parent-subsidiary arrangements. These rulings refer to administrative, management, and similar services as *corporate services*.

This outcome obviously was welcome news for organizations desiring to utilize joint operating agreements. But, from the larger perspective, the development was a transformative one for many other tax-exempt organizations. Inasmuch as the tax law rationale underlying these agreements could not fairly be confined to that context, it meant that, in any situation in which a tax-exempt organization had a parent-subsidiary relationship with another exempt organization, the provision of corporate services could be protected from unrelated business taxation by reason of this rationale. It also meant that the matter-of-accounting rationale could be extended to any arrangement where the relationship between two tax-exempt organizations was analogous to that of parent and subsidiary.

The first time this parent-subsidiary rationale was used outside the healthcare setting was in connection with a typical situation: where a tax-exempt social welfare organization provided corporate services to its related foundation.[258] This arrangement was held to not generate unrelated

---

[256] In constructing this rationale, the IRS applied this accounting concept previously reserved for use only in the context of the feeder organization rules (IRC § 502) and the unrelated debt-financed income rules (IRC § 514). For example, the IRS ruled that a debt owed to a tax-exempt labor union by its wholly owned title-holding company was not an acquisition indebtedness (it was termed an *interorganizational indebtedness*) because the "very nature of the title-holding company as well as the parent-subsidiary relationship show this indebtedness to be merely a matter of accounting between the organizations rather than an indebtedness" contemplated by the unrelated debt-financed income rules (Rev. Rul. 77-72, 1977-1 C.B. 157, 158).

[257] E.g., Priv. Ltr. Rul. 9651047. Many more rulings of this nature have subsequently been issued.

[258] Priv. Ltr. Rul. 200022056.

business income because of the "close structural relationship" between the two organizations. Thus, where this type of in-tandem relationship is in place, the matter-of-accounting rationale is applicable, and the provision of corporate services is not an unrelated business—a complete reversal as to what the state of the law was prior to the advent of the joint operating agreement.

As to arrangements where the relationship is analogous to that of parent and subsidiary, the first illustration was provided in the case of two charitable organizations that managed healthcare facilities; they entered into a management agreement with a third such organization. Each of these entities was independent of the others. By reason of the agreement, these two charitable organizations were found by the IRS to have ceded to the third organization "significant financial, managerial and operational authority over their affairs, including exclusive authority over capital and operating budgets, strategic plans, managed care contracting, the ability to allocate or reallocate services among the health care facilities [they] manage, and the ability to monitor and audit compliance with directives." The IRS ruled that these two organizations were "effectively under the common control" of the third organization. Therefore, the IRS held that these organizations are "within a relationship analogous to that of a parent and subsidiary," so that the provision of these corporate services would not result in unrelated business income.[259]

The IRS usually does not explain why certain corporate services are considered exempt functions and when to use the exempt-function rationale and when to use the matter-of-accounting rationale.[260]

§ 2.3 EXCEPTIONS

The unrelated business rules amply include exceptions, many of which are of import in the context of communications by means of the Internet. Some of these exceptions are found in a set of rules termed *modifications* of the unrelated business laws. Others are stated as exceptions as such. Thus, notwithstanding the fact that an activity may constitute an unrelated trade or business that is regularly carried on, the income generated by the activity

---

[259] Priv. Ltr. Rul. 200108045.

[260] E.g., Priv. Ltr. Rul. 200108048.

may escape federal unrelated business income taxation pursuant to one or more exceptions.

(a) Modifications

In determining unrelated business income, both gross income derived from an unrelated business and related expense deductions are computed, taking into account certain modifications.[261]

(i) Concept of Passive Income. The unrelated business rules were enacted to ameliorate the effects of competition between tax-exempt organizations and taxable organizations by taxing the net income of exempt organizations from unrelated business activities.[262] The concept underlying this statutory scheme is that the business endeavors must be *active* ones for competitive activity to result. Correspondingly, income derived by a tax-exempt organization in a *passive* manner generally is income that is not acquired as the result of competitive activity; consequently, nearly all forms of passive income are not taxed as unrelated business income.[263]

(ii) Excluded Income in General. The modifications rules exclude from unrelated business income taxation certain stated forms of passive income. These include dividends, interest, annuities, royalties, rent, and capital gain.[264] The legislative history of these rules reflects the belief of Congress that passive income should not be taxed in this context "where it is used for exempt purposes because investments producing incomes of these types have long been recognized as proper for educational and charitable organizations."[265]

There may be forms of passive income incurred by tax-exempt organizations that are not strictly within the technical meaning of one of the

---

[261] IRC § 512(b).

[262] See *supra* § 1(a).

[263] Two significant exceptions to this generalization concern passive income derived from unrelated debt-financed property and passive income received from controlled corporations (IRC § 512(b)(4), (13)).

[264] IRC § 512(b)(1)–(3), (5).

[265] H. Rep. No. 2319, *supra* note 4 at 38; S. Rep. No. 2375, *supra* note 4 at 30–31.

specific terms referenced in the passive income rules yet that are nonetheless outside the framework of unrelated income taxation. This is evidenced in the legislative history of the unrelated business rules, which stated: "Dividends, interest, royalties, most rents, capital gains and losses and *similar items* are excluded from the base of the tax on unrelated income because . . . [the Senate Finance Committee] believes that they are 'passive' in character and are not likely to result in serious competition for taxable businesses having similar income."[266]

(iii) Royalties. In the context of Internet communications, the exclusion from unrelated business income taxation for royalties[267] is the most important of these modifications. Until recently, the law as to the definition of the term *royalty* in this setting was vague. (This state of affairs is to be contrasted with the fact that, for the most part, terms such as *dividend*, *interest*, *annuity*, *rent*, and *capital gain* are solidly defined in the federal tax law.)

Essentially, a royalty is a payment by a person to another person for the use of a valuable intangible property right owned by the latter person, such as a trademark, trade name, service mark, or copyright.[268] In the tax-exempt organizations context, however, an ongoing issue is the extent to which an exempt organization—that is, the recipient of the income that assertedly is royalty income—may engage in activities, usually termed *services*, that stimulate the flow of the income in question. For example, an exempt organization may have an affinity card program, which generates income for the organization in proportion to use of the cards by the organization's membership; the organization may engage in activities, such as articles in its publications and a booth at its annual convention, intended to induce its members to purchase goods and services by means of the affinity cards. As to this example, the question becomes: At what point does the extent of these activities by the organization defeat the characterization of the income paid to the exempt organization (such as

---

[266] S. Rep. No. 2375, *supra* note 4 at 30–31 (emphasis supplied). Also H. Rep. No. 2319, *supra* note 4 at 36–38.

[267] IRC § 512(b)(2).

[268] E.g., *Fraternal Order of Police Illinois State Troopers Lodge No. 41* v. *Commissioner*, *supra* note 145; *Disabled American Veterans* v. *United States*, *supra* note 197.

by a financial institution) as a royalty (assuming it qualified for royalty treatment at all)?

At the outset of litigation on this issue, the parties (like most litigants) assumed polarized positions. The exempt organizations asserted that a royalty is a payment for the use of valuable intangible property rights, period. That is, this view holds that whether the income is passive or not is irrelevant. It had been the position of the IRS that monies should be taxed, even if characterized as royalties, where the tax-exempt organization is actively involved in the enterprise that generates the revenue, such as through the provision of services.[269] Indeed, the IRS may contend that the relationship between the parties is that of joint venturers.[270] A common instance of this treatment is the insistence by the IRS that the funds an exempt organization receives for an endorsement are taxable as unrelated business income, while the organization asserts that the monies are royalties paid for the use of its name and logo.[271]

The contemporary litigation on this issue commenced in the U.S. Tax Court. One case concerned affinity card program payments; the other, payments for the use of mailing lists. In the mailing list case, the court held that, if the arrangement was otherwise properly structured, the mailing list payments are royalties and thus that they are excludable from unrelated business income taxation even if they are not forms of passive income—that is, even if the exempt organization is providing services in an effort to stimulate the list rentals.[272] The court also so held in the case of affinity card program payments.[273] The essence of this view is that, although Congress *believed* this type of income to be passive,[274] that does not necessarily mean that this

---

[269] E.g., *National Water Well Association, Inc. v. Commissioner*, 92 T.C. 75 (1989).

[270] E.g., Priv. Ltr. Rul. 9450028. In one instance, the IRS asserted (without success) that a tax-exempt organization that raised funds in a lawful gambling operation, by the placement of "tip jars" in various bars and lounges, should be taxed on the gambling income on the theory that the exempt organization was in a joint venture with the taverns (*Vigilant Hose Company of Emmitsburg v. United States, supra* note 28).

[271] E.g., Tech. Adv. Mem. 9509002.

[272] *Sierra Club, Inc. v. Commissioner*, 65 T.C.M. 2582 (1993).

[273] *Sierra Club, Inc. v. Commissioner*, 103 T.C. 307 (1994).

[274] See the text accompanied by *supra* note 265.

form of income always *must be* passive.[275] Stated in the reverse, this view holds that a statutorily classified item of excludible income remains excludible irrespective of whether the income is passive or derived from the conduct of activities.

These two cases were appealed on a consolidated basis. The mailing list case was affirmed; the affinity card case was remanded. The appellate court developed a compromise definition of the term *royalty* in this context. It adopted the Tax Court definition, albeit with the admonition that a royalty "cannot include compensation for services rendered by the owner of the property."[276] This intermediate position is seen in the court of appeals' observation that, to the extent that the IRS "claims that a tax-exempt organization can do nothing to acquire such fees," the agency is "incorrect."[277] Yet, this court continued, "to the extent that . . . [the exempt organization involved] appears to argue that a 'royalty' is any payment for the use of a property right—such as a copyright—regardless of any additional services that are performed in addition to the owner simply permitting another to use the right at issue, we disagree."[278] In other words, a tax-exempt organization may provide *some* services in this regard and not thereby disqualify the payment as a royalty, but if the services are *substantial* the royalty exclusion is forfeited.

The Tax Court held, on the remand, that the payments were royalties, even under the appellate court's definition of the term.[279] The IRS's position was further eroded when the Tax Court again held, in three opinions, that mailing list payments qualified as royalties. [280] The denouement of the

---

[275] This view is based on language in the legislative history indicating that the exception for dividends, interest, annuities, royalties, and the like "applies not only to investment income [a concept broader than passive income], but also to such items as business interest on overdue open accounts receivable" (S. Rep. No. 2375, *supra* note 4, at 108; H. Rep. No. 2319, *supra* note 4, at 110).

[276] *Sierra Club, Inc.* v. *Commissioner*, 86 F.3d 1526, 1532 (9th Cir. 1996).

[277] *Id*. at 1535.

[278] *Id*.

[279] *Sierra Club, Inc.* v. *Commissioner*, 77 T.C.M. 1569 (1999).

[280] *Common Cause* v. *Commissioner*, 112 T.C. 332 (1999); *Planned Parenthood Federation of America, Inc.* v. *Commissioner*, 77 T.C.M. 2227 (1999); *Mississippi State University Alumni, Inc.* v. *Commissioner*, 74 T.C.M. 458 (1999).

government's stance in this regard arrived when two other appellate courts ruled against it.[281]

By the close of 1999, the IRS was forced to conclude that this series of defeats was insurmountable—that is, that the courts were not going to accede to its interpretation of the scope of the tax-excludible royalty. The IRS National Office, late in that year, communicated with its exempt organizations specialists in the field, essentially capitulating on the point; a memorandum distributed to them stated bluntly that "[c]ases should be resolved in a manner consistent with the existing court cases."[282] This memorandum added that "it is now clear that courts will continue to find the income [generated by activities such as mailing list rentals and affinity card programs] to be excluded royalty income unless the factual record clearly reflects more than unsubstantial services being provided." Two factors were highlighted by the IRS as establishing nontaxable royalty income: where the involvement of the exempt organization is "relatively minimal"[283] and where the exempt organization "hired outside contractors to perform most services associated with the exploitation of the use of intangible property."[284]

This is not to say that the government is losing every case on this point. Where the tax-exempt organization participates in and maintains control over significant aspects of the activities that generate the income, the courts will reject the contention that the revenue is an excludible royalty.[285]

---

[281] *Oregon State University Alumni Association, Inc.* v. *Commissioner; Alumni Association of University of Oregon, Inc.* v. *Commissioner*, 193 F.3d 1098 (9th Cir. 1999), *aff'g* 71 T.C.M. 1935 (1996), 71 T.C.M. 2093 (1996).

[282] This memorandum is dated December 16, 1999.

[283] While difficult to quantify as a general standard, this characterization of the permitted threshold probably is too stringent. More accurate terminology is *insubstantial* or *insignificant*. At any rate, the involvement of the exempt organization in the provision of services may not be *substantial* if royalty treatment is to be achieved.

[284] This technique may not be of utility from a tax perspective if the contract involved casts the "outside contractor" as an agent of the tax-exempt organization (see the text accompanied by *supra* note 93).

[285] E.g., *Arkansas State Police Association, Inc.* v. *Commissioner*, 81 T.C.M. 1172 (2001), *aff'd*, 2002-1 U.S.T.C. ¶ 50, 269 (8th Cir. 2002).

An issue under consideration at the IRS is whether there should be an allocation of a single payment as between compensation for the use of intangible property (a royalty) and compensation for services that are more than insubstantial. Some tax-exempt organizations engage in the practice, making partial use of the royalty exclusion by the use of two contracts: one for the royalty arrangement and one for the taxable services.[286]

(b) Exceptions

In addition to those provided in the rules concerning the modifications and other exceptions referenced above, there are various other exceptions to the rules concerning unrelated business income taxation. Those that are of particular pertinence in the Internet communications context are summarized next.

(i) Businesses Conducted by Volunteers. Exempt from the scope of taxable unrelated trade or business is a business in which substantially all of the work in carrying on the business is performed for the tax-exempt organization without compensation.[287] An example of this exception is a tax-exempt orphanage operating a secondhand clothing store and selling items to the general public, where substantially all of the work in running the store is performed by volunteers.[288] Another illustration is the production and sale of phonograph records by a medical organization, where the services of the performers were provided without compensation.[289] Still another illustration concerned a trade association that sold advertising in a commercial, unrelated manner but avoided income taxation of the activity because the work involved was provided solely by volunteers.[290] In

---

[286] There is some support for this approach in *Texas Farm Bureau, Inc.* v. *United States*, 53 F.3d 120 (5th Cir. 1995).

[287] IRC § 513(a)(1).

[288] S. Rep. No. 2375, *supra* note 4, at 108.

[289] *Greene County Medical Society Foundation* v. *United States*, 345 F. Supp. 900 (W.D. Mo. 1972).

[290] Priv. Ltr. Rul. 9302023.

another case, a court found that a tax-exempt religious order that operated a farm was not taxable on the income it derived from the farming operations because the farm was maintained by the uncompensated labor of the members of the order.[291]

A court ruled that this exemption was defeated, in part, because free drinks provided to the collectors and cashiers in connection with the conduct of a bingo game by a tax-exempt organization were considered "liquid compensation."[292] That position was, however, rejected on appeal.[293] The court nonetheless subsequently held that this exception was not available, in the case of an exempt organization that regularly carried on gambling activities, because the dealers and other individuals received tips from patrons of the games.[294]

(ii) Convenience Businesses. Also excluded is a business, in the case of a tax-exempt charitable organization or a state college or university, that is carried on by the organization primarily for the convenience of its members, students, patients, officers, or employees.[295] An example of this exception is a laundry operated by a tax-exempt college for the purpose of laundering dormitory linens and the clothing of students.[296] As another illustration, the provision by an exempt hospital of mobile services to its patients by means of specially designed vans was ruled to be a convenience business.[297]

Read literally, this exception pertains only to the classes of persons who have the requisite relationship directly with the tax-exempt organization; for example, it applies with respect to services carried on by a hospital for the convenience of *its* patients. The IRS ruled, however, that the doctrine

---

[291] *St. Joseph Farms of Indiana Brothers of the Congregation of Holy Cross, Southwest Province, Inc.* v. *Commissioner*, 85 T.C. 9 (1985), *appeal dismissed* (7th Cir. 1986).

[292] *Waco Lodge No. 166, Benevolent & Protective Order of Elks* v. *Commissioner*, 42 T.C.M. 1202 (1981).

[293] 696 F.2d 372 (5th Cir. 1983).

[294] *Executive Network Club, Inc.* v. *Commissioner*, 69 T.C.M. 1680 (1995).

[295] IRC § 513(a)(2).

[296] Reg. § 1.513-2(6).

[297] Priv. Ltr. Rul. 9841049.

was available when an exempt organization's activities were for the convenience of patients of another, albeit related, exempt entity.[298] The IRS refused to extend the doctrine to embrace spouses and children of students of a university.[299]

(iii) Sales of Gift Items. Unrelated trade or business does not include a business that constitutes the selling of merchandise, substantially all of which has been contributed to the tax-exempt organization.[300] This exception is available for thrift shops that sell donated clothes, books, and the like to the general public.[301] Yet the exception is not confined to business conducted by these shops; it may be utilized, for example, in connection with the conduct of frequent auctions, as long as substantially all of the goods or services auctioned were given to the organization.

§ 2.4 OTHER RULES

(a) Partnership Rules

If a trade or business regularly carried on by a partnership, of which a tax-exempt organization is a member, is an unrelated trade or business with respect to the organization, in computing its unrelated business taxable income the organization must include its share (whether or not distributed and subject to the modifications rules[302]) of the gross income from the partnership from the unrelated business and its share of the partnership deductions directly connected with the gross income.[303] This rule—a *look-through rule*—applies irrespective of whether the tax-exempt organization is a general partner or limited partner in the partnership.[304]

---

[298] Priv. Ltr. Rul. 9535023.

[299] Tech. Adv. Mem. 9645004.

[300] IRC § 513(a)(3).

[301] Rev. Rul. 71-581, 1971-2 C.B. 236.

[302] See *supra* § 3(a).

[303] IRC § 512(c)(1); Reg. § 1.512(c)-1.

[304] Rev. Rul. 79-222, 1979-2 C.B. 236.

(b) Limited Liability Company Rules

A tax-exempt organization may establish or participate in a limited liability company which conducts a business that is an unrelated business with respect to the organization. If the exempt organization is not the only member of the limited liability company, the tax treatment of the income to the organization from the business operation is determined using the look-through rules utilized in the partnership context. If, however, the exempt organization is the sole member of the limited liability company, the company is disregarded for tax purposes[305] and the exempt organization is regarded as having conducted the unrelated business directly.

(c) Deduction Rules

Generally, the term *unrelated business taxable income* means the gross income derived by a tax-exempt organization from an unrelated business that is regularly carried on by the organization, less business deductions that are directly connected with the carrying on of the business.[306] For purposes of computing unrelated business taxable income, both gross income and business deductions are computed using the modifications rules.[307]

To be *directly connected with* the conduct of an unrelated business, generally an item of deduction must have a proximate and primary relationship to the carrying on of that business. In the case of an organization that derives gross income from the regular conduct of two or more unrelated businesses, unrelated business taxable income is the aggregate of gross income from all unrelated business activities, less the aggregate of the deductions allowed with respect to all unrelated business activities.[308] Expenses, depreciation, and similar items attributable solely to the conduct of unrelated business are proximately and primarily related to that business

---

[305] Ann. 99-102, 1999-2 C.B. 545.

[306] IRC § 512(a)(1).

[307] See *supra* § 3(a).

[308] Reg. § 1.512(a)-1(a).

and therefore qualify for deduction to the extent they meet the requirements of relevant provisions of the federal income tax law.[309]

A loss incurred in the conduct of an unrelated activity may be offset against the net gain occasioned by the conduct of another unrelated activity only where the activity generating the loss is a *business* in the first instance. That is, the activity must be carried on with a profit motive.[310] An activity that consistently yields losses may be regarded by the IRS as something other than a business, in which case the loss cannot be offset against gross income from an unrelated business.

Where facilities and/or personnel are used both to carry on tax-exempt activities and to conduct unrelated business, the expenses, depreciation, and similar items attributable to the facilities and/or personnel, such as overhead and salary, must be allocated between the two uses on a basis that is reasonable.[311] Despite the statutory rule that an expense must be directly connected with an unrelated business, the regulations merely state that the portion of the expense allocated to the unrelated business activity is, where the allocation is on a reasonable basis, proximately and primarily related to the business activity.[312] Once an item is proximately and primarily related to a business undertaking, it is allowable as a deduction in computing unrelated business income in the manner and to the extent permitted by federal income tax law generally.[313]

Gross income may be derived from an unrelated business that exploits an exempt function.[314] Generally, in these situations, expenses, depreciation, and similar items attributable to the conduct of the tax-exempt function are not deductible in computing unrelated business taxable income. Since the items are incident to a function of the type that is the chief purpose of the organization to conduct, they do not possess a proximate and

---

[309] E.g., IRC §§ 162 (business expenses), 167 (depreciation). Reg. § 1.512(a)-1(b).

[310] See *supra* § 1(b)(ii).

[311] Reg. § 1.512(a)-1(c).

[312] *Id.*

[313] *Id.*

[314] See *supra* § 1(d)(v).

primary relationship to the unrelated trade or business. Therefore, they do not qualify as being directly related to that business.[315]

A tax-exempt organization will be denied business expense deductions in computing its unrelated business taxable income if it cannot adequately substantiate that the expenses were incurred or that they were directly connected with the unrelated activity. In one instance, the IRS successfully disallowed nearly all of an exempt organization's claimed deductions because it did not maintain adequate books and records, failed to accurately allocate expenses among accounts, and had insufficient accounting practices.[316]

(d) Tax Structure

Even though a nonprofit organization achieves exemption from the federal income tax,[317] it nonetheless remains potentially taxable on any unrelated business income.[318]

The unrelated income tax rates applicable to most tax-exempt organizations are the corporate rates.[319] Some exempt organizations, such as trusts, are subject to the individual income tax rates.[320]

The tax law features the following three-bracket structure for corporations: a 15 percent tax rate on taxable income of $50,000 or less, a 25 percent rate on income between $50,000 and $75,000, and a 34 percent rate on income over $75,000. An additional 5 percent surtax is imposed on taxable income between $100,000 and $335,000, causing a marginal tax rate of 39 percent on taxable income in that range.[321]

Tax-exempt organizations must make quarterly estimated payments of the tax on unrelated business income, under the same rules that require

---

[315] Reg. § 1.512(a)-1(d).

[316] *CORE Special Purpose Fund* v. *Commissioner*, 49 T.C.M. 626 (1985).

[317] IRC § 501(a).

[318] IRC § 501(b).

[319] IRC § 11.

[320] IRC § 1(d).

[321] IRC § 11(b).

quarterly estimated payments of corporate income taxes.[322] Revenue and expenses associated with unrelated business activity are reported to the IRS on a tax return (Form 990-T).[323]

§ 2.5 INTERNET COMMUNICATIONS

Unrelated business activity by tax-exempt organizations can be and is being conducted on the Internet. Products and goods are being advertised and sold, in unrelated business activities, by this means. The Internet, being a medium of communication, offers to exempt organizations (and others) a magnificent opportunity to create business, market goods and services, and sell these goods and services to the general public. As is the case in other contexts, however, the federal tax law does not provide any unique treatment to transactions or activities of tax-exempt organizations involving related or unrelated business activity simply because the Internet is the medium of communication.

(a) Internet Unrelated Business Activity in General

As the IRS saliently observed, the "use of the Internet to accomplish a particular task does not change the way the tax laws apply to that task." The IRS continued: "Advertising is still advertising and fundraising is still fundraising."[324] The agency also could have written: "Unrelated business activity is still unrelated business activity." Indeed, the IRS stated in 1999 that "it is reasonable to assume that as the Service position [on exempt organization Web merchandising, advertising, and publishing] develops it will remain consistent with our position with respect to advertising and merchandising and publishing in the off-line world."[325] Thus, the rules as to unrelated business activity by tax-exempt organizations embrace this type of activity by means of the Internet.

---

[322] IRC § 6655(a)–(d).

[323] IRC § 6012(a)(2), (4).

[324] IRS FY 2000 CPE Text on Exempt Organizations and Internet Use at 64.

[325] *Id.* at 74.

There are four forms of Internet communications in this setting:

1. A communication published on a publicly accessible Web page
2. A communication posted on a password-protected portion of a Web site
3. A communication on a listserv (or by means of other methods such as a newsgroup, chat room, and/or forum)
4. A communication by means of e-mail

The IRS observed that "[m]any tax-exempt organizations now have a web page that describes their purpose, discusses their activities, provides lists of upcoming events, lists local affiliates, provides contact information, and more." The IRS also noted, in the Announcement, that, "[b]y publishing a webpage on the Internet, an exempt organization can provide the general public with information about the organization, its activities, and issues of concern to the organization, as well as immediate access to websites of other organizations."[326]

(i) Business Activities. As discussed, the federal tax law views—by application of the fragmentation rule—a tax-exempt organization as a cluster of businesses, with each discrete activity evaluated independently from the others.[327] Again, the fundamental statutory definition of the term, in the unrelated business setting, is that a business includes "any activity which is carried on for the production of income from the sale of goods or the performance of services."[328] Thus, nearly everything that an exempt organization engages in by means of the Internet is a *business*. Indeed, utilization of the Internet by a tax-exempt organization entails either the operation of one or more businesses or is a component of one or more businesses.

The Web site of a typical tax-exempt organization primarily, if not exclusively, contains information concerning the organization's programs.[329] Its operations and purposes are described, often in some detail. In some instances, substantive information is provided pertaining to its

---

[326] *Id.* at 70.

[327] See *supra* § 1(b)(v).

[328] IRC § 513(c).

[329] See § 1.6.

area or areas of interest. Some collateral information may be on the site: Photographs, maps, membership lists, and staff directories are common. Many charitable organizations include information about giving opportunities. Some tax-exempt organizations discuss their advocacy activities. Rarely, however, are unrelated business endeavors openly reflected on an exempt organization's Web site.

It is not, as noted, common for a Web site to function wholly as one or more discrete businesses. Rather, these various postings are extensions of offline programs and other activities. A university's site, for example, summarizes its undergraduate and graduate programs, describes its various schools, and offers information as to how and when to apply for admission. A scientific research institution's site inventories the research projects in process and perhaps highlights the work of a particular scientist. An association's site enumerates its various programs, perhaps contains information about its advocacy efforts, and includes information about its other efforts, such as certification and enforcement of its code of ethics. Usually all of this information is also available elsewhere.

One of the major difficulties in this regard is the allocation of time and expenditures to these Web site offerings.[330] There are, of course, expenses of building and maintaining a Web site. The costs of posting the information, however, are negligible. Thus, an unanswered question is: How are Web site establishment and maintenance costs allocated to a tax-exempt organization's various programs and other activities?

There may be an alternative approach. Perhaps the fragmentation rule should be applied in such a way that Web site establishment and maintenance itself is a business, or perhaps two or more businesses. Certainly the matter of determination and allocation of expenses would be simplified. For most tax-exempt organizations, this approach would mean that Web site creation and maintenance is wholly a related business. For other exempt organizations, even with this approach, however, the expenses of activities such as fundraising, advocacy, and unrelated business would have to be factored out for reporting and other purposes.

(ii) Regularly Carried On. For the most part, activities reflected on a tax-exempt organization's Web site are regularly carried on. Organizations,

---

[330] See § 1.8(a).

from time to time, change the content of the site, of course, but usually the categories of information (programs, directories, fundraising, advocacy, certification, ethics enforcement, and the like) remain the same.

(iii) Substantially Related. As noted, nearly everything on a tax-exempt organization's Web site—often, *everything*—consists of information and material that is related to the organization's exempt purposes. The biggest exception is fundraising activities. Many organizations that are involved in unrelated business do not, as noted, openly reflect that fact on their Web site. Likewise, the participation by an exempt organization in a joint venture (such as a partnership or limited liability company) usually is not mentioned on the site; the same is true with the use of a for-profit subsidiary.

(iv) Advertising in General. One of the major uses by tax-exempt organizations of the Internet is for *advertising*—of themselves. Today one of the principal purposes of an exempt organization's Web site is advertising of its programs—services, products, and facilities. Visits to Web sites lead to invitations to apply to a college, join an association, explore a museum, tour a scientific research facility, and much more. Some Web sites are entirely bastions of advertising, with headings such as "Who we are," "What we do," "FAQs about us," and so forth.

Usually, advertising[331] by tax-exempt organizations of the products or services of other persons is considered to be an unrelated activity. Pre-Internet, rare was the situation where advertising was considered a related function.

The advent of the Internet has not changed the rules as to commercial advertising, however. From this perspective, three categories of information dissemination are in the realm of advertising: related advertising, commercial (unrelated) advertising, and acknowledgments in the context of corporate sponsorships.[332] As between related and unrelated advertising, the Supreme Court instructed that a tax-exempt organization can "control its publication of advertisements in such a way as to reflect an intention to contribute importantly to its...[exempt] functions."[333] This

---

[331] See *supra* § 2(a)(i).

[332] See *supra* § 2(b).

[333] *United States* v. *American College of Physicians, supra* note 153, at 849.

can be done, wrote the Court, by "coordinating the content of the advertisements with the editorial content of the issue, or by publishing only advertisements reflecting new developments."[334]

One of the issues of the day in this regard is whether a communication that would otherwise be an acknowledgment is transmuted into advertising because of a link between the exempt organization and its corporate sponsor. An IRS private letter ruling suggests that a link causes conversion of the communication to advertising.[335]

(v) Compensation for Advertising. The IRS observed that the advertising rates charged by a tax-exempt organization "will vary considerably based on its area of concern, the quality of its web site and the user traffic it generates."[336] The IRS includes as advertising the display of a "banner, graphic, or statement of sponsorship." The agency noted that exempt organizations generally favor the "less obtrusive" sponsorship statements rather than the banner advertisement, in that the latter is "perceived as more appropriate to commercial sites and potentially more offensive to potential donors." Also, a moving banner is "probably more likely" to be considered taxable advertising than other approaches.

One way for an exempt organization to be compensated for Web site advertising is by means of a flat fee. An organization may offer pay-per-view advertisements, where it earns a credit each time a site visitor views the advertisement. A related form of compensation is the click-through charge, where the advertiser pays only when an individual clicks through the banner or corporate logo and visits the advertiser's site.

The IRS addressed the fact that many exempt organization Web sites include links to related, affiliated, or similarly recommended sites. Some organizations exchange banners or links. The IRS wrote that it is presently "unclear" whether it will treat link or banner exchanges as "similar to a

---

[334] *Id.* at 849–850.

[335] Priv. Ltr. Rul. 9723046, where it was written that "[a]dvertising spots differ from mere expressions of recognition in that they may contain additional information about an advertiser's product, services or facilities, or function as a hypertext link to the advertiser."

[336] IRS FY 2000 CPE Text on Exempt Organizations and Internet Use at 74. All quotations of the IRS in this section and the 8 following ones are from this text.

mailing list exchange or whether an organization that participates in such a program may incur liability for unrelated business income." The agency added that, in analyzing these exchange mechanisms, their *purpose* is critical, in that it must be determined "whether the link [or banner] exchange is an exchange of advertising or rather merely an attempt to refer the site visitor to additional information in furtherance of the organization's exempt purposes and activities."

(vi) Online Corporate Sponsorship. The IRS has recognized that the "differences between an advertisement and corporate sponsorship is [*sic*] further complicated in the Internet environment."[337] The agency noted that it is "not uncommon" for a tax-exempt organization to have all or part of its Web site corporately sponsored. This financial support may be acknowledged through display of a corporate logo, notation of the sponsor's Web site address and/or 800 number, a moving banner, or hypertext link.

In an understatement, the IRS stated that, "[g]enerally, exempt organizations prefer to view payments as corporate sponsorship rather than advertising income, which is more likely to be subject to unrelated business income tax." The agency wrote that the "use of promotional logos or slogans that are an established part of a sponsor's identity" is not, alone, advertising. It was also noted that display or sale of a sponsor's product by an exempt organization as a sponsored event is an acknowledgment, not advertising.

A payment cannot be a qualified sponsorship payment if the amount is contingent, by contract or otherwise, on the level of attendance at one or more events, broadcast ratings, or other factors indicating the degree of public exposure to an activity. Although the IRS did not say so, this rule seems to preclude pay-per-view or click-through arrangements from constituting qualified corporate sponsorship arrangements.

It is because of the evolution of this aspect of the law that nonprofit organizations now have their first inkling as to the position of the IRS as to the tax law import of links. It came in the final regulations concerning corporate sponsorships, where the agency considered whether the use of a link in what would otherwise be an acknowledgment changes the character of a

---

[337] The corporate sponsorship rules in general are the subject of *supra* § 2(b).

payment from a qualified (nontaxable) corporate sponsorship to taxable advertising. The essence of the IRS position is that the mere presence of a link by a tax-exempt organization to the site of a corporate sponsor does not defeat characterization of the payment as a nontaxable sponsorship. If, however, the sponsor's Web site contains advertising in the nature of an endorsement of a product or service by an exempt organization, the protections of the qualified corporate sponsorship rules may fall away, at least in part.[338]

(vii) Virtual Trade Shows. One of the issues of the day is whether the trade show rules[339] apply in connection with what the IRS referred to as the "trade show in the virtual reality format." The IRS has signaled that the answer is no, writing that it is "highly questionable whether income from a year round virtual trade show would be accorded exclusion from unrelated business income tax" (and it should not).

The agency noted that some of these trade shows "merely consist of a listing of HyperText links to industry suppliers' websites for which remuneration is received by the website host trade association." Others have "displays including educational information related to issues of interest to industry members." Virtual trade shows are "sometimes timed to coincide with the sponsoring organization's annual meeting or regular trade show in order to increase participation by industry members who are unable to attend the actual events." It looks like application of the trade show exclusion rules will be confined to shows that are *regular* and *actual*, not merely *virtual*.

(viii) Online Storefronts. The IRS has mused about the proper tax treatment of "[o]nline storefronts complete with virtual shopping carts." Not surprisingly, the agency is relying on its "traditional" assessment of sales activities by tax-exempt organizations, particularly museum shop sales.[340]

Once again, the determination of ultimate causal relationship and its importance is based on the facts and circumstances of each case. As with

---

[338] See § 1.8(b).

[339] See *supra* § 2(d).

[340] E.g., Tech. Adv. Mem. 9720002.

museums, the IRS will determine relatedness of sales based on the non-profit organization's primary purpose for selling the item. If the purpose underlying the production and/or sale of the item is furtherance of the organization's exempt purposes, the sale will be considered a related one. Where, however, the primary purpose for a sale is utilitarian, ornamental, or only generally educational in nature, or amounts to the sale of a souvenir, it is not likely to be regarded as related. Various factors are considered by the IRS in analyzing this primary purpose, as the agency probes the "nature, scope, and motivation" for these sales. The factors include the degree of connection between the item being sold and the purpose of the exempt organization and the "overall impression" conveyed by the article; if the "dominant impression" leads to the conclusion that "non-charitable use or function predominates," the sale would be an unrelated one. The fact that an item could, in a different context, be held related to the exempt purpose of another tax-exempt organization does not make the sale by the organization under review a related activity.

Thus, the IRS is comparing Internet merchandising to sales made in stores and through catalogs and similar vehicles. Merchandise will be evaluated on an item-by-item basis—the fragmentation rule[341] again—to determine whether the sales activity furthers the accomplishment of an organization's exempt purposes or is "simply a way to increase revenues."

(ix) Online Auctions. The IRS is looking at online auctions in part from the standpoint as to how they are conducted. Some tax-exempt organizations conduct their own; others use outside service providers. Some online auction Web sites provide services for exempt organizations only; some sites and search engines also operate auctions for individuals and for-profit organizations. The advantages to utilization of an outside auction service provider include provision of a larger auction audience than might be available if the exempt organization conducted it itself and avoidance of credit card fraud problems. Yet, as the IRS delicately phrased the matter, "entering into an agreement with an outside service provider might have tax implications."

One of the factors considered by the IRS is the degree of control (if any) the tax-exempt organization will exercise over the marketing and

---

[341] See *supra* § 1(b)(v).

conduct of the auction. The IRS wants the event to be "sufficiently segregated from other, particularly non-charitable auction activities" (whatever that may mean) and the exempt organization to retain "primary responsibility" for publicity and marketing. Otherwise, the agency "may be more likely to view income from such auction activities as income from classified advertising rather than as income derived from the conduct of a fundraising event."

Also, the IRS has characterized these service providers as "essentially professional fundraisers." It is not clear what the point of that analogy is, but nonetheless the IRS will scrutinize their functions and fees "using traditional [private] inurement and private benefit principles."[342] The agency might have mentioned that the intermediate sanctions rules[343] also are applicable in this setting.

(x) Online Charity Malls. Internet sites may permit online member shoppers to shop at affiliated vendors through links on the site. For each purchase, the vendor agrees to remit, through a charity mall operator, an agreed-on percentage of the purchase price to a designated charity. A few of the charity mall operators represent that they use volunteers and pass on all of the funds raised to the designated charities. Others retain a percentage of the proceeds for site maintenance and development. Some malls solicit paid advertisements. The mall operator credits the charity with the contribution upon receipt of the rebate from the vendor.[344]

A nonprofit organization that operates one of these malls as its primary purpose probably cannot qualify as a tax-exempt charitable organization "since the marketing and operation of the virtual mall is a trade or business ordinarily [regularly] carried on for profit." Among the concerns the IRS has about virtual charity mall operations are (1) that the beneficiary organizations "do not appear to have any agreement with the virtual mall operators and do not appear to be entitled to any record of member designations or transactions" and (2) the exempt organization "has little recourse if it finds its name used in association with such mall operators, who may or may not prove reputable."

---

[342] See §§ 7.4, 7.5.

[343] See § 7.6.

[344] See § 7.8(b) for a discussion of the deductibility of these rebates.

(xi) Merchant Affiliate Programs. Affiliate and other co-venture pro-grams are growing in popularity—online and off—with many variations. Probably the most ubiquitous of these programs on the Internet involve co-ventures with large, online booksellers, although art galleries, toy mer-chants, and event credit report providers have these programs. Organiza-tions are offered the option of making book recommendations that may be "displayed" or listed on the organization's Web site or simply using a logo or other link to the bookseller. The exempt organization earns a percentage of sales of recommended materials as well as a commission on other purchases sold as the result of the referring link. The exempt organi-zation receives a periodic report detailing link activity.

The controversy over the tax treatment of income received by tax-exempt organizations from affinity card programs[345] may have an impact on the taxation of income generated by these ventures.

The IRS noted that a "distinct advantage that these programs have over the virtual mall type operations from the point of view of the charity is that the exempt organization itself enters into an agreement with the merchant and is provided an activity report in order to ensure that it [is] credited with the appropriate royalty."

In this context, then, the IRS seems to have conceded that these pay-ments qualify as a tax-excludible royalty.[346] Indeed, the payments discussed in some of the preceding sections constitute excludible royalties.

(xii) Professional and Trade Associations. Many professional and trade associations[347] have Web sites accessible by the general public, along with material that is restricted to members. Many of these member-only sections "provide access to research services, continuing education oppor-tunities, employment listings, membership directories, links to various organization benefit programs, legislative alerts, publications, etc."

The IRS issued this caution: "Organizations and web designers must be aware that the traditional rules with respect to prohibitions on providing

---

[345] See *supra* § 3(a)(iii).

[346] *Id.*

[347] These generally are organizations that are tax-exempt pursuant to IRC § 501(a) by reason of description in IRC § 501(c)(6).

particular services, treatment of advertising income, [and] sales activity, as well as lobbying restrictions [,] still apply to website activities."

(xiii) Web Sites and Rules as to Periodicals. The corporate sponsorship rules intertwine with the general unrelated business rules as applicable in the Internet communications context in several instances. Again, the fundamental issue is whether the communication by the sponsored organization, in response to receipt of the corporate support, is merely an acknowledgment of the support or is a communication that amounts to advertising.

This dichotomy between acknowledgments and advertising becomes irrelevant if the communication involved appears in a periodical. That is, in this circumstance, the exception for corporate sponsorship payments is not available. Technically, the exception for the qualified corporate sponsorship does not apply to a payment that entitles the payor (sponsor) to the use or acknowledgment of the name or logo (or product line) of the payor's business in a periodical of a tax-exempt organization.[348]

A *periodical* is regularly scheduled and *printed* material published by or on behalf of the payee (sponsored) organization that is not related to and primarily distributed in connection with a specific event conducted by the payee organization.[349] Thus, the exception does not apply to payments that lead to acknowledgments in a monthly journal but applies if a sponsor received an acknowledgment in a program or brochure distributed at a sponsored event. Read literally, this rule denying the exception cannot apply in the Internet communications context because of the reference to *printed* material, which presumably is confined to hard copy. Yet it is difficult to believe that this is, or will be, the state of the law. Surely, at least under certain circumstances, a Web site will be regarded as a periodical.[350] (In a comparable situation, where the statutory law makes reference to

---

[348] IRC § 513(i)(2)(B)(ii)(I).

[349] *Id.*

[350] When the IRS published the corporate sponsorship regulations in proposed form, the agency solicited comments as to how the exception to the exception for periodicals is to apply in the context of Internet communications.

printed material,[351] the IRS promulgated a regulation providing that the term includes material that is published electronically.[352])

Moreover, should a Web site be considered a periodical, the rules for determining unrelated business taxable income from the publishing of advertising in periodicals would apply.[353]

One observer pointed out that the IRS took an "interesting, and perhaps controversial, position" concerning this matter of a Web site amounting to a periodical.[354] In 1999 the IRS wrote that "[m]ost of the materials made available on exempt organization Web sites are clearly prepared in a manner that is distinguishable from the methodology used in the preparation of periodicals."[355] This means that most Web sites maintained by exempt organizations will not be considered by the IRS as periodicals, which in turn means that the corporate sponsorship payment rules will be available to shelter the income from taxation—as long as all of the other requirements of these rules are present (basically, no advertising).

The IRS continued in this analysis, however, to say that, in considering how to treat potential income from Web site materials for unrelated business income tax purposes, the agency "will look closely at the methodology used in the preparation of" Web site materials. It added that the IRS "will be unwilling to allow the exempt organization to take advantage of the specialized rules available to compute unrelated business income from periodical advertising income unless the exempt organization can clearly establish that the on-line materials are prepared and distributed in substantially the same manner as a traditional periodical." That means that, if there is advertising, the special rules for calculating unrelated business taxable income in the case of periodicals will not be available.

This observer astutely pointed out a "leap" in reasoning by the IRS.[356] The corporate sponsorship payment rules make reference to "regularly

---

[351] IRC § 513(i)(2)(B)(ii)(I).

[352] Reg. § 1.513-4(b). See § 2.2(b), text accompanied by note 186.

[353] See *supra* § 2(a)(iv).

[354] Livingston at 422.

[355] IRS FY 2000 CPE Text on Exempt Organizations and Internet Use at 77.

[356] Livingston at 422.

scheduled and printed material."[357] This led this commentator to offer these useful guidelines and distinctions:

- "Bulletins distributed by e-mail on an occasional but unscheduled basis should not be considered periodicals any more than they would be if they were in hard copy distributed by U.S. mail."

- The "fact that a Web site may contain certain discrete factual information, like the date or key news items, that are [*sic*] updated on a regularly scheduled basis should not cause the site to be treated as a periodical to the extent the bulk of the site's content does not change on any regularly scheduled basis."

- "That the technology makes it possible to make frequent updates to what functions effectively as a brochure, overview, or educational text, should not dictate the characterization of the site as a periodical."

- This analysis "may be a bit complicated for certain Internet-based publications that change chunks of content on a rolling but regularly scheduled basis."

- "If the intent is to revise all of the content on a regularly scheduled basis, then it seems likely the publication will be characterized as a periodical."[358]

As this observer noted, the statutory "definition" of the word *periodical* does not contain any "reference to the process."[359] Yet this IRS analysis emphasized the "methodology used in the preparation of periodicals."[360] This observer also noted, in decrying this methodology test, that the "process of writing, editing, and producing publications, in hard copy or electronic form, varies greatly from organization to organization"; that "[c]ontent come from staff, professional writers, members, volunteers, unsolicited submissions, and other sources"; and that some materials "are heavily revised and edited," while other organizations "simply go through the mechanical process of laying out and printing submissions as the

---

[357] IRC § 513(i)(2)(B)(ii)(I).

[358] Livingston at 423.

[359] *Id.* at 422.

[360] IRS FY 2000 CPE Text on Exempt Organizations and Internet Use at 77.

author has written them." Therefore, this observer concluded, "no one can say what methodology an organization must show the Service to prove a Web-based item is or is not a periodical."[361]

In fact, the operative element in the definition of the word *periodical* is the scheduling of the publication; these materials are regularly compiled and distributed to the public on a *periodic* basis. This observer opined that the IRS "should rethink its view on this point."[362] Indeed, it was reported that a representative of the IRS subsequently acknowledged that this view of the agency "may be in error."[363]

Unrelated business taxable income that is earned from advertising on a Web site that is not a periodical is determined by the general rules,[364] namely, by adding the gross income from the advertising to the gross income generated from any other unrelated business activity (other than advertising in periodicals) and subtracting the expenses that are directly connected with carrying on the unrelated business or businesses.[365] The reference to an expense that is *directly connected* to the conduct of unrelated business means an expense (to be deductible) that is an item of deduction that has a "proximate and primary relationship" to the carrying on of an unrelated business.[366]

If the "facility" is used both to carry on exempt activities and to conduct unrelated activities, the expenses attributable to these activities (as, for example, items of overhead) are to be allocated between the two uses on a basis that is reasonable.[367] The same rule applies with respect to the expenses associated with personnel (as, for example, salaries). It is common to make these allocations on the basis of time expended on the various activities.[368]

---

[361] Livingston at 422.

[362] *Id.* at 422–423.

[363] *Id.* at 423.

[364] See *supra* § 2(a)(ii).

[365] Reg. § 1.512(a)-1(a).

[366] *Id.*

[367] Reg. § 1.512(a)-1(c).

[368] E.g., *Rensselaer Polytechnic Institute* v. *Commissioner*, 732 F.2d 1058 (2d Cir. 1984).

If the unrelated activity involved constitutes an exploitation of an exempt activity, the allocation rule is different. For expenses to be deductible, the unrelated business activity must have a "proximate and primary relationship" with the exempt purpose activity.[369]

(b) Questions Posed by IRS Announcement

In the Announcement, the IRS observed that tax-exempt organizations "use the Internet to carry on activities that otherwise can be conducted through other media, such as radio or television broadcasts, print publications, or direct mailings." The emphasis, then, was placed on types of media rather than types of activities. Thus, one of the major issues as to Internet communications by tax-exempt organizations is whether the advertising by means of that medium is related or unrelated business.

In this context, the determination as to the type of business—related or unrelated (taxable)—must be made in light of the fundamental purpose of the unrelated business rules.[370] In part, this means ascertaining whether the advertising activity is regularly carried on.[371] Thus, the tax regulations provide that, for purposes of determining regularity of advertising activity, the "manner of conduct of the activities must be compared with the manner in which commercial activities are normally pursued by nonexempt organizations."[372] If the advertising activity is infrequent, the net income involved is not taxable even if the advertising content is unrelated to exempt purposes.

(i) General Issues. The first of the general questions posed by the Announcement was whether a Web site maintained by a tax-exempt organization "constitute[s] a single publication or communication." A Web site presumably can be considered a single *publication,* in that a single publication can encompass many subjects and messages. A college's catalog, an association's journal, or a charity's newsletter is a single publication, notwithstanding the variety of its content.

---

[369] Reg. § 1.512(a)-(d).

[370] See *supra* § 1(a).

[371] *Id.* § 1(c).

[372] Reg. § 1.513-1(c)(2)(ii).

Aside from that point, it is highly unlikely that a Web site would be regarded as a single *communication*. If the word *communication* is defined simply as the act of imparting or transmitting information, then a Web site could be treated as a single communication. If, however, prominence is accorded the content of the communication—as it should be—a Web site is seen as a myriad of communications. As noted, the IRS correlated Internet communications to other media, such as television broadcasts. A television channel may be thought of as a single unit, but its programming is a series of communications. The same is true with a Web site. Thus, the visitor to an exempt association's site is able to stimulate a host of communications about the organization's programs, members, staff, and other matters, such as certification, ethics, and perhaps its related foundation and/or political action committee. Thus, the answer to this question should be that a tax-exempt organization's Web site may constitute a single publication but rarely should it be considered a single communication.

The IRS then asked, perhaps suggesting its view as to the answer to the first question, if a Web site is not a single publication or single communication, "how should it be separated into distinct publications or communications?" Inasmuch as application of the fragmentation rule[373] is conceptually limitless (or bottomless), one approach would be to separate the communications by category, such as program, fundraising, advocacy, related activities, and the like. For larger organizations, the category of program could be fragmented, so that there would be communications as to program A, program B, program C, certification, ethics enforcement, and the like. These exercises will be generating new and interesting applications of the fragmentation rule.

This question and the next one have a meaningful relationship. When a Web site is fragmented into multiple publications or multiple communications, each of these functions presumably carries with it expenses as to its maintenance. The amount of taxable unrelated business income (if any) that results will be affected by the number of these functions and the expenses that are associated with or assigned to each of them.

---

[373] See *supra* § 1(b)(v).

The third of the IRS questions inquired as to the proper methodology to use when allocating expenses for a Web site. Again, simply by referencing the subject of *allocation*, the IRS must be thinking that a Web site is comprised of if not more than one publication, then certainly more than one communication. Before allocating expenses of a Web site, however, the expenses themselves must be determined. There are the costs of establishing the site and the costs of maintaining the site. Much of the material on a Web site was previously created for offline use, such as articles, directories, and information about charitable giving, certification, and ethics. Thus, it appears that there must be allocation of expenses as between offline and online material and information. There may not be that much left over to allocate in the context of Internet communications.

The question presupposes that allocation is required. That, however, may not always be the case. A tax-exempt organization that uses its Web site for related purposes (that is, there is nothing on the site pertaining to fundraising or unrelated business) and not for advocacy purposes may see no reason to allocate expenses among programs. In that case, the organization may simply have a line item for Web site expenses.

When allocation is required or desired, the simplest of answers to the IRS question would be to separate a Web site into discrete communications on the basis of the amount of space each communication occupies on the site. As the IRS noted, expense allocation could be based on Web pages. This is often the approach taken in the case of print publications. In some instances, however, a *primary purpose test* is applied (or at least advocated), so that if the primary purpose of a publication is to communicate a particular message, the entire publication is deemed to have communication of that message as its purpose.

The IRS observed that, "[u]nlike other publications of an exempt organization, a website may be modified on a daily basis." The IRS then asked: "To what extent and by what means should an exempt organization maintain the information from prior versions of the organization's website?" As noted, it would be impractical, to say the least, to require a tax-exempt organization to maintain the information posted on every prior version of its Web site, whether in search of unrelated activity or otherwise.[374]

---

[374] See § 1.8(c).

This matter of expense allocations can be considered in light of these last two questions combined. Isolating the costs of various Web site communications is difficult enough, without taking into account many changes in site content in the course of a year. When the changes are factored in, expense isolation and allocation may become nearly impossible—or, in any event, more expensive than the Web site expenses themselves.[375]

As noted, an additional complicating factor is that the time and expense involved in preparing a Web site communication may be elements that the tax-exempt organization would incur in any event. The same messages may be used in other forms of communication, such as print media. That aspect of various activities, then, may well be accounted for already, leaving the cost in connection with the Web site only that of posting the material, which is negligible.

As has been suggested elsewhere, the answer to this dilemma may lie in the development of a safe harbor rule or de minimis exception to a general rule.[376]

(ii) Specific Questions. In the Announcement, the IRS asked three questions specifically pertaining to unrelated business activities on the Web sites of tax-exempt organizations. The agency is of the unassailable view that "a number of exempt organizations use the Internet as another outlet for their own sales activity."

The first of these questions is: "To what extent are business activities conducted on the Internet regularly carried on?" The answer to this question should be that regularity of business operations on an exempt

---

[375] In discussing this point in the context of lobbying by tax-exempt organizations, one commentator observed that the "cost[s] for adding the Web as a tool for lobbying communication are likely to be quite modest, and could in fact be dwarfed by the costs of accounting for them" (Livingston at 425).

[376] Following up on the previous note, this commentator continued: "It would be highly problematic if charities were deterred from using the most efficient tool available for participating in legislative debates because all of the resources gained from the increased efficiency were being consumed by the burdens of an accounting rule. To prevent that from happening, charities may consider proposing to the IRS adoption of some form of de minimis rule or safe harbor for this kind of expense allocation" (*id.*).

organization's Web site is determined using the same criteria as are applied in any other context.[377] This assessment is generally made on the basis of the particular year of the tax-exempt organization.

As a follow-up question, the IRS asked: "What facts and circumstances are relevant in determining whether these activities on the Internet are regularly carried on?"

This determination is of two parts. First, it is necessary to ascertain whether the business activities manifest the requisite *frequency* and *continuity*. Business undertakings that are *intermittent* or *discontinuous* are not regularly carried on. Thus, business activities that are reflected on a Web site only occasionally are not regularly carried on. By contrast, a business undertaking that is always represented on a site is regularly carried on. It is unlikely, however, that a tax-exempt organization would conduct an unrelated business on its Web site under circumstances where it is not regularly carried on.

The fact is that most unrelated businesses are not carried on by means of the Internet. This state of affairs is likely to change, however. Still, the tax-exempt organization that openly offers, as one of its Web pages to select, "unrelated business activities" has not, as part of this project, been found.

If income-producing activities are of a kind normally undertaken by nonexempt commercial organizations only on a seasonal basis, the conduct of the activities by a tax-exempt organization during a significant portion of the season ordinarily constitutes the regular conduct of a business.

Particular problems lurk in this setting where fundraising activities are conducted over the Internet. If services or products are being sold in a business undertaking that is not related, it is likely that that business is being regularly carried on. Even if the actual business activity on the Internet is not continuous, the matter of the preparatory time involved[378] may be an adverse factor.

The second part of this determination looks to the manner in which the business activities are pursued. Thus, a business activity of a tax-exempt

---

[377] See *supra* § 1(c).

[378] See *supra* § 1(c)(iv).

organization is likely to be considered regularly carried on if it is pursued in a manner generally similar to comparable commercial activities of nonexempt organizations. In this setting, then, a determination should be made as to how the comparable activity would be conducted on the Internet by for-profit companies.

Another IRS question is whether there are "any circumstances under which the payment of a percentage of sales from customers referred by the exempt organization to another website would be substantially related"? That question was prefaced with the observation that some tax-exempt organizations "receive payments based upon a percentage of sales for referring customers to another website, while others receive payments based upon the number of persons who use the hyperlink to go to the other webpage." Presumably at least one of the fact patterns that the IRS has in mind is the relationship between a tax-exempt organization and a commercial book-selling company, where the exempt organization refers potential customers to the bookseller to purchase books on subjects that relate to the organization's exempt purposes.

Generally, fees of this nature are unrelated income. The fact that books may be purchased which pertain to the exempt organization's exempt purpose is too tenuous a basis to sustain a claim that the payment is being made within the confines of exempt functions. If the two organizations are programmatically related, however, the book purchasing may be a related activity.

Even if a payment of this nature is deemed to be unrelated income, that does not necessarily mean that the payment is taxable. Generally, it would seem that payments of this nature are excludible from taxation as royalties.[379] Also, if the two organizations with linked Web sites are related, as in a parent-subsidiary relationship or one that is analogous to that of parent and subsidiary, the payments may be disregarded for tax purposes as being merely a matter of accounting if the referral function is viewed as a corporate service.[380]

The IRS observed that some tax-exempt organizations operate "virtual trade shows," in "an attempt to replicate trade shows on the Internet." This

---

[379] See *supra* § 3(a)(iii).

[380] *Id.* § 2(e).

led the IRS to ask: "Are there any circumstances under which an online 'virtual trade show' qualifies as an activity of a kind 'traditionally conducted' at trade shows" pursuant to the exception for trade show operations?[381]

It is difficult to see how this exception extends to online trade shows. In writing this exception, Congress had in mind the type of show conducted as part of an association's annual convention and thus lasting only a few days each year. The typical virtual trade show is conducted on a year-round basis. Also, as the IRS noted, some of these virtual trade shows "simply consist of hyperlinks to industry suppliers' websites." This appears to be unrelated activity.

Oddly, the IRS, in the Announcement, did not ask any questions concerning advertising. Generally, advertising income received by a tax-exempt organization is taxable income.[382] Nonetheless, the Announcement notes that "[m]any exempt organizations receive payment from companies to display advertising messages on the organization's website." Stated that way, those payments would be taxable, absent the unlikely circumstance that the advertising is a related activity (such as advertising by another tax-exempt organization with a similar mission) or that the advertising is not regularly carried on.

The IRS also observed in the Announcement that some exempt organizations "have banners on their websites containing information about and a link to other organizations in exchange for a similar banner on the other organization's website(s)." As noted, banners on Web sites are forms of advertising.[383] Thus, unless these banners constitute program activities (related advertising), it is inescapable that the regular running of them is unrelated activity.

Exempt organizations also, said the IRS in the Announcement, "provide hyperlinks on their websites to companies that sponsor their activities." The tax consequences of this practice are governed, at least initially, by the rules pertaining to corporate sponsorships.[384]

---

[381] *Id.* § 2(d).

[382] *Id.* § 2(a).

[383] See *supra* § 2(a).

[384] See *supra* § 2(b).

These rules concern the *qualified sponsorship payment*, which is not taxable as unrelated business income. This type of a payment is one that is made by a person engaged in a for-profit business, with respect to which there is no arrangement or expectation that the person will receive any substantive return benefit other than the use or acknowledgment of the name or logo (or product lines) of the person's business in connection with the recipient organization's activities. The regulations expand this rule a bit but, as will be discussed, in a significant manner, by stating that a qualified acknowledgment can also include reference to a sponsor's address and telephone number. This use or acknowledgment does not include advertising of the person's products or services, including messages containing qualitative or comparative language, price information or other indications of savings or value, an endorsement, or an inducement to purchase, sell, or use the products or services.

Assuming that this arrangement between a tax-exempt organization and a for-profit company does not involve advertising, the question is whether the provision of a link by the exempt entity to the for-profit sponsor is a *substantial return benefit*. The arrangement certainly amounts to more than use or acknowledgment of the company's name or logo. This question cannot be answered in isolation; it depends, at least in part, on the value to be accorded a link in general.[385] Thus, the answer is likely to be wrapped up in another facts-and-circumstances analysis. If the evidence shows that the link is an important source of income for the company or that some other benefit (other than an incidental one) is thereby provided, it is hard to avoid the conclusion that the link destroys the exception from unrelated income taxation—that is, it prevents the sponsorship payment from being a qualified one. The fact that an exempt organization intended to confer a substantial return benefit may be a factor, even if that benefit did not materialize. It may be expected that the IRS will take the position that, at least in some circumstances, this type of a linkage will be a substantial return benefit, particularly where the content on the linked Web site would cause the payment to be taxable if that content was on the exempt organization's site.

One analysis of this area of the law advances the argument that an exempt organization's link to the sponsor's Web site does not defeat

---

[385] See *supra* § 1.8(b).

applicability of the qualified sponsorship exception because of the reference in the regulations to the permissible inclusion in an acknowledgment of information such as the sponsor's address and telephone number. Thus, a link to the sponsor "would seem to be analogous in the electronic world to the street address in the physical world." Also, "there appears to be no legal basis for distinguishing between giving a link and giving a telephone number or street address."[386]

Unfortunately for tax-exempt organizations, however, that argument does not hold. A street address or a telephone number is an item of information. A link is an automatic hookup between the parties. "In all three cases," this argument continues, the "individual recipient retains the discretion to decide whether he or she wishes to contact the recommended destination organization."[387] But the difference is in the speed and ease of a link: an instant click and one is transported from one site to the other. That is far different from exercising one's discretion to get into one's car or onto an airplane and travel to the sponsor's location.

This argument persists with the thought that "no one has ever suggested that giving a telephone number for another organization will cause anything that organization says when it answers the telephone to be attributed to the organization."[388] That is undoubtedly a true statement, but it is disingenuous. The point is not attribution of content but whether the link is a return benefit that is outside the scope of the qualified sponsorship payment rules.[389]

It is not difficult to fathom the possibility that a link by an exempt organization to a corporate sponsor's Web site defeats the protection against unrelated income taxation provided by the qualified sponsorship

---

[386] Livingston at 421.

[387] *Id.* at 421–422.

[388] *Id.* at 422.

[389] The following statement in the Announcement was quoted in support of this argument: "The ease with which different Web sites may be linked electronically…raises a concern about whether the message of a linked Web site is attributable to the charitable organization." But that language is quoted out of context. That statement was made by the IRS when discussing the matter of Internet communications and attribution of content rather than the corporate sponsorship rules.

rules. Succinctly put, a link may cause the arrangement to be taxable advertising. An IRS private letter ruling suggests that the provision by an exempt organization of a link to a corporate sponsor's Web site makes the messages involved advertisements.[390]

Indeed, later, in 1998, the IRS wrote: "In determining what on the Web page is advertising a rough rule of thumb is that if it is an active or passive placard, or a running banner and income is being derived, it is advertising." Also, "[i]f the Web page shows merely a displayed link, then it may not be advertising, but only if related to activities or purposes of the organization."[391] The IRS reiterated this point of view in 1999.[392]

Yet a commentator has cryptically written that, "[i]n speeches, an IRS official who is one of the authors of these articles has rejected this analysis as erroneous."[393] It is hard to see why that is so; perhaps the true (or current) view of the IRS on this point has yet to be articulated.

This issue as to the scope of a *use or acknowledgment* and a *substantial return benefit* in the Internet communications context is not confined to the matter of links. A Web site is a powerful place to acknowledge receipt of contributions (from corporations and individuals) and grants (such as from private foundations). Yet these funds are not taxable if they are not payments for advertising and otherwise are within the framework of the qualified sponsorship payment.

Notwithstanding all of this, the qualified sponsorship rules allow for apportionment of a payment, so that a portion of it can be a qualified sponsorship payment, while the other portion is for advertising services.[394]

(c) Summary

The law as to unrelated business activities will prove to be the most difficult of the components of the law of tax-exempt organizations to apply in the Internet communications context. Fragmentation of Web site activities

---

[390] Priv. Ltr. Rul. 9723046.

[391] IRS FY 1999 CPE Text on Internet Service Providers at 64.

[392] IRS FY 2000 CPE Text on Exempt Organizations and Internet Use at 75.

[393] Livingston at 421.

[394] IRC § 513(i)(3).

into discrete businesses will often be difficult, as will the allocation of costs to them. These activities will usually be regularly carried on. Saving this area from even worse catastrophes is the fact that most of this activity will consist of related endeavors. The commerciality doctrine may be a problem, however, in that nonprofit Web sites are being operated in essentially the same fashion as for-profit Web sites.

The rules as to advertising will cause difficulties for many tax-exempt organizations, for this is an area where the IRS is likely to concentrate its efforts. Directly tied to this will be application of the corporate sponsorship rules, where line-drawing as between qualified and non-qualified payments will be exacerbated by Internet communications. Creative uses of the royalty exception may be anticipated in this setting. Related tax-exempt organizations will, however, be able to provide Web site-based services to each other without fear of unrelated business income taxation.

CHAPTER 3

Charitable Giving Programs Administration

$\mathbf{A}$s the nonprofit sector steadily grows and charitable giving steadily increases, federal and state law regulating the fundraising process steadily proliferates. Some of these developments are reflected in other chapters, particularly Chapter 4. One of the many aspects of this accretion of the law is a compounding of the burden of administering (other than gift solicitation efforts) a charitable giving program. The law that has developed, and is developing, in this area applies to charitable giving programs undertaken by means of the Internet.

§ 3.1 INTRODUCTION

Abuses of the charitable contribution deduction have inflamed the IRS and Congress. One of the trangressions that is the genesis of much law is the transfer of money to a charitable organization in a transaction that is not a gift or is only partially a gift, where the transferor claims a charitable contribution deduction for all of the money paid over to the charity. Usually this practice was engaged in innocently. Nearly everyone knows, for example, that funds paid to a school for tuition or to a hospital for healthcare services are not deductible gifts.[1] Nonetheless, for example, a

---

[1] E.g., *Sklar* v. *Commissioner*, 279 F.3d 697 (9th Cir. 2002) (tuition payments made to a religious private school held to not be deductible as charitable contributions).

patron of a charity's auction may consider, when the time comes to prepare a tax return, the payment following a winning bid to be a deductible gift, when in fact it was wholly a payment for a good or service. Worse, on some occasions the charities involved advised (again, usually out of ignorance) their patrons that these payments were deductible contributions.

The IRS, for many years, has published its views on this subject, which are, of course, that (1) payments of this nature generally are not contributions at all (let alone deductible ones) and (2) if some portion of the payment is in excess of the value of a good or service received in exchange for the payment, only that excess component of the payment is a deductible gift.[2] Transactions of this nature are, however, difficult to detect, even in the context of an IRS audit,[3] and the IRS did not have much in the way of sanctions to deploy when transgressions were found.[4]

Another issue in this regard is valuation of property. This matter can arise when a donor transfers property to a charitable organization and the issue becomes determination of the amount of the charitable deduction. On the flip side, there may have to be valuation of property received by a person in exchange for a payment, as part of the process of calculating the charitable deduction for the amount of the payment that exceeds the value of the property. Sometimes this valuation exercise was undertaken by the donor, patron, and/or charity, without benefit of assistance from a competent, independent appraiser.

A consequence of all of this is a battery of law, most of it fairly recent, designed to eliminate these abuses and punish them when they occur.

---

[2] E.g., Rev. Rul. 67-246, 1967-2 C.B. 104.

[3] In a marvelous illustration of this type of behavior, an individual had "canceled checks showing $500 to $1,000 [in] weekly payments to his church." This would seem to be, prior to the advent of the gift substantiation rules (1994), sufficient evidence of authentic charitable giving. "During an audit, an IRS agent checked with the minister to verify that the money had actually been given [transferred to] to the church. Indeed it had, but the minister added a critical piece of information: The taxpayer was a coin collector who bought the change that worshippers dropped in the collection plate each week" (48 *Kiplinger's Personal Finance Magazine* (No. 5) 140 (May 1994)).

[4] In Priv. Ltr. Rul. 8832003, the IRS conceded that there were no sanctions for violations of its disclosure requirements.

Some of this law came about by enactment of statutes, while other law is reflected in IRS regulations.

The statutory law in this connection concerns substantiation requirements and the quid pro quo contributions rules. These bodies of law are accompanied by regulations. The rules as to appraisals have been formulated by regulations.

All of this law applies with respect to contributions to charitable organizations made by means of the Internet. The IRS observed, in 1999, that the "use of the Internet to accomplish a particular task does not change the way the tax laws apply to that task." This means that "[a]dvertising is still advertising and fundraising is still fundraising."[5] It could have also written that charitable giving programs administration is still charitable giving programs administration.

§ 3.2 SUBSTANTIATION REQUIREMENTS

Most transfers of money or property that are claimed to give rise to federal tax deductions have to be *substantiated*, that is, proved.[6] Inasmuch as the burden of proof is on the taxpayer, the law requires the collection and retention of a certain amount of evidence to sustain the deduction should the IRS elect to examine it.

As to charitable contributions, however, special substantiation rules have been enacted. Under these rules, donors who make a separate charitable contribution of $250 or more in a year, for which they claim a federal income tax charitable contribution deduction, must obtain written substantiation of the gift from the donee charitable organization. The sanction: If the substantiation is not timely provided, the donor is not entitled to the charitable deduction that would otherwise be available.

More specifically, the federal income tax charitable deduction is not allowed for a *separate contribution* of $250 or more unless the donor has

---

[5] IRS FY 2000 CPE Text on Exempt Organizations and Internet Use at 64. On that occasion, however, the IRS also noted that the "nature of the Internet does change the way in which these tasks are accomplished" (*id.*).

[6] E.g., *Welch v. Helvering*, 290 U.S. 111 (1933); *Guest v. Commissioner*, 77 T.C. 9 (1981).

written substantiation from the charitable donee of the contribution in the form of a *contemporaneous written acknowledgment*.[7] Thus, donors cannot rely solely on a canceled check as substantiation for a gift of $250 or more. (A canceled check will suffice as substantiation for gifts of less than $250.[8])

An acknowledgment meets this requirement if it includes the following information:

- The amount of money and a description (but not value) of any property other than money that was contributed

- Whether the donee organization provided any goods or services in consideration, in whole or in part, for any money or property contributed

- A description and good-faith estimate of the value of any goods or services involved or, if the goods or services consist solely of intangible religious benefits, a statement to that effect[9]

The phrase *intangible religious benefit* means "any intangible religious benefit which is provided by an organization organized exclusively for religious purposes and which generally is not sold in a commercial transaction outside the donative context."[10] An *acknowledgment* is considered to be *contemporaneous* if the contributor obtains the acknowledgment on or before the earlier of (1) the date on which the donor filed a tax return for the tax year in which the contribution was made or (2) the due date (including any extension or extensions) for filing the return.[11] Even

---

[7] IRC § 170(f)(8)(A).

[8] Reg. § 1.170A-13(a), (b).

[9] IRC § 170(f)(8)(B); Reg. § 1.170A-13(f)(2).

[10] IRC § 170(f)(8)(B), last sentence.

[11] IRC § 170(f)(8)(C); Reg. § 1.170A-13(f)(3). The tax regulations are silent as to the matter of the substantiation being *written*. This is because, at the time the statute and regulations were prepared, the meaning of that word was obvious. In the context of charitable contributions made by means of the Internet, however, the use of that word is not so clear (see *infra* § 7(a)).

where a good or service is not provided to a donor, a statement to that effect must appear in the acknowledgment.

As noted, this substantiation rule applies with respect to *separate payments*. Separate payments generally are treated as separate contributions and are not aggregated for purposes of applying the $250 threshold. Where contributions are paid by withholding from wages and payment by the employer to a donee charitable organization, the deduction from each paycheck is treated as a separate payment.[12] Gifts of this nature may be substantiated by documents such as a pay receipt, Form W-2, or a pledge card.[13] The substantiation requirement does not apply to contributions made by means of payroll deduction unless the employer deducts $250 or more from a single paycheck for the purpose of making a charitable gift.

The written acknowledgment of a separate gift is not required to take any particular form. Thus, acknowledgments may be made by letter, postcard, or computer-generated form. A donee charitable organization may prepare a separate acknowledgment for each contribution or may provide donors with periodic (such as annual) acknowledgments that set forth the required information for each contribution of $250 or more made by the donor during the period.

A *good-faith* estimate is the donee charitable organization's estimate of the fair market value of any goods or services, "without regard to the manner in which the organization in fact made that estimate."[14] The phrase *goods or services* means money, property, services, benefits, and privileges.[15]

A charitable organization is considered as providing goods or services *in consideration for* a person's payment if, at the time the person makes the payment, the person receives or expects to receive goods or services in exchange for the payment.[16] Goods or services a donee charity provides

---

[12] Reg. § 1.170A-13(f)(11)(ii).

[13] Reg. § 1.170A-13(f)(11)(i).

[14] Reg. § 1.170A-13(f)(7).

[15] Reg. § 1.170A-13(f)(5).

[16] Reg. § 1.170A-13(f)(6).

in consideration for a payment by a person includes goods or services provided in a year other than the year in which the payment is made.[17]

A charitable organization, or a Principal Combined Fund Organization for purposes of the Combined Federal Campaign and acting in that capacity, that receives a contribution is treated as a donee organization for purposes of the substantiation requirements, even if the organization (pursuant to the donor's instructions or otherwise) distributes the amount received to one or more charitable organizations.[18]

Certain goods or services may be disregarded when applying these substantiation rules:

- Those that have an insubstantial value, in that the fair market value of all the benefits received is not more than 2 percent of the contribution or $50 (indexed for inflation), whichever is less.[19]

- Those that have an insubstantial value, in that the contribution is $25 or more (indexed for inflation) and the only benefits received by the donor in return have an aggregate cost of not more than a *low-cost article*, which generally is one with a cost not in excess of $5 (indexed for inflation).[20]

---

[17] A frequent question is: What to do about the situation where a charitable organization decides, months after contributions have been made, to honor a class of donors by providing them a tangible benefit, such as a thank-you dinner? The event or other benefit may be provided in a subsequent year. As to whether the fair market value of this benefit must be subtracted from the amount of the gift for deduction purposes, the answer generally is no. This is affirmed by the regulations, which require that the goods or services be provided *at the time* the payment is made, when the donor receives or expects to receive a benefit. In this instance, the donors did not receive or expect to receive a dinner or anything else at the time of their gifts. If, however, a charitable organization develops a regular pattern of providing these after-the-fact benefits, at some point expectations arise. Application of the substantiation requirements, and the quid pro quo contribution rules (see *infra* § 3), in this regard is dependent on the particular facts and circumstances.

[18] Reg. § 1.170A-13(f)(12).

[19] Reg. § 1.170A-13(f)(8)(i)(A).

[20] *Id.* The rules as to low-cost articles are the subject of IRC § 513(h)(2).

- Annual membership benefits offered to an individual for a payment of no more than $75 per year that consist of rights or privileges that the individual can exercise frequently during the membership period.[21] Examples of these rights and privileges include free or discounted admission to the organization's facilities or events, free or discounted parking, preferred access to goods or services, and discounts on the purchase of goods or services.

- Annual membership benefits offered to an individual for a payment of no more than $75 per year that consist of admission to events during the membership period that are open only to members of the donee organization.[22] For this rule to be available, the organization must reasonably project that the cost per person (excluding an allocable overhead) for each event is within the limits established for low-cost articles. The projected cost to the donee organization is determined at the time the organization first offered its membership package for the year.

- Goods or services provided by a charitable organization to an entity's employees in return for a payment to the organization, to the extent the goods or services provided to each employee are the same as those referenced in the previous two exceptions.[23] When one or more of these goods or services are provided to a donor, the contemporaneous written acknowledgment may indicate that goods or services were not provided in exchange for the donor's payment.

If a person makes a contribution of $250 or more to a charitable organization and, in return, the charity offers the person's employees goods or services (other than those that may be disregarded), the contemporaneous written acknowledgment of the person's contribution does not have to include a good-faith estimate of the value of the goods or services but must include a description of these goods or services.[24]

---

[21] Reg. § 1.170A-13(f)(8)(i)(B)(1).

[22] Reg. § 1.170A-13(f)(8)(i)(B)(2).

[23] Reg. § 1.170A-13(f)(9)(i).

[24] Reg. § 1.170A-13(f)(9)(ii).

If a partnership or S corporation makes a charitable contribution of $250 or more, the partnership or S corporation is treated as the taxpayer for gift substantiation purposes.[25] Therefore, the partnership or S corporation must substantiate the contribution with a contemporaneous written acknowledgment from the donee charity before reporting the contribution on its information return for the appropriate year and must maintain the contemporaneous written acknowledgment in its records. A partner in a partnership or a shareholder of an S corporation is not required to obtain any additional substantiation for his or her share of the partnership's or S corporation's charitable contribution.

If a person's payment to a charitable organization is matched, in whole or in part, by another payor, and the person received goods or services in consideration for the payment and some or all of the matched payment, the goods or services are treated as provided in consideration for the person's payment and not in consideration for the matching payment.[26]

It is the responsibility of the donor to obtain the substantiation document and maintain it in his or her records. (Again, as noted, the charitable contribution deduction is dependent on compliance with these rules.)

These substantiation rules do not impose on charitable organizations any requirement as to the reporting of gift information to the IRS. Charitable organizations potentially have the option to avoid these rules by filing an information return with the IRS, reporting information that is sufficient to substantiate the amount of the deductible contribution.[27]

A charitable organization that knowingly provides a false written substantiation document to a donor may become subject to the penalty for aiding and abetting an understatement of tax liability.[28]

This substantiation requirement is in addition to:

---

[25] Reg. § 1.170A-13(f)(15).

[26] Reg. § 1.170A-13(f)(17).

[27] IRC § 170(f)(8)(D). This alternative has not, however, been implemented by regulations and thus is not currently available.

[28] IRC § 6701.

- The rules that require the provision of certain information if the amount of the claimed charitable deduction for all noncash contributions exceeds $500.[29]

- The rules that apply to noncash gifts exceeding $5,000 per item or group of similar items (other than certain publicly traded securities), where the services of a qualified appraiser are required and the charitable donee must acknowledge receipt of the gift and provide certain other information.[30]

§ 3.3 QUID PRO QUO CONTRIBUTION RULES

The federal tax law imposes certain disclosure requirements on charitable organizations that receive quid pro quo contributions. A *quid pro quo contribution* is a payment "made partly as a contribution and partly in consideration for goods or services provided to the payor by the donee organization."[31] The term does not include a payment to an organization, operated exclusively for religious purposes, in return for which the donor receives solely an intangible religious benefit that generally is not sold in a commercial transaction outside the donative context.[32]

Specifically, if a charitable organization receives a quid pro quo contribution in excess of $75, the organization must, in connection with the solicitation or receipt of the contribution, provide a written statement that:

- Informs the donor that the amount of the contribution that is deductible for federal income tax purposes is limited to the excess of the amount of any money and the value of any property other than money contributed by the donor over the value of the goods or services provided by the organization, and

---

[29] Reg. § 1.170A-13(b)(3).

[30] See *infra* §4.

[31] IRC § 6115(b).

[32] *Id.*

- Provides the donor with a good-faith estimate of the value of the goods or services.[33]

It is intended that this disclosure be made in a manner that is reasonably likely to come to the attention of the donor. Therefore, immersion of the disclosure in fine print in a larger document is inadequate.

For purposes of the $75 threshold, separate payments made at different times of the year with respect to separate fundraising events generally will not be aggregated.

A charitable organization may use "any reasonable methodology in making a good-faith estimate, provided it applies the methodology in good faith."[34] A good-faith estimate of the value of goods or services that are not generally available in a commercial transaction may be determined by reference to the fair market value of similar or comparable goods or services. Goods or services may be similar or comparable even though they do not have the "unique qualities" of the goods or services that are being valued.[35]

Five types of goods or services are disregarded for purposes of these quid pro quo contributions rules.[36] A comparable rule as to goods or services provided to employees of donors is applicable in this context.[37] Also, these rules do not apply to transactions that lack a donative element, such as the charging of tuition by a tax-exempt school, the charging of healthcare fees by an exempt hospital, or the sale of items by an exempt museum.

No part of this type of payment can be considered a deductible charitable contribution unless two elements exist:

1. The patron makes a payment in an amount that is in fact in excess of the fair market value of the goods or services received, and

2. The patron intends to make a payment in an amount that exceeds that fair market value.[38]

---

[33] IRC § 6115(a). For contributions that have a value of $75 or less, the general substantiation rules apply (see the text accompanied by *supra* note 8).

[34] Reg. § 1.6115–1(a)(1).

[35] Reg. § 1.6115–1(a)(2).

[36] See the text accompanied by *supra* notes 19–23.

[37] See the text accompanied by *supra* note 24.

[38] Reg. § 1.170A–1(h)(1).

This requirement of the element of *intent* may sometimes be relatively harmless, in that the patron is likely to know the charity's good-faith estimate amount in advance of the payment and thus cannot help but have this intent. Still, proving intent is not always easy.

There is a penalty, imposed on donee charitable organizations, for violation of these requirements. It is $10 for each contribution in respect of which the organization fails to make the required disclosure; the total penalty with respect to a particular fundraising event or mailing may not exceed $5,000.[39] This penalty may not be imposed if it is shown that the failure to disclose was due to reasonable cause.[40]

§ 3.4 APPRAISAL REQUIREMENTS

Additional substantiation requirements apply with respect to deductions claimed by individuals, closely held corporations, personal service corporations, partnerships, and S corporations for charitable contributions of certain property.[41] Property to which these rules apply is termed *charitable deduction property*. If the contributed property is a partial interest in an item of property, the appraisal must be of the partial interest.[42] These substantiation requirements must be complied with if the charitable contribution deduction (otherwise permissible) is to be allowed.[43]

These requirements apply to contributions of property (other than money and publicly traded securities) if the aggregate claimed or reported value of the property is in excess of $5,000.[44] The requirements also apply with respect to all similar items of property for which deductions for charitable contributions are claimed or reported by the same donor for the same tax year, whether or not contributed to the same charitable donee.

---

[39] IRC § 6714(a).

[40] IRC § 6714(b).

[41] Reg. § 1.170A–13(c).

[42] Reg. § 1.170A–13(c)(1)(ii).

[43] Reg. § 1.170A–13(c)(2). An example of total noncompliance with these rules is in *Todd* v. *Commissioner*, 118 T.C. 334 (2002); nonetheless, a portion of the claimed deduction was allowed.

[44] Reg. § 1.170A–13(c)(1)(i).

(a) Similar Items of Property

The phrase *similar items of property* means "property of the same generic category or type," including stamp collections, coin collections, lithographs, paintings, photographs, books, nonpublicly traded stock, other nonpublicly traded securities, land, buildings, clothing, jewelry, furniture, electronic equipment, household appliances, toys, everyday kitchenware, china, crystal, or silver.[45] For example, if a donor claimed for a year deductions of $2,000 for books contributed to College A, $2,500 for books given to College B, and $900 for books given to College C, the $5,000 threshold would be exceeded.

For this type of gift, the donor must obtain a qualified appraisal and attach an appraisal summary to the tax return on which the charitable deduction is claimed.[46] In the case of nonpublicly traded stock, however, the claimed value of which does not exceed $10,000 but is greater than $5,000, the donor does not have to obtain a qualified appraisal but must attach a partially completed appraisal summary form to the tax or information return on which the deduction is claimed.[47]

As to the foregoing example, therefore, the donor would have to obtain a qualified appraisal for the books and attach to the appropriate income tax return three appraisal summaries for the books donated to the colleges.

(b) Qualified Appraisal

A *qualified appraisal* is an appraisal document that

- Relates to an appraisal that is made not earlier than 60 days prior to the date of contribution of the appraised property
- Is prepared, signed, and dated by a qualified appraiser (or appraisers)
- Contains the requisite information
- Does not involve a prohibited type of appraisal fee[48]

---

[45] Reg. § 1.170A–13(c)(7)(iii).

[46] Reg. § 1.170A–13(c)(2)(i)(A), (B).

[47] Reg. § 1.170A–13(c)(2)(ii).

[48] Reg. § 1.170A–13(c)(3)(i).

Certain information must be included in a qualified appraisal:

- A description of the property in sufficient detail for a person who is not generally familiar with the type of property to ascertain that the property that was appraised is the property being contributed
- The physical condition of the property (in the case of tangible property)
- The date of contribution of the property
- The terms of any agreement between the parties relating to any subsequent disposition of the property, including restrictions on the charity's use of the gift property
- The name, address, and tax identification number of the appraiser
- The qualifications of the qualified appraiser (or appraisers)
- A statement that the appraisal was prepared for income tax purposes
- The date or dates on which the property was appraised
- The appraised fair market value of the property on the date of contribution
- The method of valuation used to determine the fair market value of the property
- The specific basis for the valuation[49]

The qualified appraisal must be received by the donor before the due date (including extensions) of the return on which the deduction for the contributed property is first claimed or, in the case of a deduction first claimed on an amended return, the date on which the return is filed.[50]

A separate qualified appraisal is required for each item of property that is not included in a group of similar items of property.[51] One qualified appraisal is required for a group of similar items of property contributed in the same tax year, as long as the appraisal includes all of the required information for each item.[52] The appraiser may select any items the aggregate

---

[49] Reg. § 1.170A-13(c)(3)(ii).

[50] Reg. § 1.170A-13(c)(3)(iv)(B).

[51] Reg. § 1.170A-13(c)(3)(iv)(A).

[52] Id.

value of which is appraised at $100 or less, for which a group description, rather than a specific description of each item, is adequate.[53]

The appraisal must be retained by the donor "for so long as it may be relevant in the administration of any internal revenue law."[54]

(c) Appraisal Summary

The *appraisal summary* must be made on a form prescribed by the IRS,[55] signed and dated by the charitable donee and qualified appraiser (or appraisers), and attached to the donor's return on which a deduction with respect to the appraised property is first claimed or reported.[56] The signature by the charitable donee does not represent concurrence in the appraised value of the contributed property.

The following information must be included in the appraisal summary:

- The name and taxpayer identification number of the donor (such as the social security number of an individual)
- A description of the property in requisite detail
- A brief summary of the condition of the property at the time of the gift (in the case of tangible property)
- The manner and date of acquisition of the property by the donor
- The cost basis of the property
- The name, address, and taxpayer identification number of the charitable donee
- The date the donee received the property
- A statement explaining whether the charitable contribution was made by means of a bargain sale[57] and amount of any consideration received from the donee for the contribution

---

[53] *Id.*

[54] Reg. § 1.170A-13(c)(3)(iv)(C).

[55] Form 8283, Section B.

[56] Reg. § 1.170A-13(c)(4).

[57] A *bargain sale* is a transaction involving the sale of property to a charitable organization, at a price below the property's fair market value, with the difference between the sales price and fair market value a charitable contribution.

- The name, address, and taxpayer identification number of the qualified appraiser (or appraisers)
- The appraised fair market value of the property on the date of contribution
- A declaration by the appraiser[58]

The rules pertaining to separate appraisals, summarized above, also apply with respect to appraisal summaries.[59] A donor who contributed similar items of property to more than one charitable donee must, however, attach to the appropriate return a separate appraisal summary for each donee.[60]

Every donor who presents an appraisal summary to a charitable organization for signature must furnish a copy of the appraisal summary to the charitable donee.[61] If the donor is a partnership or S corporation, the donor must provide a copy of the appraisal summary to every partner or shareholder who receives an allocation of a deduction for a charitable contribution of property described in the appraisal summary.[62] The partner or shareholder must attach the appraisal summary to the partner's or shareholder's return.[63] If a donor (or partner or shareholder of a donor) fails to attach the appraisal summary to the return, a charitable deduction will not be disallowed if the donor (or partner or shareholder) submits an appraisal summary within 90 days of being requested to do so by the IRS, as long as the failure to attach the appraisal summary was a good-faith omission and certain other requirements are met, including timely completion of the appraisal.[64]

The appraisal summary form[65] must be filed by contributors where the total value of all noncash contributions exceeds $500 and is less than

---

[58] Reg. § 1.170A-13(c)(4)(ii).

[59] Reg. § 1.170A-13(c)(4)(iv)(A).

[60] Reg. § 1.170A-13(c)(4)(iv)(B).

[61] Reg. § 1.170A-13(c)(4)(iv)(E).

[62] Reg. § 1.170A-13(c)(4)(iv)(F).

[63] Reg. § 1.170A-13(c)(4)(iv)(G).

[64] Reg. § 1.170A-13(c)(4)(iv)(H).

[65] Form 8283, Section A.

$5,000. This portion of the form must also be used to report contributions of publicly traded securities, even where their value is in excess of $5,000.

Special rules apply for the substantiation of charitable deductions for gifts of nonpublicly traded securities. When a five-part test is satisfied, charitable deductions are permitted for securities that are not publicly exchanged and for which there are no published quotations.

(d) Qualified Appraiser

The term *qualified appraiser* means an individual who includes on the appraisal summary a declaration that

- He or she holds himself or herself out to the public as an appraiser or performs appraisals on a regular basis.
- Because of the appraiser's qualifications as described in the appraisal, he or she is qualified to make appraisals of the type of property being valued.
- The appraiser is not one of the persons excluded by these rules from being a qualified appraiser.
- The appraiser understands that an intentionally false or fraudulent overstatement of the value of the property described in the qualified appraisal or appraisal summary may subject the appraiser to a civil penalty for aiding and abetting an understatement of tax liability,[66] and consequently the appraiser may have appraisals disregarded.[67]

Notwithstanding these requirements, an individual is not a qualified appraiser if the donor had knowledge of facts that would cause a reasonable person to expect the appraiser to falsely overstate the value of the donated property.[68] Also, the donor, donee, or certain other related persons cannot be a qualified appraiser of the property involved in the gift transaction.[69]

---

[66] IRC § 6701.

[67] Reg. § 1.170A-13(c)(5)(i).

[68] Reg. § 1.170A-13(c)(5)(ii).

[69] Reg. § 1.170A-13(c)(5)(iv).

More than one appraiser may appraise the donated property, as long as each appraiser complies with these requirements, including signing the qualified appraisal and appraisal summary.[70] If more than one appraiser appraises the property, the donor does not have to use each appraisal for purposes of substantiating the charitable deduction.[71]

Generally, no part of the fee arrangement for a qualified appraisal can be based on a percentage of the appraised value of the property.[72] If a fee arrangement is based, in whole or in part, on the amount of the appraised value of the property that is allowed as a charitable deduction, after IRS examination or otherwise, it is treated as a fee based on a percentage of the appraised value of the property.[73]

In any situation involving a gift of property, the charitable organization that is the recipient of the gift must value the property for its own record-keeping and reporting purposes. The charitable donee, however, is not required to share that valuation with the donor.

Many of these requirements apply to the donor. Therefore, technically, compliance with these rules is the responsibility of the donor and not the charitable donee. As a matter of donor relations, however (in part because availability of the charitable deduction may depend on adherence to the rules), the charitable organization will want to be certain that its donors are made aware of, and are in compliance with, these rules.

§ 3.5 VALUATION OF PROPERTY

Charitable gifts are, of course, frequently made of property. The property may be personal property or real property, tangible property or intangible property. These gifts may be outright contributions of property to charity or of a partial interest in an item of property to charity.

Whatever the circumstances, the determination of a federal income tax charitable contribution deduction for a gift of property to charity requires

---

[70] Reg. § 1.170A-13(c)(5)(iii).

[71] *Id.*

[72] Reg. § 1.170A-13(c)(6)(i).

[73] *Id.*

valuation of the property. Sometimes the process is simple, as with contributions of publicly traded securities. Sometimes the process is complex, requiring the services of one or more appraisers. As discussed, there are appraisal requirements for large charitable contributions.[74] Also, an estimation of the value of any return benefits is an integral part of the gift substantiation requirements[75] and the rules as to quid pro quo contributions.[76]

As a general rule, the *fair market value* of an item of property is the price at which the property would change hands between a willing buyer and a willing seller, neither being under any compulsion to buy or sell and both having reasonable knowledge of relevant facts.[77] The IRS amplified this rule, holding that the "most probative evidence of fair market [value] is the prices at which similar quantities of…[the property] are sold in arm's-length transactions."[78] The IRS also stated that the fair market value of gift property is determined by reference to the "most active and comparable market place at the time of the donor's contribution."[79]

§ 3.6 VEHICLE DONATION PROGRAMS

Some charitable organizations solicit contributions of used automobiles and other motor vehicles. There is nothing inherently improper in this type of fundraising. Nonetheless, the IRS is concerned about "certain practices that occur in some car donation programs"—indeed, the agency has proclaimed this to be a "growing area of noncompliance."[80]

The IRS has said that it is not concerned about charities that solicit these vehicles for use in their programs (such as sheltered workshops and programs for refurbishment of cars to be given to the needy). The IRS also is not concerned with small charities that receive a few cars and resell

---

[74] See *supra* § 4.

[75] See *supra* § 2.

[76] See *supra* § 3.

[77] Reg. § 1.170A-1(c)(2).

[78] Rev. Rul. 80-69, 1980-1 C.B. 55.

[79] Rev. Rul. 80-233, 1980-2 C.B. 69.

[80] IRS FY 2000 CPE Text, Section T, Part I. All quotations from the IRS in this section are from this CPE Text article.

them. The focus of the IRS is on organizations "who have permitted third party entrepreneurs to use their names to solicit contributions of cars; to plan and place advertising for donations; to take delivery on the cars (or pick them up) if they are not in running condition; to complete the legal paper work; and to sell them typically at auction or to junk yards or to scrap dealers." The IRS is dismayed that some charities "perform no oversight" in this process; they have "abdicated responsibility for the things that are done in their names." These practices are referred to by the IRS as "suspect vehicle donation plans or programs."

(a) Valuation

One of the principal issues in this area is a fact one, not a law one: valuation.[81] The IRS is deeply troubled by advertisements that state or suggest that donors will be entitled to a deduction based on the full fair market value of the vehicle, such as the value stated in the Blue Book, when the vehicle is in poor or perhaps nonoperating condition. The IRS wrote that valuation methods "presume that the car is running and then evaluate it according to its condition, mileage, etc."

Therefore, the value of a used vehicle is, like the value of any item of property, based on its true condition. There may be a mere modicum of value—and hence not much of a charitable deduction. Donors need to be cautious and avoid an overstated tax deduction for the gift of a vehicle to a tax-exempt organization.

(b) Substantiation Requirements

A contribution of a used vehicle to a charitable organization is likely to trigger the substantiation requirements.[82] These rules come into play when the value of the property given is at least $250. If sufficient substantiation is not timely provided by the donee charitable organization, the donor is not entitled to any charitable deduction.

---

[81] See *supra* § 5.

[82] See *supra* § 2. In some circumstances, the quid pro quo contribution rules (see *supra* § 3) will also apply.

The recipient charity must provide the donor a contemporaneous written acknowledgment. In an instance of a gift of a used vehicle, the acknowledgment must include a description of the vehicle. Although the acknowledgment does not have to assign a value to the vehicle, the description must be truthful and sufficient so as to provide the appropriate descriptive basis for determining that value. As the IRS indelicately noted, the charity involved "must ensure that this paperwork is done accurately because there are penalties for aiding and abetting in the preparation of a false return."[83]

(c) Appraisal Requirement

A contribution of a used vehicle to a charitable organization may well require application of the appraisal requirements.[84] These rules come into play when the value of the property given is in excess of $5,000. If the requisite appraisal is not timely obtained by the donor, the charitable deduction is not allowed.

The appraisal requirements are more pointed in this regard than the substantiation rules. That is, the qualified appraisal document involving a contributed vehicle must include information such as a "description of the property in sufficient detail," the physical condition of the property, and the "specific basis" for the valuation. Similar information must be in the appraisal summary.

The IRS observation that the charity involved "must ensure that this paperwork is done accurately because there are penalties for aiding and abetting in the preparation of a false return" was also offered up in the context of the appraisal rules.

(d) Deductibility

The transfer of a vehicle for the benefit of a charitable organization may not be a charitable contribution to begin with. To be deductible, a contribution must be made *to* a charitable organization or be *for the use of* a

---

[83] This penalty is the subject of IRC § 6701.

[84] See *supra* § 4.

charitable organization. A determination as to whether a contribution is to a charitable organization is based on whether the donee entity has full control of the donated property and discretion as to its use.[85] A gift for the use of a charity essentially refers to gifts made by means of trusts and similar arrangements.[86]

A fact pattern that the IRS is focusing on is the use by a charitable organization of a professional fundraiser in this setting. The titling laws of the state involved require owners to appear in the chain of title. Owners cannot appoint agents to hold title for them. The professional fundraiser has, by contract, the right to solicit contributions of vehicles in the name of the charity, the ability to give "tax deductible receipts" in the charity's name, the right to appointment as the charity's agent to sign all documents and handle matters relating to dealer's licensing, and the right to keep proceeds from the sale of the donated vehicles. The charity is not responsible for any facet of the project, except to endorse it. Although both the charity and the fundraiser hold used vehicle dealer licenses, the donor assigns the title to the vehicle to the charity and the fundraiser, as agent of the charity, then assigns the title to itself. The charity, which never takes possession of the vehicles, is paid $4,000 a month by the fundraiser.

In this circumstance, stated the IRS (correctly), the charity does not have control over the donated vehicles, nor does it have discretion as to their use. The charity is not involved in reviewing the solicitation advertising or exercising any discretion as to the solicitations. Once the fundraiser takes possession of the vehicles, the charity does not play any role in any decision as to their use. The IRS wrote that this titling process, while nominally designed to incorporate the charity in the chain of title to satisfy the legal requirements of the state, is "insufficient to show agency." The charity does not take possession of the vehicles or even oversee that aspect of the transactions. Overall, the charity has "abdicated any oversight" of the titling process.

The IRS also noted the manner in which this charity is being compensated, as a factor "weighing against the idea that these vehicles have been donated" to it. The IRS observed that the charity, by means of one or

---

[85] Rev. Rul. 62-113, 1962-2 C.B. 10.

[86] E.g., *Davis v. United States*, 495 U.S. 472 (1990).

more employees or agents "properly delegated," could have conducted the program. With this approach, the charity would bear the risk of loss. Noting that "this one factor may not by itself be determinative, it combined with the others indicate[s] that donations of the vehicles hasn't [*sic*] been made" to the charity.

In this situation, the charity does not exercise any discretion as to disposition of the vehicles. It does not make any decisions as to whether they are sold as used cars or at auction. The IRS wrote that it is "difficult to see that disposition isn't an important part of their use."

The IRS concluded that these facts indicate that the charity does not exercise the requisite degree of control and discretion, so that the transaction is not a gift of a used vehicle to the charity. Moreover, the donations are not made in trust or similar arrangement, so they cannot be for the use of the charity. The result: no charitable deduction for these transfers.

The IRS pointed out that these relationships between charitable organizations and what the agency termed "for-profit entrepreneurs" vary from program to program. These relationships include principal and agent, joint venturers, licensor and licensee, and independent contractors. In some instances, there may be an employment relationship.

(e) Characterization of Income

If the funds received by a charitable organization are not contributions, as is the case in the above illustration, it is not clear what the characterization of the income is. The potential is that it is unrelated business income.[87]

As the IRS pointed out, when a charity receives a payment from a third party, the donated goods exception[88] is not available. Generally, a business consisting of the sale of materials donated to a charitable organization is not treated as an unrelated business. The exception is not of any utility in this setting because there has not been a donation to the charity.

The most likely possibility, if the unrelated business rules are to be sidestepped, is that the income is a royalty.[89] But, as the IRS pointed out,

---

[87] See Chapter 2.

[88] See § 2.3(b)(iii).

[89] See § 2.3(a)(iii).

"where contributions are not deductible, an exempt organization may not be able to make a claim that the income is exclusively a royalty payment if it flows from the sale of a right which the taxpayer cannot license—the right to receive deductible contributions." This denial of the applicability of the royalty exception seems to be the correct conclusion but for the wrong reason. While it is true that a charity cannot "license" the ability to receive deductible contributions, a gift to a noncharitable organization can be deductible where the organization is a conduit of gifts to the charity.[90] The problem is that a charity in this situation cannot utilize some sort of agency theory because, under this type of state law, an organization cannot be considered a vehicle *owner* by appointing an agent to hold title for it.

(f) Private Benefit Doctrine

A charitable organization may not serve private interests, other than incidentally. This rule of law is the *private benefit doctrine*.[91] The word *incidental* in this context has a qualitative and a quantitative meaning. To be incidental in a *qualitative* sense, the benefit to the public cannot be achieved without necessarily benefiting certain private individuals. Also, if an organization's activity provides a substantial benefit to private interests, even indirectly, it will negate charitability and thus tax-exempt status. The substantiality of the private benefit is measured in the context of the overall public benefit conferred by the activity.

The IRS has signaled that the private benefit doctrine will be invoked in connection with suspect vehicle donation programs. The agency wrote: "Present in vehicle donation programs, as in some other fund-raising situations [,] is the possibility that promoters can take advantage of the format, solicit vehicles publicly, do little or no charity with the primary object of enriching themselves." The IRS added: "This raises the question

---

[90] E.g., Rev. Rul. 85-124, 1985-2 C.B. 84 (charitable deduction allowed for additional amounts paid by customers of a utility company, when paying their bills to the company, where the additional amounts were earmarked for a charitable organization that assisted individuals with emergency-related energy needs).

[91] See § 7.5.

of whether the organization is operated for a private benefit in both a qualitative and a quantitative sense."

The IRS posited an example of this type of a *captive program*. An automobile dealer sees car donation programs as a way to generate revenue. He creates a charitable organization, which obtains recognition of tax-exempt status on the basis of educating the public on health issues. Thereafter, the dealer enters into a contract with the charity, which he controls, that is similar to the one in the above example. A major difference, however, is the hiring of the dealer as the "agent" of the charity to run an aspect of its overall charitable program. Under this arrangement, the dealer will create a Web page that has links to national disease prevention programs. The bulk of the Web page, however, is devoted to the solicitation of gifts of vehicles. Potential donors are offered significant premiums for participating in the program, such as discount books and tickets in new car raffles. In this arrangement, the cost of the program is increased, reducing the amount that the charity receives. While the charity retains a small percentage of the gross (as opposed to a flat fee) at the end of each month, it has yet to devote the proceeds to any charitable endeavor.

In this situation, the IRS surmised that the "true beneficiary of this suspect vehicle donation program" seems to be the automobile dealer. The dealer arranges the transaction, takes delivery on or picks up the vehicles, resells the vehicles or cannibalizes them for their parts, and turns over a prearranged percentage to the charity. In a telling statement, the IRS wrote that "[n]one of this could happen without the charity," in that if the charity did not "participate and lend its tax exempt status to the transactions, there would be no trading in donated cars."

Then the IRS posed the question: "If [the charity] does nothing with the proceeds during the years under examination, can one argue that [the charity] is not operated for private benefit during those years in a qualitative sense? Is it operated to serve a private benefit in a quantitative sense?" Of course, one can argue just about anything. It is not clear why the IRS added the fact about the charity doing nothing with the proceeds of the program. Suppose the proceeds were in fact devoted to charitable ends. Even so, given the current expansive interpretation of the private benefit doctrine by the IRS, this arrangement seems to be providing unwarranted private benefit to the charity.

(g) Private Inurement

The IRS has raised the prospect of application of the private inurement doctrine[92] in the setting of captive programs. In the above example, the doctrine clearly is in play because the automobile dealer is an insider with respect to the charity, having created the organization and manifesting ongoing control over it. The IRS observed that, if, for example, the automobile dealer understated the income to be paid to the charitable organization, that would constitute private inurement, thereby endangering the charity's tax-exempt status.

(h) Intermediate Sanctions

The intermediate sanctions rules[93] apply in this context as well. Again, using the situation of the captive program, the automobile dealer is an insider with respect to the charitable organization. An understatement of the income owed by the dealer to the charity would amount to one or more excess benefit transactions, triggering tax penalties and correction obligations on the part of the automobile dealer.

(i) Royalty Exception

True royalties paid to a tax-exempt organization are not subject to the unrelated business income tax.[94] In connection with vehicle donation programs involving payments from third parties, the payment from the promoter may well constitute a royalty. As the IRS observed, "[t]here are many different forms the arrangement between the exempt organization and the promoter can take."

The concern of the IRS, as indicated, is with the captive programs, involving a "third party broker." A fee from the broker or dealer, calculated as a percentage of gross receipts, may appear to be the most obvious of royalty arrangements. But the IRS has raised two sets of facts that may

---

[92] See § 7.4.

[93] See § 7.7.

[94] See § 2.3(a)(iii).

preclude treatment of these payments as royalties. One pertains to the fact that "[p]romoters are typically given the right to claim that contributors to the program can take deductions for their donations." The IRS said that the fact that "contributions other than to the charities or their agents are not deductible raises questions as to whether the income is a royalty." Second, by providing services in the form of the requisite written substantiation and acknowledging appraisals of property having a value in excess of $5,000, the charity may have caused the payments to not qualify as royalties.

(j) Penalties

The federal tax law contains a variety of penalties that can be applied for violation of various aspects of the law of charitable giving. These penalties are part of a broader range of *accuracy-related penalties*.[95]

The accuracy-related penalty is determined as an amount to be added to the income tax equal to 20 percent of the portion of the underpayment.[96] This body of law relates to the portion of any underpayment that is attributable to one or more specified acts, including:

- Negligence
- Disregard of rules or regulations
- Any substantial understatement of income tax
- Any substantial income tax valuation misstatement
- Any substantial estate or gift tax valuation understatement[97]

Additional penalties may be applied in the context of charitable giving. One of them is the penalty for the promotion of a tax shelter.[98]

---

[95] IRC § 6662.

[96] IRC § 6662(a).

[97] IRC § 6662(b).

[98] IRC § 6700.

Another penalty—one that the IRS loves to threaten charitable organizations with—is the penalty for aiding and abetting an understatement of tax liability.[99]

§ 3.7 INTERNET COMMUNICATIONS

Although the Announcement observed that an "increasing number of exempt organizations solicit contributions on the Internet," there is little focus by the IRS in that document on the matter of the administration of charitable giving programs. What is addressed by the Announcement is incorporated below.

(a) Substantiation Requirements

Clearly, the substantiation requirements apply with respect to contributions to charitable organizations made by means of the Internet. This is the case where (1) the gift is solicited by an Internet communication and paid or transferred to the charity in some other manner (such as by cash, check, or credit card), or (2) where the gift is both solicited and consummated by use of the Internet. In the latter circumstance, the charity may directly accept contributions by means of the Internet or do so through a third party that provides a secure connection for credit card transactions. Thus, a donor who makes a separate charitable contribution of $250 or more in a year, by means of the Internet, and intends to claim a federal income tax charitable contribution deduction, must obtain written substantiation of the gift from the charitable organization.[100]

Inasmuch as all of the elements of these requirements are applicable in instances of gifts made by use of the Internet, the only aspect of these rules that was uncertain, until early 2002, was the matter of a *written* acknowledgment. The word *written* is the past participle of the word *write*,

---

[99] IRC § 6701.

[100] See *supra* § 2.

which, among other definitions, means to form or record by a series of written characters. One dictionary states that to write means to form or produce a legible character in, upon, or by means of a suitable medium; examples given are a name written in lights on a marquee, an advertisement written by skywriting, and the drawing of letters on a frosted windowpane. Another definition states that to *write* is to set something down, especially on paper in order to record, relate, or explain.

In the Announcement, the IRS asked whether a donor satisfies these requirements for a written acknowledgment of a contribution of $250 or more with a "printed webpage confirmation or copy of a confirmation e-mail [message] from the donee organization." If a message on a medium as ephemeral as a frosted windowpane is writing, or something as transient as skywriting is writing, then presumably a copy of an e-mail message is a writing. Yet the statute probably means the setting of words down on paper by hand or machine, as an original. It may be assumed that Congress did not compose the statutory language believing that a *writing* included a printed Web page confirmation or a copy of an e-mail message. Nonetheless, these forms of communication are, using the most generous of interpretations, writings.

The IRS, then, has the inherent authority to issue an interpretation of the words *written* or *write* to include copies of Internet communications.[101] This interpretation can be in the form of a revenue ruling, revenue procedure, notice, announcement, technical advice memorandum, or private letter ruling. With the involvement of the Department of the Treasury, this interpretation can emerge as a regulation or part of one. (In a comparable situation, where the statutory law makes reference to *printed material*,[102] the IRS promulgated a regulation providing that the term includes material that is published electronically.[103]) If Congress disapproved, it would certainly let the IRS know. There certainly is no policy reason why this

---

[101] If the IRS has the authority to conjure up the initial contract exception out of the ramblings of the Seventh Circuit in *United Cancer Council v. Commissioner*, and include that exception in the intermediate sanctions regulations, the agency has the capacity to treat printed Web page confirmations and copies of email messages as writings. See § 7.6, text accompanied by note 78.

[102] IRC § 513(i)(2)(B)(ii)(I).

[103] Reg. § 1.513–4(b). See § 2.2(b), text accompanied by note 186.

interpretation of the word *written* could not be extended to printed Web page confirmations and copies of e-mail messages. Contemporary practices compel such an outcome.[104] Moreover, as one observer noted, "at a time when the IRS is trying to lessen the administrative burden of compliance, permitting electronic disclosures and acknowledgments could save substantial mailing costs and allow for better compliance through automated procedures."[105]

There is, however, another aspect of this matter: application of the Electronic Signatures Act.[106] Pursuant to this body of law, as to any transaction in or affecting interstate commerce, a "record" relating to the transaction may not be denied legal effect, validity, or enforceability solely because it is in electronic form. Assuming that a charitable contribution is a transaction "in or affecting interstate commerce," it may be substantiated by means of a record in electronic form. Certainly a contribution is a *transaction* involving the disposition of property.[107] One commentator wrote that "it appears the statute [Electronic Signatures Act] will compel the IRS to

---

[104] For example, in the first ruling of its kind by a federal appellate court, it was held (on March 22, 2002) that legal documents may, at least under certain circumstances, lawfully be sent via e-mail (*Rio Properties, Inc.* v. *Rio International Interlink*, 284 F.3d 1007 (9th Cir. 2002)). The case concerned the procedures for service of process on a foreign business entity and whether such service could be accomplished by e-mail. The court of appeals acknowledged that it was "tread[ing] upon untrodden ground" (at 1017). (That, by the way, was not entirely true; a federal bankruptcy court permitted service of process by e-mail in 2000 (*Broadfoot* v. *Diaz*, 245 B.R. 713 (Bankr. N.D. Ga. 2000).) Nonetheless, it permitted e-mail service in this case, observing that this approach "unshackles the federal courts from anachronistic methods of service and permits them entry into the technological renaissance" (at 1017). As another court noted, courts "cannot be blind to changes and advances in technology," in that "[n]o longer do we live in a world where communications are conducted solely by mail carried by fast sailing clipper . . . ships" (*New England Merchants National Bank* v. *Iran Power Generation & Transmission Co.*, 495 F. Supp. 73, 81 (S.D.N.Y. 1980)).

[105] Livingston at 432.

[106] In general, see § 7.11.

[107] See § 7.11, text accompanied by notes 139–140. Gifts made by means of a will, codicil, or testamentary trust, however, may not be made electronically (*id.*, text accompanied by note 140).

accept these acknowledgments and disclosures in electronic form."[108] In fact, the statute *does* compel the IRS to adopt the position that a contemporaneous written acknowledgment can be made in electronic form.

In any event, the IRS has attempted to resolve this matter. In early 2002, the agency—without fanfare or even notice—revised the online text of its publication on charitable contributions and the substantiation requirements.[109] In this publication, the IRS wrote that a charitable organization "can provide either a paper copy of the acknowledgment to the donor, or an organization can provide the acknowledgment electronically, such as via e-mail addressed to the donor." Thereafter, the IRS extended the deadline for providing the written acknowledgments to October 15, 2002, with respect to gifts made after September 10, 2001, and before January 1, 2002.[110] To take advantage of this extension, a donor must show a good-faith effort to obtain the documentation, such as by sending the charity a letter or an e-mail message requesting it. Once again, the IRS stated that acknowledgments can be provided by charitable organizations via e-mail.

(b) Quid Pro Quo Contributions

Just as clearly, the rules as to quid pro quo contributions apply with respect to these contributions made by means of the Internet. Again, these are payments made partly as a contribution and partly in consideration

---

[108] Livingston at 432, note 7. The reference to "acknowledgments and disclosures" was to these substantial requirements and the quid pro quo contribution rules.

It should be noted that the rules pertaining to electronic contracts involving consumers (see § 7.11, text accompanied by notes 144–145) do not apply in the case of gifts. Also, the provision of the Electronic Signatures Act pertaining to the filing of records with a federal regulatory agency (*id.*, text accompanied by note 148) does not apply because the substantial document is not filed with the IRS (nor are the disclosures mandated by the quid pro quo contributions rules (see *infra* § 3) or the fundraising disclosure rules imposed on noncharitable organizations (see § 7.3(c)).

[109] *Charitable Contributions—Substantiation and Disclosure Requirements* (IRS Pub. 1771) (revised in March, 2002).

[110] IRS Notice 2002–25, 2002–15 I.R.B. 743. See the text accompanied by *supra* note 11.

for goods or services provided to the payor by the donee charitable organization.[111] These rules require that charitable organization receiving these contributions provide *written statements* to payors containing certain information.

In the Announcement, the IRS asked whether a charitable organization meets the requirements as to quid pro quo contributions "with a webpage confirmation that may be printed out by the contributor or by sending a confirmation email [message] to the donor." This is, in essence, the same question that was asked in the gift substantiation context.

The same considerations apply in this context as in the setting of the gift substantiation rules. That is, the IRS possesses the authority to regard printed Web page confirmations and copies of e-mail messages as writings for purposes of the quid pro quo contribution rules. In the modern era, it should be expected. In any event, this conclusion is also compelled by the Electronic Signatures Act. Nonetheless, although the IRS has approved the use of electronic messages in the context of charitable gift substantiation, the agency has yet to make a similar announcement as to quid pro quo disclosures.

(c) Appraisal Requirements

Contributions of most items of charitable deduction property that have a value of more than $5,000 are subject to certain appraisal requirements.[112] These requirements are applicable in situations where property is contributed to a charitable organization in a transaction involving an Internet communication.

(d) Valuation of Property

The determination of a federal income tax charitable contribution deduction for a gift of property to charity requires valuation of the property.[113] This requirement pertains in situations where property is contributed to a charitable organization in a transaction involving an Internet communication.

---

[111] See *supra* § 3.

[112] See *supra* § 4.

[113] See *supra* § 5.

(e) Vehicle Donation Programs

The IRS wrote that "[i]t is now common to turn on your radio, television or the [I]nternet and be exposed to an advertisement encouraging you to donate your car to charity."[114] Thus, it is clear—it would be in any event—that vehicle donation programs involving Internet communications are subject to the same bodies of law that pertain to these types of gifts made otherwise.[115]

Again, this aspect of the law involves the matter of the proper valuation of the vehicle and adherence to the substantiation requirements, the appraisal requirements, the basic rules as to gift deductibility, the unrelated business rules, and application of the private benefit doctrine.

(f) Charitable Gift Planning

Sophisticated charitable giving—which basically means integration of financial and estate planning concerns into the charitable contribution decisions—often is *planned giving*. This type of giving entails use of one or more vehicles, such as a charitable remainder trust, a charitable lead trust, and/or a charitable gift annuity. These entities may be established during the donor's lifetime and/or funded at death.

Planned giving is not accomplished in a vacuum; the very concept of *planning* connotes the use, by donors, of one or more professional advisors. Successful planning requires communication. Increasingly, communication is being accomplished by e-mail. In the charitable planning setting, the IRS has characterized this type of communication, at least in this context, as a "limited" form of communication. Indeed, in this instance, communications solely by e-mail led to a "breakdown" in communications. This case, then, stands as a caution to those who attempt charitable gift planning solely by means of e-mail communications. That is, in this setting at least, there seems to be still room for—and perhaps a need for—some interpersonal communication.

This case concerned a husband and wife who, seeking retirement planning advice, sought out the services of a financial planner. One of the

---

[114] IRS FY 2000 CPE Text.

[115] See *supra* § 6.

elements of this planning was focus on use of a charitable remainder trust, to which highly appreciated stock would be given. The financial planner asked the head of planned giving at the charity involved to provide illustrations of a standard (fixed percentage) charitable remainder unitrust ("SCRUT") and a net-income make-up charitable remainder unitrust ("NIMCRUT").[116] Following a presentation by the planned giving specialist, the couple decided, after discussion with the financial planner, to fund a NIMCRUT. In an effort to pass this decision along to the planned giving specialist, the latter was told by the former that the husband and wife had decided to establish a "charitable remainder unitrust."

The specialist assumed that the couple wanted a SCRUT, and sent a copy of the charity's prototype SCRUT document to the financial planner and to the lawyer for the husband and wife. The financial planner did not review the document, relying instead on the lawyer's expertise. Throughout this process, communications among the financial planner, the planned giving specialist, and the lawyer were confined to e-mail messages. The lawyer never realized that the couple wanted a NIMCRUT. The husband and wife mistakenly executed and funded a SCRUT.

The error was discovered by the couple's accountant, when reviewing their income tax information. In a meeting involving the husband and wife, the financial planner, the planned giving specialist, and the lawyer (which must have been interesting), the parties agreed that the mistake emanated from a "breakdown in communications," caused by the sole use of e-mail messaging.

It took a reformation of the trust instrument by a court and a ruling from the IRS[117] to rectify this situation. (The IRS generously portrays a mistake of this nature as a *scrivener's error.*) Of course, this type of error cannot be blamed wholly on e-mail messaging. The problem could have been avoided, for example, if the financial planner read the draft trust document. Yet, this matter illustrates the limitations inherent in the sole use of e-mail for charitable gift planning.

---

[116] These and the other types of charitable remainder trusts are the subject of Hopkins, *The Tax Law of Charitable Giving, Second Edition* (John Wiley & Sons 2000), Chapter 12.

[117] Priv. Ltr. Rul. 200218008.

CHAPTER 4

Fundraising Programs

O f all the areas of the law concerning nonprofit organizations where Internet communications are involved, none is being more directly affected by increasing Internet use than the matter of fundraising for charitable organizations. The blend of fundraising and Internet use is generating new law, and new interpretations of preexisting law, at the federal, state, and local levels. These developments are on the rise. Some of these phenomena are reflected in other chapters, particularly Chapters 3 and 7.

As is the case with other aspects of the law concerning nonprofit organizations and Internet communications, the IRS is trying to extrapolate from existing principles. The IRS observed, in 1999, that the "use of the Internet to accomplish a particular task does not change the way the tax laws apply to that task." This means that "[a]dvertising is still advertising and fundraising is still fundraising."[1]

This aspect of the law cries out for reform far more than any of the others. This is due in part to the fact that the entire realm of state law regulation of charitable fundraising, with its panoply of differing charitable solicitation acts, needs to be scrapped and replaced. Another factor is the vagaries inherent in the state law concept of charitable *solicitation*. A third factor is the increase in charitable fundraising and gift receiving by means of the Internet.

---

[1] IRS FY 2000 CPE Text on Exempt Organizations and Internet Use at 64. On that occasion, however, the IRS also noted that the "nature of the Internet does change the way in which these tasks are accomplished" (*id.*).

§ 4.1 INTRODUCTION

Some basics about fundraising are in order. There is a common perception that there is a single type of activity called *fundraising* and that all contributions are made in cash. (Fundraising by means of the Internet is likely to exacerbate and perpetuate that belief.) Certainly the federal, state, and local approaches to regulation in this area are founded on this view. Likewise, public attitudes of charitable fundraising—both positive and negative—are largely rested on this belief.

Charitable gifts can be made with property as well as money. The contribution may be of tangible personal property, intangible personal property, and real property. A contribution may be of the donor's entire interest in the property or of a portion of the donor's interest in the property. The latter is technically termed *partial interest giving*, meaning gifts to charity by means of techniques such as charitable remainder trusts and charitable gift annuities. Gifts of money and all types of property may be solicited by means of the Internet. While gifts of money can be facilitated and received by means of the Internet, gifts of property, at least for the most part, must be formally executed and received offline.

A gift *solicitation* can be made in one or a combination of five ways: in person, by telephone, by regular mail, by facsimile, or by means of the Internet. As to the last of these, the asking for a gift can be done by e-mail or Web site communication.

Just as there are a number of ways to solicit a gift, there are a number of types of fundraising. One category—the one most suitable for the Internet—is annual giving programs. The other two overarching categories are special-purpose fundraising and the fundraising done in the context of planned giving and financial and estate planning. As to the category of annual giving fundraising, these solicitations are done by direct mail (donor acquisition or donor renewal), telephone, radio, television, advertisements in publications, door-to-door solicitations, on-street solicitations, and, of course, by use of the Internet. Special events, commemorative giving, donor clubs, and sweepstakes and lotteries can be utilized in this setting. Gifts can be solicited and received, and tickets sold, by means of the Internet.

Special-purpose programs are not likely to be enhanced much by Internet communication. This type of fundraising entails major gifts from individuals, grants from private foundations and government agencies, and capital campaigns. Certainly research in support of these undertakings can be done on the Internet, but the "ask" is not likely to be done that way and the gift acquisition is not likely to be accomplished that way either (although some elements of a capital campaign might involve Internet-made gifts).

Another basic point to be made is that fundraising is not (or almost always is not) *program*. Many individuals, including some in law and fundraising, regard fundraising as part of an organization's program activities because its purpose is to promote the organization's purposes in some fashion. This misunderstanding is fueled in part by the distinctions in law simply between exempt functions and nonexempt functions, or—more technically—between related businesses and unrelated businesses.[2] Because it is inconceivable that fundraising is a nonexempt function, it must be an exempt function—so the reasoning goes. From that position, it is an easy jump in logic to the conclusion that fundraising is the same as program (inasmuch much as neither is a nonexempt function), but such a conclusion is erroneous. (Indeed, some fundraising activities are unrelated businesses.[3])

These distinctions are mirrored in the concept of *functional accounting*, an exercise imposed by the IRS on charitable and other tax-exempt organizations as part of the annual information return preparation and filing process.[4] This method of accounting separates a tax-exempt organization's functions into three categories: program, administration, and fundraising.

This aspect of fundraising has only been lightly treated in law. Indeed, the first attempt by a court to squarely face and analyze the difference, for tax purposes, between fundraising activity and business activity engaged in by a nonprofit organization resulted in a reversal by the Supreme Court.[5] Yet the reasoning of the lower court has some continuing merit. This court wrote that, where the tax-exempt organization involved in an unrelated business case is a charitable one, the "court must distinguish between those activities that constitute a trade or business and those that are merely

---

[2] See Chapter 2.

[3] See § 2.2(c).

[4] See § 7.1.

[5] *United States v. American Bar Endowment*, 477 U.S. 105 (1986).

fundraising."[6] Admittedly, said the court, this distinction is not always readily apparent, as "[c]haritable activities are sometimes so similar to commercial transactions that it becomes very difficult to determine whether the organization is raising money 'from the sale of goods or the performance of services' [the statutory definition of a *business* activity[7]] or whether the goods or services are provided merely as an incident to a fundraising activity."[8] Nonetheless, the court held that the test is whether the activity in question is "operated in a competitive, commercial manner," which is a "question of fact and turns upon the circumstances of each case."[9] "At bottom," the court wrote, the "inquiry is whether the actions of the participants conform with normal assumptions about how people behave in a commercial context" and "[i]f they do not, it may be because the participants are engaged in a charitable fundraising activity."[10]

§ 4.2 STATE FUNDRAISING REGULATION IN GENERAL

Nearly every state regulates fundraising for charitable purposes—although the extent and intensity of enforcement varies greatly. This regulation is accomplished principally by means of statutes termed *charitable solicitation acts*. There are 41 of these laws.

(a) Summary

These laws are often intricate. In addition to their complexity, there is a considerable absence of uniformity, although the states are making some progress toward a uniform registration process. This combination of intri-

---

[6] *American Bar Endowment* v. *United States*, 84-1 U.S.T.C. ¶ 9204 (Ct. Cl. 1984).

[7] See § 2.1(b).

[8] *American Bar Endowment* v. *United States*, *supra* note 6, at 83,350. Indeed, the court observed (seemingly with the Internet in mind) that, "[o]ver the years, charities have adopted fundraising schemes that are increasingly complex and sophisticated, relying on many business techniques" (*id.*)

[9] *Id.* at 83,351.

[10] *Id.*

cacy and nonconformity makes this a body of law with which it is difficult to comply—a problem aggravated by a disparity in regulations, rules,
and forms.

More than 30 states have adopted what may be termed *comprehensive*
charitable solicitation acts. The remaining states—including the few that
lack a charitable solicitation act altogether (and the District of Columbia)—
have elected to regulate fundraising for charitable purposes by means of
differing approaches.

The various state charitable acts are, to substantially understate the situation, diverse. The content of these laws is so disparate that any implication that it is possible to neatly generalize about their assorted terms,
requirements, limitations, exceptions, and prohibitions would be mislead-
ing. Of even greater variance are the requirements imposed by the many
regulations, rules, and forms promulgated to accompany and amplify the
state statutes. Nonetheless, some basic commonalties can be found in the
comprehensive charitable solicitation acts.

The fundamental features of many of these fundraising regulation laws
are:

- A series of definitions
- Registration or similar requirements for charitable organizations
- Annual reporting requirements for charitable organizations
- Exemption of certain charitable organizations from all or a portion
  of the statutory requirements
- Registration and reporting requirements for professional fundraisers
- Registration and reporting requirements for professional solicitors
- Requirements with respect to the conduct of charitable sales promo-
  tions (also known as commercial co-ventures)
- Record-keeping and public information requirements
- Requirements regarding the contents of contracts involving
  fundraising charitable organizations
- Disclosure requirements
- A range of prohibited acts
- Registered agent requirements
- Rules pertaining to reciprocal agreements

- Investigatory and injunctive authority vested in enforcement officials
- Civil and criminal penalties
- Other sanctions[11]

(b) Meaning of *Solicitation*

Many terms in these charitable solicitation acts require definition. The most common ones are the organizations to which these laws apply (generically, *charitable* entities) and the transactions to which these laws apply (generically, charitable *contributions*). An aspect of these bodies of law that almost always guarantees inconsistency and confusion are the many meanings associated with the terms *professional fundraiser* and *professional solicitor.*

Yet, in the context of Internet communications, the key terms are the words *solicit* and *solicitation.* One of the principal questions of the day is this: When a charitable organization posts a message on its Web site that it is seeking contributions, is that a solicitation of charitable gifts? If that is a solicitation, then presumably the charity is soliciting gifts in every state, county, city, town, and hamlet in the United States (not to mention internationally). The regulatory implications associated with the answers to these questions are stupendous.

Before answering those questions, a brief review of the law on the point is appropriate. The word *solicitation* in these statutes is broadly defined. This fact is evidenced not only by the express language of the definition but also by application of these acts to charitable solicitations conducted, in terminology that is common, "by any means whatsoever." A solicitation can be oral or written. It can take place by means of an in-person request, regular mail, facsimile, advertisement, other publication, radio, television, telephone, or other medium. Also, of course, (and this is giving away the answer to the above questions) charitable solicitations can occur over the Internet.

A most encompassing, yet typical, definition of the term reads as follows: The term *solicit* means any request, directly or indirectly, for money,

---

[11] In general, Hopkins, *The Law of Fundraising, Third Edition* (John Wiley & Sons 2002), particularly Chapters 3 and 4.

credit, property, financial assistance, or other thing of any kind or value on the plea or representation that such money, property, and the like of any kind or value is to be used for a charitable purpose or benefit a charitable organization.

Usually the word *solicitation* is used in tandem with the word *contribution*. The term *solicitation* may, however, encompass the pursuit of a grant from a private foundation, other nonprofit organization, or government department or agency. About a dozen states exclude from the term *solicitation* the process of applying for a government grant. Occasionally state law will provide that the word *contribution* includes a grant from a government agency or will exclude the quest for a grant from a private foundation.

It is clear, although few charitable solicitation acts expressly address the point, that the definition of *solicitation* entails the seeking of a charitable gift. That is, there is no requirement that the solicitation be successful, which is to say that a *solicitation* can occur irrespective of whether the request actually results in the making of a gift.

One court created its own definition of the term *solicit* in this setting, writing that the "theme running through all of these cases is that to solicit means 'to appeal for something,' 'to ask earnestly,' 'to make petition to,' 'to plead for,' 'to endeavor to obtain by asking,' and other similar expressions."[12]

With this as background, it can be seen that a message on the Web site of a charitable (or other nonprofit) organization seeking contributions from the public is, literally and plainly, a solicitation of those contributions. Likewise, and even more obvious, an e-mail message sent to a prospective donor is a solicitation of a gift. One does not have to be an expert in semantics or parlance, or retain the services of a logogogue, to readily conclude that these uses of the Internet are forms of communication that amount to gift solicitations.

Yet while this is the correct outcome as a matter of word definition, it can be an absurdity in terms of its real-life consequences. The presence of a message on a charity's Web site asking for contributions, taken literally, mandates registration and reporting by the charity in each of the states (as

---

[12] *State* v. *Blakney*, 361 N.E. 2d 567, 568 (Ohio 1975). Likewise *Brown* v. *Marine Club, Inc.*, 365 N.E. 2d 1277 (Ohio 1976).

noted, most of them) that have a charitable solicitation act requiring this type of registration. It may mean that the charity is *doing business* in each of the states, requiring registration and reporting as a nonprofit corporation and/or trust. This can easily entail over 100 annual registrations or reports. Such a message also presumably means that the charity is soliciting gifts in thousands of counties, cities, and the like, all of which have ordinances purporting to regulate fundraising in their jurisdictions. This level of compliance is not only beyond a reasonable person's ability to fathom, it would annihilate any semblance of a fundraising program.

It was because of the potential of these outcomes that the Charleston Principles were devised.[13]

(c) Definition of *Professional Fundraiser*

There is—and this has little to do with the advent of the Internet— considerable confusion about the meaning of the term *professional fundraiser*. The dilemma arises from the fact that the term, and its nemesis *professional solicitor*, was developed in an era when the roles of the parties were discrete and thus much easier to identify. Basically and historically, a professional fundraiser was a consultant—an individual who or firm that did not directly participate in the charitable gift solicitation process but rather worked with the charity in designing the fundraising plan. In most cases, the charitable organization was the person that undertook the actual fundraising, using volunteers and perhaps staff. By contrast, a *professional solicitor* was a person who was paid to solicit gifts in the name of the charity.

During this era, these roles were separate and distinct. The fundraiser planned and did not solicit. Thus, the fundraiser did not have contact with prospective donors and, thus, in many if not most instances (such as with respect to direct mail efforts), lacked any nexus with the prospects' state(s) of domicile. The solicitor pursued gifts and was not involved in planning the campaign. The fundraiser was paid a flat fee by the charity; the solicitor was paid a percentage of gifts collected and often received the funds

---

[13] See *infra* § 4.

directly from the donors. In many instances today, that formal dichotomy is still being followed. Increasingly, however, these roles are blurred, usually because the professional fundraiser is undertaking one or more roles in the area of solicitation.

Most states adhere to a definition (mirroring the bygone era) such as this: A *professional fundraiser* is any person who, for a flat fixed fee under a written agreement, plans, conducts, manages, carries on, advises, or acts as a consultant, whether directly or indirectly, in connection with the solicitation of contributions for or on behalf of a charitable organization. This type of definition usually is followed by the admonition that a professional fundraiser may not actually solicit contributions as part of the services.

Often excluded from the ambit of the term *professional fundraiser* are the officers and employees of a charitable organization that is either registered with the state or is exempt from registration. Also usually excluded from the term are lawyers, investment counselors, and bankers, even if they advise a client or customer to contribute to a charitable organization.

Some states use a definition of the term *professional fundraiser* in a different manner, with some having a definition of the term that also encompasses most categories of professional solicitors. About a dozen of the states' laws lack any definition of this term.

Part of the reason for the confusion in this area is the variation in terminology among the states. In about one-fifth of the states, the person usually generically referenced as a professional fundraiser is identified by means of that term. Other states, however, intending the same meaning, use the term *professional fundraising counsel*. Still other states prefer *fundraising counsel*. Other terms used in various state laws are *fundraising consultant*, *professional fundraiser consultant*, or *professional fundraising consultant*.

Currently the state laws regarding fundraising regulation reflect considerable misunderstanding of the meaning of the term *professional fundraiser* in relation to the term *professional solicitor*. As noted, some state laws so broadly define *professional fundraiser* (or equivalent term) that the term embraces what is normally meant by *professional solicitor*. Terms used to describe a professional solicitor include such phrases as *professional fundraising firm*, *professional commercial fundraiser*, and *commercial fundraiser for charitable purposes*. A few states employ the term *professional fundraiser* to describe what is generically meant by the term *professional solicitor*.

§ 4.3 STATE FUNDRAISING REGULATION AND THE INTERNET[14]

The Internet has greatly expanded the number of charitable organizations capable of carrying out, and actually engaged in the practice of, multistate solicitation activities. Essentially, to reach potential donors in all of the states, an organization needs nothing more than a computer and an account with an Internet service provider. Once established, the organization's charitable appeal can instantly be sent or made available to the entire Internet community. The large national and international charities with the resources necessary to assure compliance with the various state regulatory regimes are thus no longer the only ones affected by state charitable solicitation laws. Instead, even the smallest organizations, operating on shoestring budgets, are beginning to tap the national contributions market. Thus, the new technology indeed is altering the nature of communication in the charitable solicitations context—it renders communication inexpensive.

One of the most difficult of contemporary issues is whether fundraising by charitable organizations by means of the Internet constitutes fundraising in every state—or, for that matter, in every locality. As discussed below, current thinking is that, technically, it does. If those states asserting jurisdiction over Internet fundraising are justified in doing so, the result will be that even the smallest organizations—those too small to afford multistate solicitation efforts by any other medium—will be required to register under numerous state charitable solicitation laws simply by virtue of utilizing the new communications technology to solicit contributions. If they do not, or cannot, assure state-law compliance, they will be forced to decide between risking legal action in several foreign states or refraining from engaging in this form of speech altogether. The question thus is whether, under this new mix of facts, state laws enforced in this fashion impermissibly restrict speech protected by the First Amendment.

---

[14] This subsection is a summary of Monaghan, Jr., "Charitable Solicitation Over the Internet and State Law Restrictions," a paper prepared under the direction of Professor John Simon, Yale Law School (1966), and adopted with permission.

There is another, perhaps equally interesting question, that must first be addressed. From a legal perspective, should Internet fundraising appeals be treated any differently solely because they take place on the Internet? (For federal tax purposes, the answer from the IRS is no.[15]) That is, should communication over this newest medium be treated as anything other than communication, for which there already is a rich regulatory scheme?

To determine whether the various state charitable solicitation regimes unduly intrude on the protected speech interest in this type of solicitation, the existing regulatory framework must be applied to the new set of facts. The first step in this analysis is to ascertain whether the act of an organization in placing an appeal for funds in a document on a computer in one state subjects the organization to the jurisdiction of one or more foreign states. There is as yet no law directly on this subject. Nonetheless, while not directly on point, a court opinion may shed some light on the matter.

A federal court of appeals, in 1996, had the opportunity to discuss the legal status of computer-borne communications in the First Amendment context. Two individuals operated an adult-oriented bulletin board service from their home in California. The site was accessible to others around the nation via modems and telephone lines.

Working with the local U.S. Attorney's office in Tennessee, a postal inspector purchased a membership in this bulletin board service and succeeded in downloading allegedly obscene images from the bulletin board. The U.S. Attorney's office filed criminal charges against these individuals for, among other things, transmitting obscenity over interstate telephone lines from their computer. By relatively conservative Memphis community standards, the images involved were found by a jury to constitute obscenity; the couple was convicted.

On appeal, this federal appellate court affirmed the convictions, holding inter alia that the crime of "knowingly us[ing] a facility or means of interstate commerce for the purpose of distributing obscene materials" did not require proof that the defendants had specific knowledge of the destination of each transmittal at the time it occurred.[16] Of interest in the Internet

---

[15] See the text accompanied by *supra* note 1.

[16] *United States v. Thomas*, 74 F.3d 701 (6th Cir. 1996).

setting, in determining that the crime occurred in Tennessee, rather than in California, the court placed considerable weight on its finding that "substantial evidence introduced at trial demonstrated that the . . . [bulletin board service] was set up so members located in other jurisdictions could access and order [obscene] files which would then be instantaneously transmitted in interstate commerce."[17]

If the reasoning of this appellate court is followed by the state courts, it appears that communication via computer constitutes sufficient contact with the foreign state to subject the communicator to local law requirements. Applied in the charitable solicitation regulation context, then, the import of this court decision is clear: Soliciting funds by means of the Internet, where users download Web pages residing in foreign jurisdictions, in all likelihood will constitute sufficient contact to subject the organization to the jurisdiction of the foreign state or states and therefore to the foreign charitable solicitation regime or regimes.

It must next be determined whether interstate communication of this nature constitutes *solicitation* encompassed by the fundraising regulation laws of the states. Although no definite answer can be divined from the language of any one statute, a brief survey of some state statutes strongly indicates that Internet solicitation will be held in many jurisdictions to be subject to regulation. For example, in one state, solicitation covered by the charitable solicitation act is defined as the making of a fundraising request "through any medium," regardless of whether any contribution is received. In another state, the charitable solicitation law applies to all "request[s] of any kind for a contribution." In another state, the law embraces "each request for a contribution." The statutory scheme in another state applies to "any request, plea, entreaty, demand or invitation, or attempt thereof, to give money or property, in connection with which . . . any appeal is made for charitable purposes." In still another state, the law applies to organizations "soliciting or collecting by agents or solicitors, upon ways or in any other public places within the commonwealth to which the public have a right of access."

Certainly it is difficult to see how Internet fundraising is not caught by any of these strikingly broad provisions. As currently written, then, the

---

[17] *Id.* at 709.

statutes of at least five states can easily be construed to reach Internet charitable fundraising.

Indeed, it is likely that most, if not all, of the state charitable fundraising regulation regimes may be so construed and that those statutes that fail as currently written can be appropriately amended without much trouble.

§ 4.4 CHARLESTON PRINCIPLES

If the assumption is that the solicitation of funds by charitable and other nonprofit organizations by means of the Internet constitutes fundraising in every state (and municipality), then, as suggested, the charitable community is facing an enormous burden. Many in the regulatory sector realize that, if this technically is the law, some form of relief for charities that solicit gifts is warranted.

To this end, the National Association of State Charity Officials (NASCO) developed guidelines to assist charitable organizations that solicit contributions, and their fundraisers, in deciding whether it is necessary to register fundraising efforts in the states when the solicitations are made by e-mail or on the organizations' Web sites.

The guidelines are a product of discussion that was initiated at NASCO's 1999 annual conference in Charleston, South Carolina. Hence the guidelines are termed the "Charleston Principles" ("Principles"). The Principles are not law but rather nonbinding guidance to NASCO members.[18]

The Principles rest on this true proposition: "Existing registration statutes generally, of their own terms, encompass and apply to Internet solicitations." An unstated proposition is that it is untenable to require registration of all charities soliciting gifts by means of the Internet, and their fundraisers, in all states with registration requirements. Thus, the scope of potential registration must be narrowed or, as the Principles put it, state charity officials should "address the issue of who has to register where."

---

[18] Nonetheless, the concept underlying the Principles is similar to the "sliding scale" analysis, by which Web sites were characterized on a continuum from active to passive, used in *Zippo Mfg. Co.* v. *Zippo Dot Com Inc.*, 952 F. Supp. 1119 (W.D. Pa. 1997).

(a) General Principles

The Principles differentiate between entities that are domiciled in a state and those that are domiciled outside the state. (An entity is domiciled in a state if its principal place of business is in that state.)

An entity that is domiciled in a state and uses the Internet to conduct charitable solicitations in that state must, according to the Principles, register in that state. This reflects the prevailing view that the Internet is a form of communication, and the law does not make a distinction between that form of communication and another (such as use of regular mail). The rule applies "without regard to whether the Internet solicitation methods it uses are passive or interactive, maintained by itself or another entity with which it contracts, or whether it conducts solicitations in any other manner."

Matters become more complex in cases where an entity is fundraising in a state in which it is not domiciled. Registration in the state is nonetheless required if:

- The organization's non-Internet activities alone are sufficient to require registration;
- It solicits contributions through an interactive Web site; and
- Either the entity—
  - Specifically targets persons physically located in the state for solicitation, or
  - Receives contributions from donors in the state on a repeated and ongoing basis or a substantial basis through its Web site; or
  - The entity solicits contributions through a site that is not interactive but either specifically invites further offline activity to complete a contribution or establishes other contacts with that state, such as sending e-mail messages or other communications that promote the Web site, and the entity engages in one of the foregoing two activities.

Obviously, often considerable line-drawing will be required in the actual application of these rules. The matter becomes even more interesting when some definitions are factored in.

(b) Definitions

An *interactive Web site* is a site that "permits a contributor to make a contribution, or purchase a product in connection with a charitable solicitation, by electronically completing the transaction, such as by submitting credit card information or authorizing an electronic funds transfer." These sites include those through which a donor "may complete a transaction online through any online mechanism processing a financial transaction even if completion requires the use of linked or redirected sites." A Web site is considered *interactive* if it has this capacity, irrespective of whether donors actually use it.

The phrase *specifically target persons physically located in the state for solicitation* means to engage in one of two practices:

1. Include on the Web site an express or implied reference to soliciting contributions from persons in that state; or

2. Otherwise affirmatively appeal to residents of the state, such as by advertising or sending messages to persons located in the state (electronically or otherwise) when the entity knows, or reasonably should know, that the recipient is physically located in the state.

Charities operating on a "purely local basis," or within a "limited geographic area," do not target states outside their operating area if their Web site makes clear in context that their fundraising focus is limited to that area, even if they receive contributions from outside that area on less than a repeated and ongoing basis or on a substantial basis.

To receive contributions from a state on a *repeated and ongoing basis* or a *substantial basis* means "receiving contributions within the entity's fiscal year, or relevant portion of a fiscal year, that are of sufficient volume to establish the regular or significant (as opposed to rare, isolated, or insubstantial) nature of these contributions."

States are encouraged to set, and communicate to the regulated entities, "numerical [*sic*] levels at which it [*sic*] will regard this criterion as satisfied." These levels should, the Principles say, define *repeated and ongoing* in terms of a number of contributions and *substantial* in terms of a total dollar amount of contributions or percentage of total contributions received by or on behalf of the charity. The meeting of one of these thresholds would give rise to a registration requirement but would not limit an enforcement action for deceptive solicitations.

(c) Other Principles

Another Principle is that an entity that solicits via e-mail in a particular state is to be treated the same as one that solicits by means of telephone or direct mail, if the soliciting party knew or reasonably should have known that the recipient was a resident of or was physically located in that state.

The Principles address the circumstance as to whether a charity is required to register in a particular state when the operator of a Web site, through which contributions for that charity are solicited or received, is required to register but the charity does not independently satisfy the registration criteria. If the law of the state does not universally require the registration of all charities on whose behalf contributions are solicited or received through a commercial fundraiser, commercial co-venturer, or fundraising counsel who is required to register, then the state should independently apply the criteria to each charity and only require registration by charities that independently meet the tests. If, however, the law of the state universally requires registration of all charities under these circumstances, the state should consider whether, as a matter of "prosecutorial discretion, public policy, and the prioritized use of limited resources," it would take action to enforce registration requirements as to charities that do not independently meet the criteria.

Still another Principle is that solicitations for the sale of a product or service that include a representation that some portion of the price shall be devoted to a charitable organization or charitable purpose (*commercial co-venturing, charitable sales promotion,* or *cause-related marketing*) shall be governed by the same standards as otherwise set out in the Principles governing charitable solicitations.

(d) "Exclusions"

There are two exclusions from the registration requirements (although they really are not "exclusions" at all). One is that maintaining or operating a Web site that does not contain a solicitation of contributions but merely provides program services by means of the Internet does not, by itself, invoke a requirement to register. This is the case even if unsolicited contributions are received.

The other "exclusion" is for entities that solely provide administrative, supportive, or technical services to charities without providing substantive content or advice concerning substantive content; they are not required to register. These entities include Internet service providers and organizations that do no more than process online transactions for a separate firm that operates a Web site or provide similar services. This exclusion does not, of course, encompass professional fundraisers, fundraising counsel, or commercial co-venturers.

(e) Responsibilities for Multistate Filers

The Principles provide that state charity officials "recognize that the burden of compliance by charitable organizations and their agents, professional fundraisers, commercial co-venturers and/or professional fundraising counsel should be kept reasonable in relation to the benefits to the public achieved by registration." Projects to create "common forms," such as the unified registration statement, are "strongly encouraged."

State charity offices are also "strongly encouraged" to publish their registration and reporting forms, their laws and regulations, and other related information on the Internet to facilitate registration and reporting by charitable organizations and their agents.

The Principles encourage development of information technology infrastructure to facilitate electronic registration and reporting. Also encouraged is Internet posting by charitable organizations of their application for recognition of exempt status, the IRS ruling, the most recent annual information returns, and their state registration statement(s). (This latter practice, of course, is also encouraged by the federal tax law, which obviates the need to provide hard copies of these federal documents to requestors when they are made available on the Internet.[19])

---

[19] See § 7.3.

§ 4.5 INTERNET COMMUNICATIONS

There should be little doubt that those comprising the state regulatory community, and probably most in the local regulatory community, believe—at least as a matter of pure law—that fundraising by charitable and other nonprofit organizations by means of the Internet amounts to fundraising in every state and every locality. That is, the charities are *soliciting* contributions in those jurisdictions by means of this form of communication, whether it be by e-mail or Web site posting. The Charleston Principles, for example, say just that.

While the deployment of the language is accurate and the logic impeccable, the outcome, of course, is, as a matter of real-world functioning, absurd. Only the largest of charities can afford to be and stay in compliance with such a massive regulatory system—and even in this setting, dollars are unnecessarily being diverted from charitable ends to the coffers of the regulators. The Charleston Principles are a nice first step, an attempt to frame a construct for enforcement of existing law. The Principles themselves are not, as noted, law, and there is no guarantee that a particular state will adhere, in whole or in part, to the guidelines.

Moreover, as has been pointed out, the Principles "may be problematic to apply."[20] This is because charities fundraising by means of the Internet frequently will not know where those who contribute to them are located. E-mail addresses obviously do not reveal that information. Unless the donor provides a street address, the "charity will not be able to determine the donor's location from his or her name, credit card number, or e-mail address."[21]

There is another aspect of all this. The Principles do not reflect the fact that, once a person has contributed to a charitable organization by means of the Internet, that charity is almost certain to follow up that gift with a request for another one. That request may be by letter or telephone call, and not electronic, so that the Principles do not apply. At that point, of course, the charity is now soliciting in the states by other means—and

---

[20] Livingston at 432.

[21] *Id.*

would be required to register, annually report, and otherwise comply with charitable solicitation acts.

One remedial approach would be to jettison this statutory system, with its crazy-quilt of differing laws, and replace it with a federal rule. It is safe to say, however, that federal preemption of this or any other aspect of state law regulation of charitable fundraising is not imminent.[22] (In this setting, uniform statutes or uniform reports would not fully solve the problem, even if such miracles could be accomplished.)

Another approach would be to amend the state charitable solicitation acts to exempt Internet communications from regulation. That is, definitions of the term *solicit* could be trimmed to exclude gift solicitations by e-mail or Web site posting. There is no reasonable likelihood of that happening either.

There may be hope that some aspects of this matter can be resolved by the courts—holding that states (and localities) lack jurisdiction to regulate charities and fundraising professionals when the only nexus is Internet communications. As far as is known, the Commonwealth of Pennsylvania is the only state to have formally asserted, through its attorney general's office, that Internet fundraising may require registration and reporting in that jurisdiction by both the charitable organization involved and the Internet company facilitating the fundraising.[23]

There has been one development in this regard. A federal district court has held that a county ordinance regulating charitable fundraising is inapplicable to fundraising consultants who lack minimal contacts with the county.[24] (This decision does not pertain to charitable organizations that are the entities soliciting the contributions.) The case essentially concerns

---

[22] It is interesting to compare this set of circumstances with those prevailing before the Electronic Signatures Act (see § 7.11) was enacted. In the latter case, Congress smartly—under comparable and compelling conditions—preempted state law except where a certain form of uniform act was in place. This approach lends itself nicely as a solution to the burdens imposed by the multifarious state charitable solicitation acts.

[23] Livingston at 432–433.

[24] *American Charities for Reasonable Fundraising Regulation, Inc. et al.* v. *Pinellas County*, 189 F. Supp. 2d 1319 (M.D. Fla. 2001), on remand, 221 F.3d 1211 (11th Cir. 2000).

the matter of *jurisdiction*. The argument, which the court ultimately accepted, was that direct mail consultants do not have the requisite contact with citizens of the county.

This decision is a due process case. To be subject to jurisdiction of a government, a person has to have at least "minimum contacts" with that jurisdiction. As the appellate court stated the matter, the "regulated party must have performed some act by which it purposefully avails itself of the privilege of conducting activities within" the jurisdiction. The "unilateral act of a third party is not sufficient to create the requisite contacts."[25] Also: "An abstract, indirect, and unaimed level of involvement with the [c]ounty would not be sufficient for the [c]ounty to regulate" the fundraising consultants.[26]

The specific point of the case is that direct mail and comparable consultants, who are not involved in the solicitation of charitable gifts in a jurisdiction and do not have any contacts with that jurisdiction, cannot constitutionally be compelled to comply with the fundraising regulation law of that jurisdiction. The court agreed with the argument that the consultants "are not aware of where solicitations are mailed, they do not advise charities on where to send solicitations, and they do not control where solicitations are sent."[27] It was found that "no agency relationship exists" and that the consultants "do not exercise a sufficient level of control because the facts clearly indicate that the [charitable] client has final approval."[28] The court went on to find that the consultants "are not sufficiently involved in the solicitation process to justify [the county's] exercise of legislative jurisdiction" and that "sufficient contacts" do not exist between the consultants and the county.[29] This led to the conclusion that the county's application of the ordinance to the consultants is "unreasonable and violates due process."[30]

---

[25] *Id.*, 221 F.3d at 1216.

[26] *Id.* at 1217.

[27] *Id.*, 189 F. Supp. 2d at 1329.

[28] *Id.* at 1331.

[29] *Id.*

[30] *Id.*

If this decision is correct, it means that individuals who and companies that consult with nonprofit organizations as to fundraising campaigns by mail are not subject to regulation by a government if they are not involved in the direction of the solicitations or control the fundraising program of the charitable organization. This rule of law applies equally where the government involved is a state, a county, or a city.[31] It also should apply in the context of solicitations of charitable gifts by means of the Internet. Indeed, this rule of law may be extended to charities in the Internet setting.[32]

Otherwise, assuming that the law cannot be meaningfully altered, the only feasible approach to resolution of this dilemma is to change the way the law is complied with. The power of the Internet can be harnessed to facilitate filing with the states by fundraising charities online. It does not appear that it would be that difficult, relatively speaking, to construct a

---

[31] "There is no legal or logical reason that the same rationale would not apply to regulation by a state of fundraisers in other states with which the regulating state has no contact" (Peters, "The Meaning of the *American Charities for Reasonable Fundraising Regulation v. Pinellas County* Decision," 34 *Philanthropy Monthly* (Nos. 3 & 4) 6, 7 (2002).

[32] This matter of *e-jurisdiction* is festering in other contexts, such as litigation for libel. A federal district court has held, for example, that newspapers published in Connecticut can be sued for libel in Virginia, even though there is little print circulation of them in Virginia, because of statements made in articles available on the Internet; the plaintiff suing for defamation read the articles in Virginia (*Young v. New Haven Advocate et al.*, 184 F. Supp. 2d 498 (W.D. Va. 2002), on appeal to U.S. Court of Appeals for the Fourth Circuit). The court framed the issue as being the "interesting question of where acts or omissions conducted in cyberspace actually occur" (at 503). In reaching its conclusion, the court observed, echoing a central theme of this book, that the "law in the area of personal jurisdiction based upon an Internet presence is still evolving" (at 507). An article about this litigation stated that "[a]dvocates of free speech and news media lawyers worry that if the district court decision stands, online publishers could be sued for defamation in any state or country that an online article is read" (Kaplan, "A Libel Suit May Establish E-Jurisdiction," *The New York Times*, May 27, 2002, at C1). Yet that is the problem that advocates of free speech and fundraising charitable organization lawyers have been worried about for years.

system where charities could register with all of the states online.[33] (This should be done irrespective of whether the charity is fundraising via the Internet.) Rather than regard Internet technology as exacerbating the problem, the technology should be seen as resolving it. All of this may have a turnout of some irony: The very technology (the Internet) that is bringing state fundraising regulation to the brink of collapse (if enforced) may be the very same technology that keeps it in place and enhances it.

---

[33] "Many of the problems charities now face with state registration would disappear if a simple single registration form were available on-line, and if a single annual filing would satisfy all of the states requiring an annual filing" (Livingston at 432). That is not asking too much.

CHAPTER 5

Lobbying Activities

Throughout recent decades, there has been an uneasy relationship between the operation of tax-exempt organizations, particularly those that are charitable ones, and the practice of attempting to influence legislation. Chiefly, the issue is whether the federal tax system should be used—some would say manipulated—to subsidize forms of lobbying. Many believe that lobbying is a necessary means to the achievement of exempt ends. Others are of the view that tax-exempt organizations should not be involved in attempts to influence legislation on the ground that the government is then subsidizing the viewpoints of specific individuals (such as donors). The advent of lobbying by means of the Internet has exacerbated this clash of beliefs.

The law in this regard is the most extensive when public charities are concerned, although the law as applicable to private foundations also certainly is relevant. Some tax-exempt organizations, such as social welfare organizations, are free to attempt to influence legislation without constraint. Other organizations are not restricted from a pure exempt organizations law standpoint but other aspects of the tax law can prove disadvantageous, such as the extent of deductibility of dues paid to trade, business, and professional associations (business leagues).

The Internet obviously can be used by charitable and other tax-exempt organizations to attempt to influence legislation. This form of communication is an effective—in terms of both cost and impact—way to pursue these types of advocacy efforts. As with other aspects of Internet communications by nonprofit organizations, this type of use is raising new legal issues and new interpretations of existing law.

Yet, as has been noted previously, the IRS observed, in 1999, that the "use of the Internet to accomplish a particular task does not change the way the tax laws apply to that task." This means that "[a]dvertising is still advertising and fundraising is still fundraising."[1] The IRS might have also written that "lobbying is still lobbying."

§ 5.1 INTRODUCTION

(a) Scope of Law

Federal law contains seven discrete bodies of law that pertain to attempts to influence legislation by tax-exempt organizations. These are two sets of rules applicable to public charities,[2] rules applicable to private foundations, rules pertaining to membership associations, law regulating attempts to influence legislation in the U.S. Congress,[3] law concerning lobbying by recipients of federal grants and similar payments,[4] and rules established by the Office of Management and Budget concerning the use of federal funds for lobbying by nonprofit organizations.[5] These various sets of rules contain law by which terms such as *legislation* and *attempts to influence* it are defined and costs associated with lobbying are ascertained. While there is considerable overlap as to the content of the rules, in several instances there are varied definitions of the concepts.

Most of the law in this area is that applicable to public charities. These organizations may engage in attempts to influence legislation as long as lobbying is not a *substantial* part of their overall activities.[6] The rules

---

[1] IRS FY 2000 CPE Text on Exempt Organizations and Internet Use at 64. On that occasion, however, the IRS also noted that the "nature of the Internet does change the way in which these tasks are accomplished" (*id.*).

[2] See § 7.7.

[3] 2 U.S.C. § 1601 et seq. ("Lobbying Disclosure Act of 1995").

[4] 31 U.S.C. § 1352 ("Byrd Amendment").

[5] Circular A-122, "Cost Principles for Nonprofit Organizations," 45 Fed. Reg. 46,022 (July 8, 1980), particularly Revised Transmittal Memorandum No. 2 (May 19, 1987).

[6] IRC § 501(c)(3).

applicable to public charities are termed the *substantial part test* and the *expenditure test*. The essence of these tests is the basis by which *substantiality* in this context is measured. A charitable organization is subject to the substantial part test, unless the expenditure test is elected.

(b) Definition of *Lobbying*

As discussed below,[7] the federal tax law concerning charitable organizations differentiates between *direct* lobbying and *indirect* lobbying. The substantial part test, however, does not place as much emphasis on this distinction as does the expenditure test.

(c) Definition of *Legislation*

A threshold concept in this setting is the meaning of the term *legislation*. In the law of tax-exempt organizations, there are three sources of the law on the point.

(i) Substantial Part Test. The term *legislation*, as defined for purposes of the substantial part test, includes action by Congress, a state legislature, a local council or similar governing body, and the general public in a referendum, initiative, constitutional amendment, or similar procedure.[8]

Legislation generally does not include action by an executive branch of a government, such as the promulgation of rules and regulations, nor does it include action by independent regulatory agencies. Appropriations bills are items of legislation for federal tax purposes. Also, the term *legislation* includes proposals for the making of laws in countries other than the United States.[9]

It is the view of the IRS that an attempt to influence the confirmation, by the U.S. Senate, of a federal judicial nominee constitutes, for these purposes, an attempt to influence legislation.[10] This position is based on the

---

[7] See *infra* §§ (d), (e).

[8] Reg. § 1.501(c)(3)-1(c)(3)(ii).

[9] Rev. Rul. 73-440, 1973-2 C.B. 177.

[10] Notice 88-76, 1988-2 C.B. 392.

definition of the term *legislation* used in connection with the expenditure test, where the term is defined to include resolutions and similar items.[11]

(ii) Expenditure Test. The expenditure test provides by statute that the term *legislation* includes "action with respect to Acts, bills, resolutions, or similar items by the Congress, any State legislature, any local council, or similar governing body, or by the public in a referendum, initiative, constitutional amendment, or similar procedure."[12] The term *action* is "limited to the introduction, amendment, enactment, defeat, or repeal of Acts, bills, resolutions, or similar items."[13]

The position of the IRS that an attempt to influence the confirmation, by the Senate, of a federal judicial nominee constitutes an attempt to influence legislation is reflected in the expenditure test, in examples in the regulations.[14]

(iii) Associations' Dues Deductibility Test. The term *legislation*, as defined for purposes of the rules concerning the deductibility of dues paid to tax-exempt associations by their members, means the same as is the case with respect to the expenditure test.[15] Thus, the term includes any action with respect to acts, bills, resolutions, or other similar items by a legislative body.[16] Also, legislation includes a "proposed treaty required to be submitted by the President to the Senate for its advice and consent from the time the President's representative begins to negotiate its position with the prospective parties to the proposed treaty."[17]

Because of the breadth of these rules, however, legislative bodies are "Congress, state legislatures, and other similar governing bodies, excluding local councils (and similar governing bodies), and executive, judicial, or

---

[11] IRC § 4911(e)(2).

[12] *Id.*; Reg. § 56.4911-2(d)(1).

[13] IRC § 4911(e)(3); Reg. § 56.4911-2(d)(2).

[14] Reg. § 56.4911-2(b)(4)(ii)(B), Example (6). Also Reg. § 53.4945–2(d)(2)(iii), Examples (5)–(7).

[15] IRC § 162(e)(4)(B).

[16] Reg. § 1.162-29(b)(4).

[17] *Id.*

administrative bodies."[18] The term *administrative bodies* includes "school boards, housing authorities, sewer and water districts, zoning boards, and other similar Federal, State, or local special purpose bodies, whether elective or appointive."[19] (In the charitable organization context, these bodies are not normally considered legislative bodies.)

(d) Definition of *Direct Lobbying*

The term *direct lobbying* means a direct lobbying communication with a member of a legislature, a member of a legislator's staff, a legislative committee, or a member of the staff of a legislative committee. This type of lobbying includes communication by means of meetings, correspondence, facsimiles, reports and other publications, videos, presentation of testimony, e-mail, and Web sites.

Pursuant to the tax regulations, an organization is regarded as attempting to influence legislation if it (1) contacts members of a legislative body for the purpose of proposing, supporting, or opposing legislation or (2) advocates the adoption or rejection of legislation.[20]

One of the ways the rules of the expenditure test define the term *influencing legislation* is any attempt to influence any legislation through communication with any member or employee of a legislative body[21] or with any other governmental official or employee who may participate in the formulation of the legislation.[22] This is known as a *direct lobbying communication.*

A communication with a legislator or governmental official is a direct lobbying communication only where the communication refers to *specific legislation* and reflects a view on the legislation.[23] Where a communication refers to and reflects a view on a measure that is the subject of a referendum, ballot initiative, or similar procedure, and is made to the members of

---

[18] Reg. § 1.162-29(b)(6).

[19] *Id.*

[20] Reg. § 1.501(c)(3)-1(c)(3)(ii).

[21] This term is defined in Reg. § 56.4911–2(d)(3).

[22] IRC § 4911(d)(1)(B); Reg. § 56.4911-2(b)(1)(i).

[23] Reg. § 56.4911–2(b)(1)(ii).

the general public in the jurisdiction where the vote will occur, the communication is a direct lobbying communication (unless certain exceptions apply).[24]

A communication between an organization and any bona fide member of the organization made to directly encourage the member to engage in direct lobbying is itself considered direct lobbying.[25]

There are rules for treating, as a direct lobbying expenditure, transfers for less than fair market value from a public charity that has elected the expenditure test to any noncharity that makes lobbying expenditures.[26]

The rules pertaining to lobbying by associations define the term *influencing legislation* as any attempt to influence any legislation through communication with any member or employee of a legislative body, or with any government official or employee who may participate in the formulation of legislation.[27]

(e) Definition of *Indirect Lobbying*

The term *indirect lobbying*—or, as it is often known, *grassroots lobbying*—means appeals to the general public, or segments of the general public, to contact legislators or take other specific action as regards legislative matters.[28] Thus, an organization is regarded as attempting to influence legislation if it urges the public to contact members of a legislative body for the purpose of proposing, supporting, or opposing legislation.[29]

One of the ways the rules of the expenditure test define the term *influencing legislation* is any attempt to influence any legislation through an

---

[24] Reg. § 56.4911–2(b)(1)(iii). This type of communication may be treated as nonpartisan analysis, study, or research; see *infra* § 2(e), text accompanied by note 82.

[25] IRC § 4911(d)(3)(A).

[26] Reg. § 56.4911–3(c)(3).

[27] IRC § 162(e)(4)(A).

[28] In certain circumstances, grassroots lobbying also is political campaign activity (e.g., Priv. Ltr. Rul. 9652026); an activity of this nature is said to have a *dual character* (see § 6.3(b), text accompanied by note 98).

[29] Reg. § 1.501(c)(3)–1(c)(3)(ii).

attempt to affect the opinions of the general public or any segment of the public.[30] This is known as a *grassroots lobbying communication*.

A communication is regarded as a grassroots lobbying communication only where it refers to *specific legislation*, reflects a view on the legislation, and encourages the recipient of the communication to take action with respect to the legislation.[31] The phrase *encouraging the recipient to take action* with respect to legislation (also known as a *call to action*) means that the communication—

- States that the recipient should contact a legislator or an employee of a legislative body, or should contact any other government official or employee who may participate in the formulation of legislation (but only if the principal purpose of urging contact with the government official or employee is to influence legislation);
- States the address, telephone number, or similar information of a legislator or an employee of a legislative body;
- Provides a petition, tear-off postcard or similar material for the recipient to communicate with a legislator or an employee of a legislative body, or with any other government official or employee who may participate in the formulation of legislation (but only if the principal purpose of so facilitating contact with the government official or employee is to influence legislation); or
- Specifically identifies one or more legislators who will vote on the legislation as opposing the communication's view with respect to the legislation, being undecided with respect to the legislation, being the recipient's representative in the legislature, or being a member of the legislative committee or subcommittee that will consider the legislation.[32]

A naming of the main sponsor(s) of the legislation for purposes of identifying it is not encouraging the recipient to take action.[33]

---

[30] IRC § 4911(d)(1)(A); Reg. § 56.4911-2(b)(2)(i).

[31] Reg. § 56.4911–2(b)(2)(ii).

[32] Reg. § 56.4911-2(b)(2)(iii).

[33] *Id.*

The IRS considers this definition of the term *grassroots lobbying communication* to be "very lenient," because it "will permit many clear advocacy communications to be treated as NONlobbying."[34]

A communication between an organization and any bona fide member of the organization made to directly encourage the member to urge persons other than members to engage in direct or grassroots lobbying is considered grassroots lobbying.[35]

A transfer is a grassroots expenditure to the extent that it is earmarked[36] for grassroots lobbying purposes.[37] A transfer that is earmarked for direct lobbying purposes, or for direct lobbying and grassroots lobbying purposes, is regarded as a grassroots expenditure in full, unless the transferor can demonstrate that all or part of the amounts transferred were expended for direct lobbying purposes, in which case that portion of the amounts transferred is a direct lobbying expenditure by the transferor.[38]

Expenses incurred for nonlobbying communications can subsequently be characterized as grassroots lobbying expenditures where the materials or other communications are later used in a lobbying effort. For this to occur, the materials must be *advocacy communications or research materials*, where the primary purpose of the organization in undertaking or preparing the communications or materials was for use in lobbying. In the case of subsequent distribution of the materials by another organization, there must be "clear and convincing" evidence of collusion between the two organizations to establish that the primary purpose for preparing the communication was for use in lobbying. In any event, this subsequent use

---

[34] 55 *Fed. Reg.* 35580 (Aug. 31, 1990) (emphasis in original). The IRS commentary on this definition added: "This is part of the Service's attempt to maintain a careful balance between the statutory limits on electing public charities' lobbying expenditures and the desire of those organizations to involve themselves in the public policy making process to the greatest extent consistent with those statutory limits" (*id.*).

[35] IRC § 4911(d)(3)(B).

[36] Reg. § 56.4911-4(f)(4).

[37] Reg. § 56.4911-3(c)(1).

[38] Reg. § 56.4911-3(c)(2).

rule applies only to expenditures paid less than six months before the first use of the nonlobbying material in the lobbying campaign.[39]

There are rules for treating, as a grassroots lobbying expenditure, transfers for less than fair market value from a public charity that has elected the expenditure test to any noncharity that makes lobbying expenditures.[40]

(f) Definition of *Specific Legislation*

The term *specific legislation* means legislation that has already been introduced in a legislative body and a specific legislative proposal that the organization supports or opposes.[41] In the case of a referendum, ballot initiative, constitutional amendment, or other measure that is placed on the ballot by petitions, an item becomes specific legislation when the petition is first circulated among the voters for signature.[42]

(g) Educational Activities

A nonprofit organization can have an impact—perhaps a substantial one—on a legislative process and not be involved in *lobbying* with respect to the legislation. The activity involved can instead be *educational* in nature. It may be, what is termed in a more formal way, nonpartisan analysis, study, or research.[43]

This distinction was nicely illustrated—and in the Internet communications setting—by the role of a nonprofit organization's Web site in relation to consideration by the U.S. Senate of a controversial farm bill. During debate on whether there should be limitations on subsidies to wealthy farmers, senators were referring to information found on "the Web site." The site is that created by the Environmental Working Group, a nonprofit entity funded principally by private foundations, the annual

---

[39] Reg. § 56.4911-2(b)(2)(v).

[40] Reg. § 56.4911-3(c)(3).

[41] Reg. § 56.4911-2(d)(1)(ii).

[42] *Id.*

[43] See *infra* § 2(d).

budget of which is devoted to development of computer databases and utilization of large computer servers. According to one report, the site "not only caught the attention of lawmakers, it also helped transform the farm bill into a question about equity and whether the country's wealthiest farmers should be paid to grow commodity crops while many smaller family farms receive nothing and are going out of business." This Web site, having influenced the bill's outcome, "has become unusual in the crowded world of special-interest politics, where it is hard to get noticed in Washington, much less heard."[44]

In the future, it is likely that this type of influencing of legislative processes will not be so "unusual."

§ 5.2 GENERAL RULES

(a) Introduction

One of the fundamental criteria for qualification as a tax-exempt charitable organization[45] is that "no substantial part of the activities" of the organization may constitute "carrying on propaganda, or otherwise attempting, to influence legislation."[46] A charitable organization that violates this rule is termed an *action organization* and thus becomes in danger of losing (or perhaps never acquiring) tax-exempt status.

One form of action organization is one as to which a "substantial part of its activities is attempting to influence legislation by propaganda or otherwise."[47] Another type of action organization is one as to which its "main or primary objective or objectives (as distinguished from its incidental or secondary objectives) may be attained only by legislation or a defeat of proposed legislation," and "it advocates, or campaigns for, the attainment of such main or primary objective or objectives as distinguished from

---

[44] Becker, "Web Site Helped Change Farm Policy," *The New York Times*, Feb. 24, 2002, at 22.

[45] That is, an organization that is tax-exempt pursuant to IRC § 501(a) as an organization described in IRC § 501(c)(3).

[46] IRC § 501(c)(3).

[47] Reg. § 1.501(c)(3)-1(c)(3)(ii).

engaging in nonpartisan, analysis, study or research and making the results thereof available to the public."[48]

It is irrelevant, for purposes of classification of an organization as a charity entity under federal tax law, that the legislation that is advocated or opposed would advance the charitable purposes for which the organization was created to promote.[49]

The rules concerning legislative activities by charitable organizations contain three essential elements: the meaning of the term *legislation*,[50] the meaning of the phrase *influencing legislation*, and the concept of a *substantial part* of the activities of a charitable organization.

(b) Substantial Part Test Basics

A determination as to whether a specific activity or category of activities of a charitable organization is *substantial* is basically a factual one, based on all of the pertinent facts and circumstances. There is no formula in this context for computing the substantiality of legislative undertakings. Consequently, this element of the substantial part test is ephemeral. Comments from the Senate Committee on Finance are illustrative of the state of this law. In 1969 the Committee stated that the "standards as to the permissible level of [legislative] activities under the present law are so vague as to encourage subjective application of the sanction."[51] In 1976 the Committee portrayed the dilemma in this fashion: "Many believe that the standards as to the permissible level of [legislative] activities under present law are too vague and thereby tend to encourage subjective and selective enforcement."[52]

An obvious approach to measuring substantiality in this context is to determine the portion of an organization's expenditures that is devoted on an annual basis to efforts to influence legislation. Yet this limitation of the

---

[48] Reg. § 1.501(c)(3)-1(c)(3)(iv).

[49] Rev. Rul. 67-293, 1967-2 C.B. 185. Also *Cammarano* v. *United States*, 358 U.S. 498 (1959).

[50] See *supra* § 1(c).

[51] S. Rep. No. 552, 91st Cong., 1st Sess. 47 (1969).

[52] S. Rep. No. 938 (Part 2), 94th Cong., 2d Sess. 80 (1976).

substantial part test refers to *activities*, so presumably there is more to the rule than the amount of money spent on lobbying for a particular period. The portion of an organization's activities devoted to the influencing of legislation may well be regarded as more important, for this purpose, than the organization's financial outlays for lobbying.[53]

Yet percentage standards may not embrace the totality of *substantiality*. (It was once suggested that as much as 5 percent of an organization's time and effort that involves legislative activities is not substantial.[54]) A tax-exempt organization enjoying considerable prestige and influence may have a substantial impact on a legislative process solely on the basis of a single official position statement—a negligible effort when measured in terms of a percentage of funds or time expended.[55] A standard such as this, however, may tend to place undue emphasis on whether or not a particular legislative effort was successful.[56]

The revocation of the tax-exempt status of a ministry organization was upheld by the courts, with a federal court of appeals finding the following substantial legislative activities: articles constituting appeals to the public to react to certain issues, support of or opposition to specific terms of legislation and laws, and efforts to cause members of the public to contact Congress on various matters.[57] This court rejected a percentage test in determining substantiality, writing that this approach obscured the "complexity of balancing the organization's activities in relation to its objectives and circumstances."[58] The appellate court observed that the "political [i.e., legislative] activities of an organization must be balanced in the context of

---

[53] *League of Women Voters* v. *United States*, 180 F. Supp. 379 (Ct. Cl. 1960), *cert. den.*, 364 U.S. 822 (1960).

[54] *Seasongood* v. *Commissioner*, 227 F.2d 907 (6th Cir. 1955).

[55] *Kuper* v. *Commissioner*, 332 F.2d 562 (3d Cir. 1964), *cert. den.*, 379 U.S. 920 (1964).

[56] *Haswell* v. *United States*, 500 F.2d 1133 (Ct. Cl. 1974), *cert. den.*, 419 U.S. 1107 (1974); *Dulles* v. *Johnson*, 273 F.2d 362 (2d Cir. 1959), *cert. den.*, 364 U.S. 834 (1960).

[57] *Christian Echoes National Ministry, Inc.* v. *United States*, 470 F.2d 849 (10th Cir. 1972), *cert. den.*, 414 U.S. 864 (1973).

[58] *Id.*, 470 F.2d at 855.

the objectives and circumstances of the organization to determine whether a substantial part of its activities was to influence or attempt to influence legislation."[59]

Another court opinion offers authority for the proposition that *substantiality* is not always measured by means of money spent or time devoted to lobbying. The court, in this instance evaluating the substantiality of program activities, wrote that "[w]hether an activity is substantial is a facts-and-circumstances inquiry not always dependent upon time or expenditure percentages."[60]

Thus, the substantial part test remains today one of the most indistinct and elusive concepts in the law pertaining to tax-exempt organizations. Although an organization's tax-exempt status can depend on the determination, *substantiality* remains a facts-and-circumstances inquiry, with the IRS and the courts free to inject and interrelate whatever elements are deemed, in the particular setting, appropriate.

(c) Expenditure Test Basics

Out of the vagaries of the substantial part test emerged the expenditure test. The expenditure test utilizes a mechanical approach to measure permissible and impermissible ranges of expenditures for lobbying by eligible charitable organizations, and does so in terms of the expenditure of funds and sliding scales of percentages.[61] (The basic rule that legislative activities cannot be a substantial portion of the undertakings of a charitable organization was not eliminated by enactment of the expenditure test rules.)

These standards are formulated in terms of declining percentages of total *exempt purpose expenditures*.[62] In general, an expenditure is an exempt purpose expenditure for a tax year if it is paid or incurred by an electing

---

[59] *Id.*

[60] *The Nationalist Movement* v. *Commissioner*, 102 T.C. 558, 589 (1994), *aff'd*, 37 F.3d 216 (5th Cir. 1994).

[61] IRC § 4911(c)(1); Reg. § 1.501(h)–3(c)(1).

[62] IRC § 4911(e)(1); Reg. § 56.4911–4(a).

public charity to accomplish the organization's exempt purposes.[63] These expenditures include

- Those expended for one or more charitable purposes, including most grants made for charitable ends
- Amounts paid as employee compensation (current or deferred) in furtherance of a charitable purpose
- The portion of administrative expenses allocable to a charitable purpose
- All lobbying expenditures
- Amounts expended for nonpartisan analysis, study, or research
- Amounts expended for examinations of broad social, economic, and similar problems
- Amounts expended in response to requests for technical advice
- Amounts expended pursuant to the *self-defense exception*
- Amounts expended for communications to members that are not lobbying expenditures
- A reasonable allowance for straight-line depreciation or amortization of charitable assets[64]
- Certain fundraising expenditures[65]

The phrase *exempt purpose expenditure* does not include

- Amounts expended that are not for purposes described in the preceding items (other than the penultimate one)
- The amount of transfers to members of an affiliated group,[66] made to artificially inflate the amount of exempt purpose expenditures, or to certain noncharitable organizations
- Amounts paid to or incurred for a *separate fundraising unit* of the organization or an affiliated organization
- Amounts paid to or incurred for any person who is not an employee or any organization that is not an affiliated organization, if paid

---

[63] IRC § 4911(e)(1)(A).

[64] IRC § 4911(e)(4).

[65] IRC § 4911(e)(1)(B); Reg. § 56.4911-4(b). Cf. Reg. § 56.4911-3(a)(1).

[66] See *infra* § 3(e).

primarily for fundraising, but only if the person or organization engages in fundraising, fundraising counseling, or the provision of similar advice or services

- Amounts paid or incurred that are properly chargeable to a capital account with respect to an unrelated trade or business

- Amounts paid or incurred for a tax that is not imposed in connection with the organization's efforts to accomplish charitable purposes (such as the tax on unrelated business income)

- Amounts paid or incurred for the production of income, where the income-producing activity is not substantially related to exempt purposes (such as the costs of maintaining an endowment)[67]

For these purposes, the term *fundraising* embraces three practices:

1. The solicitation of dues or contributions from members of the organization, from persons whose dues are in arrears, or from the general public;

2. The solicitation of gifts from businesses or gifts or grants from other organizations, including charitable ones; or

3. The solicitation of grants from governmental units or any agency or instrumentality of the units.[68]

A *separate fundraising unit* of an organization "must consist of either two or more individuals a majority of whose time is spent on fundraising for the organization, or any separate accounting unit of the organization that is devoted to fundraising." In addition, "amounts paid to or incurred for a separate fundraising unit include all amounts incurred for the creation, production, copying, and distribution of the fundraising portion of a separate fundraising unit's communication."[69]

The basic permitted annual level of expenditures for legislative efforts (the *lobbying nontaxable amount*[70]) is determined by using a sliding scale percentage of the organization's exempt purpose expenditures, as follows: 20 percent of the first $500,000 of an organization's expenditures for an

---

[67] IRC § 4911(e)(1)(C); Reg. § 56.4911–4(c).

[68] Reg. § 56.4911–4(f)(1).

[69] Reg. § 56.4911–4(f)(2).

[70] Reg. §§ 1.501(h)–3(c)(2), 56.4911–1(c)(1).

exempt purpose, plus 15 percent of the next $500,000; 10 percent of the next $500,000; and 5 percent of any remaining expenditures. These calculations generally are made on the basis of a four-year average.[71] The total amount spent for legislative activities in any one year by an eligible charitable organization, however, may not exceed $1 million.[72] A separate limitation—up to 25 percent of the foregoing amounts—is imposed on attempts to influence the general public on legislative matters[73] (the *grassroots nontaxable amount*).[74]

Attempts to influence legislation by individuals who are doing so as volunteers are disregarded for this purpose.[75]

(d) Substantial Part Test Exceptions

In a real sense, there are no exceptions to the substantial part test. That is, the activities involving charitable organizations relating to the legislative process which are sometimes referred to as activities that are "excepted" from the definition of attempts to influence legislation are not forms of lobbying in the first instance.

One of these "exceptions" is for activities that constitute engaging in nonpartisan analysis, study, and research; this type of activity is an educational undertaking, not lobbying. Thus, a charitable organization can engage in this type of activity and publish the results of it, where some of the plans and policies formulated can be carried out only through legislative enactment, without being an action organization, as long as it does not advocate the adoption of legislation or other legislative action to implement its findings.[76] That is, an organization may evaluate a subject of proposed legislation or a pending item of legislation and present to the

---

[71] IRC § 501(h)(1). This averaging is used as a consequence of the word *normally*; the general measuring period is termed the *base years* (Reg. § 1.501(h)-3(c)(7)).

[72] IRC § 4911(c)(2); Reg. § 56.4911-1(c)(1).

[73] IRC § 4911(c)(3); Reg. §§ 56.4911-1(c)(2), 1.501(h)-3(c)(4).

[74] IRC § 4911(c)(4); Reg. §§ 1.501(h)-3(c)(5), 56.4911-1(c)(2).

[75] Reg. § 56.4911-3(a)(1).

[76] Reg. § 1.501(c)(3)–1(c)(3)(iv). Also *Weyl* v. *Commissioner*, 48 F.2d 811 (2d Cir. 1931).

public an objective analysis of it, as long as it does not participate in the presentation of bills to the legislature and does not engage in any campaign to secure enactment of the legislation.[77] If, however, the organization's primary objective can be attained only by legislative action, it is an action organization.[78] In general, promoting activism instead of promoting educational activities can lead to denial or revocation of an organization's classification as a tax-exempt charitable entity.[79]

Another "exception" is that a charitable organization that does not initiate any action with respect to pending legislation but merely responds to a request from a legislative committee to testify is not, solely because of this activity, an action organization.[80] As to this rule, the IRS observed that (1) proscribed attempts to influence legislation "imply an affirmative act and require something more than a mere passive response to a Committee invitation," and (2) "it is unlikely that Congress, in framing the language of [the substantial part test], intended to deny itself access to the best technical expertise available on any matter with which it concerns itself."[81] This is known as the *technical advice exception.*

(e) Expenditure Test Exceptions

Five categories of activities are excluded, by statute, from the phrase *influencing legislation* for purposes of the expenditure test:

1. Making available the results of nonpartisan, analysis, study, or research[82]

---

[77] Rev. Rul. 64–195, 1964–2 C.B. 138.

[78] Rev. Rul. 62–71, 1962–1 C.B. 85. Also *Haswell* v. *United States, supra* note 56, at 1143–1145.

[79] Rev. Rul. 60–193, 1960–1 C.B. 195, as modified by Rev. Rul. 66–258, 1966–2 C.B. 213.

[80] Rev. Rul. 70–449, 1970–2 C.B. 111.

[81] *Id.* It is also unlikely that the IRS has any interest in being in the position of, once Congress or another legislature sought and obtained the technical expertise of a charitable organization, revoking the tax-exempt status of the organization because it responded by providing that expertise.

[82] IRC § 4911(d)(2)(A); Reg. § 56.4911-2(c)(1). See *supra* § 1(g).

2. Providing technical advice or assistance to a governmental body or legislative committee in response to a written request by the body or committee[83]

3. Appearances before or communications to any legislative body with respect to a possible decision of that body that might affect the existence of the organization, its powers and duties, its tax-exempt status, or the deduction of contributions to it (the *self-defense exception*)[84]

4. Communications between the organization and its bona fide members[85] with respect to legislation or proposed legislation of direct interest to it and them, unless the communications directly encourage the members to influence legislation or directly encourage the members to urge nonmembers to influence legislation[86]

5. Routine communications with government officials or employees[87]

Again, in a real sense, only the third of these categories of activities is an exception to the expenditure test. That is, the other activities involving charitable organizations relating to the legislative process which are sometimes referred to as activities that are "excepted" from the definition of attempts to influence legislation are not forms of lobbying in the first instance.

In amplification of the fourth exception, expenditures for a communication that refers to, and reflects a view on, specific legislation are not lobbying expenditures if the communication satisfies all of the following four requirements:

1. The communication is directed only to members of the organization

2. The specific legislation the communication refers to, and reflects a view on, is of direct interest to the organization and its members

---

[83] IRC § 4911(d)(2)(B); Reg. § 56.4911-2(c)(3). See text accompanied by *supra* notes 80–81.

[84] IRC § 4911(d)(2)(C); Reg. § 56.4911-2(c)(4).

[85] Reg. §§ 56.4911–5(f)(1)–(4).

[86] IRC § 4911(d)(2)(D).

[87] IRC § 4911(d)(2)(E).

3. The communication does not directly encourage the member to engage in direct lobbying[88]

4. The communication does not directly encourage the member to engage in grassroots lobbying[89]

An expenditure that meets all of these requirements, other than the third one, is treated as an expenditure for direct lobbying.[90] An expenditure that satisfies all of these requirements, other than the fourth one, is treated as an expenditure for grassroots lobbying.[91] There are rules for treatment, as expenditures for direct or grassroots lobbying, of expenditures for any written communication that is designed primarily for members of an organization and that refers to, and reflects a view on, specific legislation of direct interest to the organization and its members.[92]

The regulations create a sixth "exception," removing from the ambit of direct lobbying communications and grassroots lobbying communications examinations and discussions of broad social, economic, and similar problems, even if the problems are of the type with which government would be expected to deal ultimately.[93]

§ 5.3 OTHER RULES

(a) Definition of *Propaganda*

The term *propaganda*, as used in this setting, is not as expansive as merely spreading particular beliefs, opinions, or doctrines. Rather, the word *propaganda* "connotes public address with selfish or ulterior purpose and characterized by the coloring or distortion of facts."[94] To avoid stigmatization

---

[88] Reg. § 56.4911–5(f)(6).

[89] Reg. § 56.4911–5(b).

[90] Reg. § 56.4911–5(c).

[91] Reg. § 56.4911–5(d).

[92] Reg. § 56.4911–5(e).

[93] Reg. § 56.4911–2(c)(2).

[94] *Seasongood* v. *Commissioner, supra* note 54, at 910-912. Also *Cochran* v. *Commissioner,* 78 F.2d 176 (4th Cir. 1935).

as propaganda, therefore, a presentation should be fairly well balanced as to stating alternative viewpoints and solutions, and be motivated more by a purpose to educate than to advocate—certainly not by a "selfish" purpose.[95]

(b) Paid Mass Media Advertisements

A *mass media advertisement* that is not a grassroots lobbying communication under the general rules may nonetheless be a grassroots lobbying communication by reason of a special rule. For this purpose, the term *mass media* means "television, radio, billboards and general circulation newspapers and magazines."[96] General circulation newspapers and magazines do not include newspapers or magazines published by a charitable organization for which the expenditure test election is in effect, unless the total circulation of the newspaper or magazine is greater than 100,000 and fewer than one-half of the recipients are members of the organization.[97] Where an electing charitable organization is itself a mass media publisher or broadcaster, all portions of that organization's mass media publications or broadcasts are treated as *paid advertisements* in the mass media, except those portions that are advertisement paid for by another person.[98]

There is a rebuttable presumption that a *paid mass media advertisement* is a form of grassroots lobbying if it

- Is made within two weeks before a vote by a legislative body, or committee of a legislative body, on highly publicized legislation[99]
- Reflects a view on the general subject of the legislation
- Either refers to the legislation or encourages the public to communicate with legislators on the general subject of the legislation[100]

---

[95] Rev. Rul. 68-263, 1968-1 C.B. 256.

[96] Reg. § 56.4911-2(b)(5)(iii)(A).

[97] *Id.* The definition of *member* is in Reg. § 56.4911-5(f). See *supra* § 2(e).

[98] Reg. § 56.4911-2(b)(5)(iii)(B).

[99] The term *highly publicized* is defined in Reg. § 56.4911-2(b)(5)(iii)(C).

[100] Reg. § 56.4911-2(b)(5)(ii).

This presumption is rebutted either by a showing that the charitable organization regularly makes similar mass media communications without regard to the timing of legislation or that the timing of the communication was unrelated to the upcoming vote.[101]

(c) Making the Election

An eligible charitable organization[102] that desires to avail itself of the expenditure test must elect to come within those standards and can do so on a year-to-year basis.[103] Charitable organizations that may not or that choose not to make the election remain governed by the substantial part test.[104] Churches, conventions or associations of churches, integrated auxiliaries of churches, certain supporting organizations of noncharitable entities, and private foundations may not elect to come under these rules.[105]

If a charitable organization has its tax-exempt status revoked by reason of the expenditure test and thereafter is again recognized as an exempt charitable organization, it may again elect the expenditure test.[106]

(d) Record Keeping

An electing public charity must keep a record of its lobbying expenditures for the tax year. These records must include:

- Expenditures for grassroots lobbying
- Amounts paid for direct lobbying

---

[101] *Id.*

[102] Reg. §§ 1.501(h)-2(b), 2(e).

[103] IRC §§ 501(h)(3), (4); Reg. § 1.501(h)-6. This election, and any revocation or reelection of it, is made by filing Form 5768 with the IRS. Reg. §§ 1.501(h)-2(a), (c), (d).

[104] Reg. § 1.501(h)-1(a)(4).

[105] IRC § 501(h)(5). Private foundations are subject to more stringent regulation in this regard (see *infra* § 4(c)).

[106] Reg. § 1.501(h)-3(d)(4).

- The portion of amounts paid or incurred as compensation for an employee's services for direct lobbying
- Amounts paid for out-of-pocket expenditures incurred on behalf of the organization and for direct lobbying
- The allocable portion of administration, overhead, and other general expenditures attributable to direct lobbying
- Expenditures for publications or for communications with members to the extent the expenditures are treated as expenditures for direct lobbying
- Expenditures for direct lobbying of a controlled organization to the extent included by a controlling organization[107] in its lobbying expenditures

Identical record keeping requirements apply with respect to grassroots lobbying expenditures.[108]

There are no specific record-keeping requirements imposed on organizations subject to the substantial part test. There are, however, questions about lobbying posed in the annual information return, and charitable organizations should, of course, prepare and maintain the records needed to answer those questions.

(e) Affiliated Organizations

The expenditure test contains methods of aggregating the expenditures of related organizations, so as to forestall the creation of numerous organizations for the purpose of avoiding the limitations of the test. Where two or more charitable organizations are members of an affiliated group[109] and at least one of the members has elected coverage under the expenditure test, the calculations of lobbying and exempt purpose expenditures must be

---

[107] See *infra* § 3(e).

[108] Reg. § 56.4911–6(b).

[109] Reg. § 56.4911–7(e).

made by taking into account the expenditures of the group.[110] If these expenditures exceed the permitted limits, each of the electing member organizations must pay a proportionate share of the penalty excise tax, with the nonelecting members treated under the substantial part test.[111]

Generally, under these rules, two organizations are deemed *affiliated* where

- One organization is bound by decisions of the other on legislative issues, pursuant to its governing instrument[112] or
- The governing board of one organization includes enough representatives of the other (an *interlocking governing board*[113]) to cause or prevent action on legislative issues[114] by the first organization.[115]

If a group of autonomous organizations controls an organization but no one organization in the controlling group alone can control that organization, the organizations are not considered an affiliated group by reason of the interlocking directorates rule.[116]

There are no comparable rules in connection with the substantial part test.

(f) Reporting

The annual information returns filed by tax-exempt organizations solicit information about the legislative activities of electing charitable organizations so as to make that information available to the public.[117] Thus, an electing organization must disclose in its information return the amount of its lobbying expenditures (total and grassroots), together with the

---

[110] IRC § 4911(f)(1); Reg. §§ 56.4911-8, 56.4911-10.

[111] IRC § 4911(f)(1)(B).

[112] Reg. § 56.4911–7(c).

[113] Reg. § 56.4911–7(b).

[114] Reg. § 56.4911–7(a)(3).

[115] IRC § 4911(f)(2); Reg. § 56.4911–7(a)(1).

[116] IRC § 4911(f)(3).

[117] Form 990, Schedule A, Part VI-A.

amount that it could have expended for legislative purposes without becoming subject to the 25 percent excise tax. An electing organization that is a member of an affiliated group must provide this information with respect to itself and the entire group.[118]

Organizations that are under the substantial part test also must include with their annual information returns information concerning any lobbying activities they may have undertaken during the reporting period.[119]

(g) Allocation Rules

There are two allocation rules, in the expenditure test context, for communications that have a lobbying purpose and a bona fide nonlobbying purpose.

One rule requires that the allocation be *reasonable.* This rule applies to an electing public charity's communications primarily with its bona fide members. More than one-half of the recipients of the communication must be members of the electing public charity for this rule to be available.[120]

The other allocation rule is for nonmembership communications. Where a monmembership lobbying communication also has a bona fide nonlobbying purpose, an organization must include as lobbying expenditures all costs attributable to those parts of the communication that are on the same specific subject as the lobbying message. The rules define the phrase *same specific subject.*[121]

If a communication (other than to an organization's members) is both a direct lobbying communication and a grassroots lobbying communication, the communication is treated as a grassroots lobbying expenditure, unless the electing public charity demonstrates that the communication was made primarily for direct lobbying purposes, in which case a reasonable allocation is permitted.[122]

---

[118] IRC § 6033(b)(8).

[119] Form 990, Schedule A, Part VI-B.

[120] Reg. § 56.4911-3(a)(2)(ii).

[121] Reg. § 56.4911-3(a)(2)(i).

[122] Reg. § 56.4911-3(a)(3).

(h) Associations' Dues Rules

From the standpoint of tax-exempt status, an association may lobby without restriction, as long as the lobbying is in furtherance of its exempt purposes. Another body of federal tax law is implicated, however, in that there generally is no business expense deduction available for amounts paid or incurred in connection with the influencing of legislation.[123]

This business expense deduction denial rule is applicable to dues paid to associations, which generally are deductible. Thus, if an association engages in lobbying, a ratio of these expenses to total expenses must be created, with the portion of the dues that is considered allocable to the lobbying effort rendered nondeductible.[124]

§ 5.4 SANCTIONS

(a) Nonelecting Public Charitable Organizations

Charitable organizations that have not elected the expenditure test, and thus remain under the auspices of the substantial part test, are subject to two discrete sanctions for engaging in too much lobbying activity. The IRS has the discretion as to which sanction to impose. The IRS also has the discretion to utilize both sanctions in a particular case.

(i) Revocation of Tax-Exempt Status. A public charity that is subject to the substantial part test (that is, it has not elected the expenditure test) and that engages in excessive lobbying activities can have its tax-exempt status revoked by the IRS. More specifically, if a substantial part of a tax-exempt charitable organization's activities consists of attempts to influence legislation, the organization is denominated an *action organization* and hence cannot continue to qualify as a tax-exempt charitable entity.[125] (Likewise, significant legislative activities will preclude tax exemption.)

---

[123] IRC § 162(e)(1). There is an exception for attempts to influence local legislation (IRC § 162(e)(2)).

[124] IRC § 162(e)(3).

[125] Reg. § 1.501(c)(3)–1(c)(3)(ii).

For an organization to be denied or lose tax-exempt status because of lobbying activity, the legislative activities must be undertaken as an act of the organization itself. Thus, for example, the IRS recognized that the legislative activities of a student newspaper were not attributable to the sponsoring university.[126] Likewise, during the course of the anti–Vietnam war efforts on many college and university campuses, which included legislative activities, the principle was established that the activities by students and faculty were not official acts of the institutions involved.[127]

(ii) Penalty Taxes. If a charitable organization that has not elected to come under the expenditure test or that is ineligible to make the election fails to meet the substantial part test, a tax in the amount of 5 percent of the lobbying expenditures may be imposed, for each year involved, on the organization.[128] A *lobbying expenditure* is any amount paid or incurred by a charitable organization in carrying on propaganda or otherwise attempting to influence legislation.[129]

A separate tax is applicable to each of the organization's managers (basically, its officers and directors) who agreed to the making of the lobbying expenditures, knowing that they were likely to result in revocation of its exemption, unless the agreement was not willful and was due to reasonable cause.[130] This tax also is an amount equal to 5 percent of the lobbying expenditures. It can be imposed only where the tax on the organization is imposed.

(iii) Both Sanctions. The IRS has the authority, in the case of a public charity under the substantial part test which has engaged in excessive lobbying, to revoke the tax-exempt status of the organization and impose the penalty taxes.[131]

---

[126] Rev. Rul. 72-513, 1972-2 C.B. 246.

[127] American Council on Education Guidelines, CCH Stand. Fed. Tax Rep. ¶ 3033.197.

[128] IRC § 4912(a).

[129] IRC § 4912(d)(1).

[130] IRC § 4912(b).

[131] There is a parallel structure in the political campaign activities context (see the discussion at § 6.4(a)).

(b) Electing Public Charitable Organizations

A charitable organization that has elected the expenditure test and that exceeds one or both of these limitations (the *lobbying ceiling amount*[132] or the *grassroots ceiling amount*[133]) becomes subject to an excise tax in the amount of 25 percent of the excess lobbying expenditures[134]; this tax falls on the greater of the two excesses.[135]

If an electing organization's lobbying expenditures normally (that is, on an average over a four-year period[136]) exceed 150 percent of either limitation, it will lose its tax-exempt status as a charitable entity.[137] A charitable organization in this circumstance is not able to convert to a tax-exempt social welfare organization.[138]

(c) Private Foundations

The rules as to charitable organizations and lobbying are much different in the case of private foundations.[139] Essentially, private foundations may not engage in attempts to influence legislation.[140] That is, they are not accorded the standard of insubstantiality granted to public charities.

Nonetheless, private foundations are permitted to make available the results of nonpartisan analysis, study, or research.[141] Also, they can provide technical advice or assistance to a legislative body in response to a written request for the advice or assistance.[142]

---

[132] Reg. § 1.501(h)-3(c)(3).

[133] Reg. § 1.501(h)-3(c)(6).

[134] IRC § 4911(a); Reg. §§ 56.4911-1(a), 1.501(h)-1(a)(3).

[135] IRC § 4911(b); Reg. § 56.4911-1(b).

[136] Reg. § 1.501(h)-3(c)(7).

[137] IRC § 501(h)(1), (2); Reg. § 1.501(h)-3(b).

[138] IRC § 504; Reg. §§ 1.504-1, 1.504-2. A social welfare organization is the subject of IRC § 501(c)(4). Cf. Reg. § 1.501(c)(3)-1(c)(3)(v).

[139] See § 7.7.

[140] IRC § 4945(d)(1), (e).

[141] See *supra* § 1(g).

[142] See *supra* § 2(d), text accompanied by notes 80–81.

Further, private foundations can, without limitation, engage in self-defense lobbying. That is, a private foundation can appear before or otherwise communicate to a legislative body with respect to a possible decision of that body that might affect the existence of the foundation, its powers and duties, its tax-exempt status, or the deductibility of contributions to the foundation.[143]

If a private foundation violates the legislative activities constraint, it can have its tax-exempt status revoked. Also, an attempt to influence legislation generally is a *taxable expenditure*, which would subject the foundation to a tax of 10 percent of the expenditure[144] and perhaps trigger a companion tax on those managing the foundation.[145]

(d) Other Tax-Exempt Organizations

The federal tax law does not limit the ability of tax-exempt organizations other than charitable ones to attempt to influence legislation. Thus, entities such as social welfare organizations and membership associations may lobby with tax law impunity—as far as tax-exempt status is concerned. Some dues-based organizations, however, can cause the dues paid to them to lose deductibility as a business expense, in whole or in part, because of legislative activities.[146]

§ 5.5 INTERNET COMMUNICATIONS

(a) Internet Lobbying in General

Lobbying is a form of communication, and the Internet is a medium of communication. Thus, lobbying by tax-exempt organizations (and other persons) can be undertaken by means of the Internet. As is the case in other contexts, however, the federal tax law does not provide any unique treatment to transactions or activities of tax-exempt organizations involving attempts to influence legislation simply because the Internet is the

---

[143] IRC § 4945(e).

[144] IRC § 4945(a)(1).

[145] IRC § 4945(a)(2).

[146] See *supra* § 3(h).

medium of communication. Thus, the rules of the substantial part test and the expenditure test embrace lobbying by means of the Internet.

There are four forms of Internet communications in this setting:

1. A communication published on a publicly accessible Web page
2. A communication posted on a password-protected portion of a Web site
3. A communication on a listserv (or by means of other methods such as a news group, chat room and/or forum)
4. A communication by means of e-mail

The IRS recognized, in the Announcement, that, "[b]y publishing a web-page on the Internet, an exempt organization can provide the general public with information about the organization, its activities, and issues of concern to the organization, as well as immediate access to websites of other organizations." The agency added: "An exempt organization can provide information to subscribers about issues of concern to the organi-zation as well as enable people with common interests to share informa-tion via the Internet through a variety of methods," referencing mailing lists and the methods referred to above in the third category of Internet communication.

An e-mail communication from a tax-exempt organization clearly can constitute an attempt to influence legislation. If the lobbying message is sent to a legislator, a member of the staff of a legislator, a member of the staff of a legislative committee, and the like, it constitutes direct lobbying. Likewise, a lobbying message can amount to indirect (or grassroots) lob-bying where the elements of that definition are met.

A tax-exempt organization may post a lobbying message on the por-tion of its Web site that is publicly accessible. For public charities, it is not always clear as to whether this is an attempt to influence legislation in the tax law sense of the phrase. (It is, of course, an attempt to influence legisla-tion in a generic sense or it would not be placed on the site in the first instance.) The answer turns in part on whether the posting of the message is considered a communication for purposes of direct lobbying or indirect lobbying. For charities under the substantial part test, the law simply is vague on the point.

For charities that have elected the expenditure test, the law in this regard is much clearer. Where a charitable organization posts a lobbying message on a publicly accessible portion of its Web site and takes a position with respect to specific legislation, the message is not a direct lobbying communication. This conclusion can be extrapolated from existing law. An example is the monthly newsletter of a public charity that contains an editorial column that refers to and reflects a view on specific pending legislation. The organization sends the newsletter to 10,000 non-member subscribers, including a senator. The newsletter containing the lobbying message is not a direct lobbying communication because the newsletter was sent to the senator in his or her capacity as a subscriber rather than as a legislator.[147] Consequently, the possibility that a legislator may visit the Web site of a public charity and read a lobbying message that is intended for all Web site visitors should not convert the message into a form of direct lobbying.

Another example illustrates some of the subtleties in this area.[148] In expansion of the prior example, one of the senator's staff members sees the senator's copy of the newsletter, reads the editorial, and writes to the public charity requesting additional information. The charity responds with a letter that refers to and reflects a view on specific legislation. This letter likely is a direct lobbying communication.[149]

Returning to the example immediately prior to the previous one, the editorial column may be an indirect (grassroots) lobbying communication if it encourages recipients to take action with respect to the pending legislation it refers to and on which it reflects a view.[150]

Substantiality in the expenditure test context is, as noted, measured solely in terms of expenditures of funds. The Internet is far more cost-effective than other forms of communication. Consequently, it is obvious

---

[147] Reg. § 56.4911-2(b)(4)(i), Example (7).

[148] *Id.*, Example (8).

[149] It is possible that this letter is within an exception to these rules, such as the exception for nonpartisan analysis, study, or research (see *supra* § 1(g)). The letter is not within the scope of the exception for responses to written requests from a legislative body or committee for technical advice (see *supra* § 2(d), text accompanied by notes 80–81) inasmuch as the letter is not in response to a written request from such a body or committee.

[150] See Reg. § 56.4911-2(b)(2).

that a charitable organization that has elected the expenditure test is in a position to engage in considerably more lobbying activity when the attempts to influence legislation are made by means of the Internet. This advantage can be compounded when coupled with the fact that lobbying by volunteers is not taken into account under the expenditure test at all.[151]

Private foundations have unique concerns in this setting. Certainly more so than is the case with tax-exempt charitable organizations generally, a private foundation should not place material on its Web site that constitutes an attempt to influence legislation. A private foundation self-defense can, however, post material in conjunction with self-defense lobbying.[152]

A private foundation may make a grant to an organization—most likely only a charitable one—that subsequently violates the constraint on legislative activities. Indeed, the foundation may have made the grant for the specific purpose of funding development and/or maintenance of a Web site, and it was the site that contained the material with the lobbying content. Nonetheless, the foundation should not be penalized for transgressions of this nature by the grantee unless the grant was earmarked for the forbidden purposes. A private foundation grant is *earmarked* for legislative purposes if it is made "pursuant to an agreement, oral or written, that the grant will be used for specific purposes."[153]

If a private foundation violates the political campaign prohibition rules, it could have its tax-exempt status revoked. Also, if funds were involved, it would have made a taxable expenditure and thus be liable for the 10 percent excise tax.[154]

(b) Questions Posed by Announcement

The IRS wrote, with considerable understatement, that "[w]hen a charitable organization engages in advocacy on the Internet, questions arise as to whether it is conducting . . . lobbying activity, and if so, to what extent."

---

[151] See the text accompanied by *supra* note 75.

[152] See *supra* § 4(c).

[153] Reg. § 53.4945–2(a)(5)(i), (6).

[154] See *supra* § 4(c), the text accompanied by note 145.

The agency added: "This situation is further complicated by the affiliation of charitable organizations with other organizations engaging in . . . lobbying activities on the Internet. The ease with which different websites may be linked electronically (through a 'hyperlink') raises a concern about whether the message of a linked website is attributable to the charitable organization."

(i) General Issues. The Announcement posed six general questions that have relevance with respect to the conduct of lobbying activities, with the IRS reiterating that tax-exempt organizations "use the Internet to carry on activities that otherwise can be conducted through other media, such as radio or television broadcasts, print publications, or direct mailings."

The first of these general questions is whether a Web site maintained by a tax-exempt organization "constitute[s] a single publication or communication." It is conceivable that a Web site could constitute a single *publication*, in that a single publication can encompass many subjects and messages. (Many publications, however, such as a book or journal, are devoted to a single subject.)

It is highly unlikely, however, that a Web site would constitute a single *communication*. In the lobbying setting, for example, even if a charity posted a message in an attempt to influence legislation, presumably it would also have messages about its purposes and exempt programs, and perhaps also fundraising and unrelated business activity. Thus, the answer to this question should be that a tax-exempt organization's Web site may constitute a single publication but that it is rare, if ever, that a Web site would constitute a single communication. (Certainly it could prove inadvisable for a charitable organization to maintain a Web site devoted solely to lobbying messages.)

The IRS then asked, suggesting the answer to the first question, if a Web site is not a single publication or single communication, "[H]ow should it be separated into distinct publications or communications?" This has been discussed; it is an application of the fragmentation rule.[155]

This segued into the third of the general questions, which inquired into the proper methodology to use when allocating expenses for different

---

[155] See § 2.1 (b)(v).

communications on a Web site. The simplest of answers would be to separate a Web site into discrete communications on the basis of the amount of space each communication occupies on the site. This is often the approach taken in the case of print publications. In some instances, however, a *primary purpose test* is applied (or at least advocated), so that if the primary purpose of a publication is to communicate a particular message, the entire publication is deemed to have communication of that message as its purpose. (There obviously could be a problem as to tax-exempt status for a charitable organization if the primary or exclusive purpose of its Web site was considered to be for lobbying.)

The IRS posed the question as to whether expense allocation should be based on Web pages, noting that, unlike print publications, they may not be of equal size. This may be one of several factors to take into account. Once again, the cost-effectiveness of Web site publishing comes into play, in that the costs involved may be relatively small to begin with.[156] (Moreover, from the standpoint of lobbying, a message posted in an attempt to influence legislation is likely to be a small component of the overall communications.)

The expenditure test rules include guidance on the allocation of *mixed purpose expenditures*.[157] This relates to "lobbying expenditures for a communication that also has a bona fide nonlobbying purpose." The guidance here is not particularly helpful and is a bit old-fashioned. For example, some of the illustrations pertain to print publications; allocation is made in terms of "pages."[158] It is safe to assume that the regulation writers did not have Web pages in mind when crafting these rules.

The IRS observed that, "[u]nlike other publications of an exempt organization, a website may be modified on a daily basis." The IRS then asked: "To what extent and by what means should an exempt organization maintain the information from prior versions of the organization's website?" Although the question is a legitimate one, it seems impractical to require a charitable or other tax-exempt organization to maintain the information posted on every prior version of its Web site.

---

[156] See § 1.8(a).

[157] Reg. § 56.4911–3(a)(2)(i).

[158] E.g., Reg. § 56.4911–3(b), Example (2).

The matter of expense allocations can be considered in light of these last two questions combined. Isolating the costs of a Web site lobbying communication is difficult enough, without taking into account many changes in site content in the course of a year. When the changes are factored in, expense isolation and allocation may become nearly impossible—or, in any event, more expensive than the Web site expenses themselves.[159]

An additional complicating factor is that the time and expense involved in preparing a Web site communication may be elements that the tax-exempt organization would incur in any event. The same message may be used in other forms of communication, such as print media. That aspect of lobbying, then, may well already be accounted for, leaving the cost in connection with the Web site only that of posting the material, which is negligible.

As has been suggested, the answer to this dilemma may lie in the development of a safe harbor rule or de minimis exception to a general rule.[160]

The last of these general questions, which is highly significant in connection with lobbying, was: "To what extent are statements made by subscribers to a forum, such as a listserv or newsgroup, attributable to an exempt organization that maintains the forum?" Existing law[161] indicates that the general answer to this question must be that attribution is not appropriate (or fair). At least, attribution should not be the case in the lob-

---

[159] A commentator wrote: "Theoretically, one might want to use the server capacity needed to hold the site as the base and allocate [expenses] based on the amount of the total capacity used for any particular part of the site. That would allow for the greater demands of certain video or graphic material and the lesser demands of text in a neutral way. However, in practice, this can become quite complicated quite quickly, especially where lots of material on the site changes with great frequency." (Livingston at 425)

[160] "It would be highly problematic if charities were deterred from using the most efficient tool available for participating in legislative debates because all of the resources gained from the increased efficiency were being consumed by the burdens of an accounting rule. To prevent that from happening, charities may consider proposing to the IRS adoption of some form of de minimis rule or safe harbor for this kind of expense allocation." (*id.*)

[161] See *supra* § 4(a)(i), text accompanied by notes 127–128.

bying context, where the tax-exempt organization cannot (or should not) be held responsible for the speech of others. As noted previously, for an organization to be denied or lose tax-exempt status because of lobbying activity, the legislative activities must be undertaken as an act of the organization itself.

This question has a follow-up component: "Does attribution vary depending on the level of participation of the exempt organization in maintaining the forum (e.g., if the organization moderates discussion, acts as editor, etc.)?" Generally, the answer to this question should continue to be that there is no attribution. For example, if a public charity maintains a chat room and initiates a discussion of a pending item of legislation, and an individual sends a message in support of or in opposition to that legislation, that message should not be attributed to the organization.

At some point, of course, the answer to this question would have to be that attribution is appropriate. As an illustration, if a charitable organization announced that it was opposed to an item of legislation and requested those who participate in a forum to send messages in opposition to the legislation so that the organization could compile them and send them to legislators, that aspect of maintenance of the forum would constitute an attempt to influence legislation.

(ii) Specific Questions. The Announcement posed seven questions specifically pertaining to lobbying by tax-exempt organizations by means of the Internet.

The first of these questions certainly was a pertinent one, highlighting as it did the fact that the substantial part test essentially is a facts-and-circumstances test.[162] The IRS inquired as to the facts and circumstances that are relevant, in the case of charitable organizations that are subject to the substantial part test, in "determining whether lobbying communications made on the Internet are a substantial part of the organization's activities." As discussed, this element of *substantiality* is vague; it may partake of expenditures, time, influence, and/or some other factor(s). There is, therefore, an odd situation here: The IRS may be seeking to articulate facts and circumstances that may cause Internet lobbying to be substantial, when

---

[162] See *supra* § 2(b).

there is a basic lack of understanding as to these facts and circumstances when any other form of communication is used to influence legislation.

As discussed in the context of the general questions, in separating a Web site into distinct communications, the simplest approach would be to make the separation on the basis of the amount of space a communication occupies on the site. While that approach might work as to the separation of communications, it cannot alone work when assessing the *effectiveness* of each of the communications. The IRS suggested two other factors, both of which are clearly relevant to the inquiry. One is location of the communication on the Web site (main page or a subsidiary page). The other is the number of hits on the site. The fact is that, in some fashion, the factor of effectiveness must be measured—either by means of a rule or left to the circumstances of each case—or disregarded as being impossible to measure. While the latter is not likely, it is far from clear as to how one "values" content on a Web site.

Another question of considerable import was alluded to above: "Does providing a hyperlink [by a charitable organization] to the website of another organization that engages in lobbying activity constitute lobbying by [the] charitable organization?" Surely, as long as the link itself is all that is involved in the analysis, the answer to this question must be no. This is because a link from one organization to another does not generally, by itself, cause any activity of the linked organization to be attributed to the linking organization.[163] It is common, for example, for a public charity to be closely related to a tax-exempt social welfare organization or an exempt business league. Web site lobbying by these types of organizations should not automatically be attributed to the charitable entity. Thus, an answer to this question to the contrary would be impractical, not to say unfair.

In the lobbying context, the no answer is reflected in existing law. Generally, for an organization to be denied or lose tax-exempt status because of lobbying activity, the legislative activity must be undertaken as an act of the organization itself; there generally is no attribution rule.[164] Moreover, in connection with the expenditure test, specific rules dictate

---

[163] See § 1.8(b).

[164] See *supra* § 4(a)(i), text accompanied by notes 127–128.

when the lobbying expenditures of an organization are to be attributed to another organization.[165] A mere link between organizations is insufficient to trigger these rules.

In furtherance of this question, the IRS also asked: What "facts and circumstances are relevant in determining whether the charitable organization has engaged in lobbying activity" by providing such a link? This aspect of the question not-so-subtlely answers the first part of the question: The sheer existence of a link does not automatically cause attribution of any lobbying, yet attribution can arise under certain sets of circumstances. Certainly, for example, if a charitable organization was opposed to an item of legislation and were to expressly request visitors to its Web site to link with another organization's Web site for the purpose of viewing an explanation as to why the legislation should be defeated, the provision of the link would constitute lobbying by the charitable organization. Also, if the charitable organization controlled the organization to which it provided the link, that would be a major factor indicating lobbying by the charitable organization. The IRS asked whether it would make any difference if lobbying activity is on the specific Web page to which the charitable organization provides the link rather than elsewhere on the other organization's Web site. The answer to that question is yes, in that such a linkage would be a factor leading to the conclusion that the provision of the link constitutes lobbying by the charitable organization.

Another question concerned charitable organizations that have elected the expenditure test. The IRS asked, when determining whether such a charitable organization has engaged in grassroots lobbying on the Internet, what facts and circumstances are relevant as to whether the organization made a *call to action*? A communication is regarded as a grassroots communication only where three requirements are satisfied; one of them is that the communication encourages the recipients to take action with respect to the legislation.[166] This question is peculiar because the phrase *encouraging the recipient to take action* with respect to legislation is given a detailed definition.[167] Thus, for example, if the communication on an

---

[165] See *supra* § 3(e).

[166] See *supra* § 1(e), text accompanied by note 31.

[167] *Id.*, text accompanied by note 32.

electing charity's Web site states that the reader should contact a legislator or an employee of a legislative body; provides the address, telephone number, or similar information about a legislator or an employee of a legislative body; or identifies one or more legislators who will vote on the legislation as opposing the communication's view with respect to the legislation, the communication is a call to action. If a Web site communication is not within one of the four types of ways to encourage recipients to take action, the communication cannot be a grassroots lobbying communication.

Still another question posed by the IRS was whether publication of a Web page on the Internet by a charitable organization that has elected the expenditure test constitutes an appearance in the mass media. The answer is: generically yes but technically no. (As to the former, the Internet (or the Web) obviously is a form of mass media—indeed, it is the largest form of mass media.) This is because the term *mass media* is defined for these purposes to mean "television, radio, billboards and general circulation newspapers and magazines."[168] The term should include the Internet but it does not.

This type of mass media publication may be a grassroots lobbying communication if it meets the three-part grassroots lobbying definition.[169] By posing this question, however, the IRS is exploring the possibility of invocation of the special rule for certain *paid mass media advertisements.* There is a rebuttable presumption—utilizing a three-part test[170]—that such an advertisement is a form of grassroots lobbying. This presumption can be overcome by a charitable organization.[171] Thus, those rules would have to be applied in a particular case to see whether the mass media publication amounts to a grassroots lobbying communication. But this analysis would be required only if the Internet were to be found to be a form of *mass media* for this purpose—which, as noted, it is not.[172] As the regulations

---

[168] Reg. § 56.4911–2(b)(5)(iii)(A).

[169] See *supra* § 3(b).

[170] *Id.*; see the text accompanied by *supra* notes 99–100.

[171] *Id., supra* note 101.

[172] The regulation states that the term *mass media* "means" ...; it does not use the usual word "includes." The IRS could easily have added the Internet to this definition but that medium was not thought of in this context when this regulation was finalized in 1990.

state, this special rule "generally applies only to a limited type of paid advertisements that appear in the mass media."[173]

The IRS did not ask whether a charitable organization with a Web site is a *publisher* or *broadcaster*. As noted, generally, where a charitable organization is itself a mass media publisher or broadcaster, all portions of the organization's mass media publications or broadcasts are treated as paid advertisements in the mass media.[174] Those terms are not defined.

Once again, the cost-effectiveness of the Internet comes into play.[175] While an organization with a Web site is a publisher or broadcaster in a generic sense, it may not be such in this context. This argument has been well and succinctly stated by a commentator who made much of the cost differential: The "resources needed to post a Web site are dramatically smaller than those needed to publish a mass circulation newspaper or broadcast from a radio or television station." With a Web site, "[n]o licenses, transmitters, printing presses, distribution systems, or advertising departments are needed." Then this argument gets notched up; it hypothecates a free Web hosting service and a volunteer with Web programming skills. With all that, "it seems sound to conclude that a charity sponsoring a Web site that is freely available to all Internet users should not be considered a publisher." If this conclusion holds true, "the paid mass media rule would not apply to communications an organization posts on its freely accessible Web site—regardless of how many hits the Web site gets or what the organization pays to develop or post the site."[176]

This is, as noted, a good argument but it may not always hold. An organization that devotes considerable resources to creating and maintaining a Web site looks and acts a lot like a publisher or broadcaster.[177] The fact that recipients of the information do not have to pay for it may not

---

[173] Reg. § 56.4911-2(b)(5)(i).

[174] See *supra* § 3(b), the text accompanied by note 98.

[175] See § 1.8(a).

[176] Livingston at 424.

[177] The organization referenced in *supra* note 44 spent its "$2 million annual budget on computer database experts, large computer servers and salaries for the 20 people who work at the group's offices." Perhaps, then, it is a small publisher for this purpose.

change that. The point that the Internet is not technically mass media—at least not yet—trumps the no-publisher contention.[178]

The IRS asked: "Does an email or listserv communication by the [charitable] organization constitute an appearance in mass media if it is sent to more than 100,000 people and fewer than half of those people are members of the organization?" This reference is to an aspect of the definition of the term *mass media*.[179] Thus, if the e-mail communication or listserv communication were to be deemed the equivalent of a general circulation newspaper or magazine, the answer to this question would be yes. These communications, however, are more analogous to regular mail, which is not considered a mass media communication. As discussed, moreover, Internet communications are not mass media communications for expenditure test purposes to begin with, so the answer to this question must no, for these two reasons.

The IRS asked: "What facts and circumstances are relevant in determining whether an Internet communication (either a limited access website or a listserv or email communication) is a communication directly to or primarily with members of the organization" for a charitable organization that is under the expenditure test? This question relates to the exception in this body of law for communications between the organization and its bona fide members.[180] The facts and circumstances are the following:

- The communication must be directed only to members of the organization. Thus, the communication cannot be posted on the organization's general Web site but must be published in a manner that makes it accessible only by members. This would be done, as the IRS suggested, by placing the communication on the Web site where only the members have access to it (by password) or make it available only to the members by means of a listserv or e-mail.[181]

---

[178] A site may be a mass media if it is the "electronic equivalent of a mass circulation print periodical" (Livingston at 424).

[179] See *supra* § 3(b), the text accompanied by note 96.

[180] See *supra* § 2(e), text accompanied by notes 85–86.

[181] A communication is considered as directed primarily to members if more than one-half of the recipients are members; Reg. § 56.4911-5(e).

- The specific legislation the communication refers to, and reflects a view on, must be of *direct interest* to the organization and its members. The presence of the requisite direct interest is determined on a facts-and-circumstances basis. An organization in this circumstance would be well advised to explain, as part of the communication, why the legislation is of direct interest to the organization and its members (although, in many instances, that nexus will be obvious).

- The communication may not directly encourage the organization's members to engage in direct lobbying with respect to the legislation.

- The communication may not directly encourage the organization's members to engage in grassroots lobbying.

The IRS did not ask any questions about lobbying activities by any other category of tax-exempt organization.

CHAPTER 6

Political Campaign Activities

Tax-exempt organizations generally are not permitted to engage in political campaign activities. This is either because the federal tax laws expressly forbid this type of advocacy, as is the case with charitable organizations, or because other laws, usually those pertaining to political campaign financing, prohibit the practice. The major exception in this regard is the tax-exempt political organization.[1]

Nonetheless, tax-exempt organizations, from time to time, engage in political campaign activities. Also, there may be uncertainty as to whether a particular form of advocacy or support is political campaign activity. Some activities are not considered political campaign activities, in that all of the elements of the definition are not met (for example, the individual benefited is not a candidate) or the activity is considered to be educational. Also, an activity can be a political activity without being a political campaign activity.

The Internet obviously can be used by nonprofit organizations to engage in political campaign activity. This form of communication is an effective—in terms of both cost and impact—way to pursue these types of advocacy efforts. As with other aspects of Internet communications by nonprofit organizations, this type of use is raising new legal issues and new interpretations of existing law.

Yet, as will be noted one more time, the IRS observed, in 1999, that the "use of the Internet to accomplish a particular task does not change the

---

[1] That is, an organization that is tax-exempt by reason of, and to the extent of, IRC § 527.

way the tax laws apply to that task. This means that "[a]dvertising is still advertising and fundraising is still fundraising."[2] The IRS might have also written that "political campaign activity is still political campaign activity."

§ 6.1 INTRODUCTION

(a) Scope of Law

Federal law contains five discrete bodies of law that pertain to involvement in political campaign activities by tax-exempt organizations:

1. A set of rules applicable to public charities
2. Rules applicable to private foundations
3. Rules applicable to political organizations
4. Rules pertaining to certain other categories of tax-exempt organizations
5. Law concerning political elections and political campaign financing

These various sets of rules contain law by which terms such as *candidate* and *political campaign activity* are defined and costs associated with political campaign activity are ascertained. While there is some overlap as to the content of the rules, in several instances there are varied definitions of the concepts.

Most of the tax law in this area is that applicable to public charities. These organizations are forbidden to participate in or intervene in political campaigns where a public office is involved. The law regarding other categories of tax-exempt organizations, other than political organizations, is unclear.

(b) A Definition of *Political Campaign Activity*

The phraseology that is used in the case of tax-exempt charitable organizations is that the organizations may not participate in or intervene in any political campaign on behalf of or in opposition to any candidate for public

---

[2] IRS FY 2000 CPE Text on Exempt Organizations and Internet Use at 64.

office. This definition of *political campaign activity* contains five elements of legal significance: the meaning of the words *participate, intervene, campaign, candidate,* and *public office.*

The requirement that a charitable organization not engage in political campaign activities is relatively clear as to meaning—certainly more so than the meaning and scope of the concept of *lobbying.*[3] Because of this relative clarity, the matter has been the subject of discussion in court opinions or in IRS rulings only infrequently. Nonetheless, these are the principal ways that a tax-exempt organization (or any other person) can involve itself in a political campaign:

- Make one or more contributions of money or property to the political campaign of a candidate for public office

- Endorse the candidacy of an individual who is campaigning for a public office

- Lend personnel, supplies, equipment, or facilities to an individual who is a candidate for public office for use in the campaign

- Publish and/or distribute statements on behalf of or in opposition to a candidate for public office

Efforts of this nature by public charities are clearly prohibited by the federal tax law.[4] While the federal tax law regarding other types of tax-exempt organizations is far less clear, the federal election laws generally prohibit this type of advocacy by tax-exempt (and other) organizations.

The little law there is on this point illustrates that, in the tax-exempt organizations context, the law regarding political campaign activity goes far beyond the above four conventional ways of supporting or opposing political candidates. For example, the IRS ruled that a charitable organization could not evaluate the qualifications of potential candidates in a

---

[3] See § 5.1(d), (e).

[4] An IRS revocation of the tax-exempt status of a church as the result of its involvement in the 1992 presidential election campaign was upheld in court; the church intervened in the campaign by means of newspaper advertisements questioning the position of one of the candidates on certain social issues (*Branch Ministries, Inc.* v. *Rossotti,* 40 F. Supp. 2d 15 (D.C.C. 1999), *aff'd,* 211 F.3d 137 (D.C. Cir. 2000)).

school board election and then support particular slates in the campaign.[5] Also, the IRS ruled that a charitable organization violated the prohibition on political campaign activities when it made an interest-bearing loan to an organization that used the funds for political purposes.[6] Further, a charitable organization was held to have improperly intervened in a political campaign because its direct mail fundraising letters were signed by an individual who was a candidate for political office at the time; language in the letters was found to be "very much like [the candidate's] campaign statements, positions, and rhetoric."[7]

The IRS Chief Counsel's office "reluctantly" concluded in 1989 that an organization "probably" did not intervene in a political campaign on behalf of or in opposition to a candidate for public office, even though the organization ran a political advertising program that

1. Was, in the words of the IRS, "mostly broadcast during a two week period around the Reagan/Mondale foreign and defense policy debate on October 21, 1984"

2. Contained statements that "could be viewed as demonstrating a preference for one of the debating candidates"

3. "Could be viewed" as having content such that "individuals listening to the ads would generally understand them to support or oppose a candidate in an election campaign"

4. Involved statements that were released so close to the November vote as to be "troublesome"

5. Was clearly in violation of the IRS's voter education rules[8]

Despite the requirement of a political campaign and a candidate for public office, the IRS denominated as an action organization (and thus denied tax exemption to) an organization formed for the purpose of implementing an orderly change of administration of the office of governor of a state, in the most efficient and economical fashion possible, by assisting the governor-elect during the period between his election and

---

[5] Rev. Rul. 67-71, 1967-1 C.B. 125.

[6] Tech. Adv. Mem. 9812001.

[7] Tech. Adv. Mem. 200044038.

[8] Tech. Adv. Mem. 8936002.

inauguration.[9] The IRS ruled that the organization's "predominant purpose is to effectuate changes in the government's policies and personnel which will make them correspond with the partisan political interests of both the Governor-elect and the political party he represents."[10]

A federal court of appeals denied tax-exempt status to a religious ministry organization, in part for intervening in political campaigns.[11] The organization, by means of publications and broadcasts, attacked candidates and incumbents (presidents and members of Congress) that it considered to be too liberal and endorsed conservative officeholders. The court summarized the offense: "These attempts to elect or defeat certain political leaders reflected . . . [the organization's] objective to change the composition of the federal government."[12] A court held that an organization established with the dominant aim of bringing about world government as rapidly as possible did not qualify as an exempt charitable organization.[13]

The IRS ruled that a university did not intervene in a political campaign by conducting a political science course that required participation by the students in political campaigns of their choice.[14] The IRS so ruled in the case of provision of faculty advisors and facilities for a campus newspaper that published the students' editorial opinions on political matters.[15] Also, a tax-exempt broadcasting station that provided equal air time

---

[9] Rev. Rul. 74-117, 1974-1 C.B. 128.

[10] *Id.* This ruling is surely incorrect, in that the proscription on political campaign activity could not apply, because the matter did not involve a candidate or a campaign. The appropriate rationale (which would have led to the same result) would have been to find the presence of a substantial amount of nonexempt activity. For example, the IRS ruled (albeit without any statement of its reasoning) that a presidential inaugural committee that sponsored inaugural activities, some of which were open to the public and some by invitation only, where donations to it were commingled with the proceeds from various fundraising events, was not an organization organized and operated exclusively for charitable purposes (Rev. Rul. 77-283, 1977-2 C.B. 72).

[11] *Christian Echoes National Ministry, Inc.* v. *United States*, 470 F.2d 849 (10th Cir. 1972), *cert. den.*, 414 U.S. 864 (1973).

[12] *Id.* at 856.

[13] *Estate of Blaine* v. *Commissioner*, 22 T.C. 1195 (1954).

[14] Rev. Rul. 72-512, 1972-2 C.B. 246.

[15] Rev. Rul. 72-513, 1972-2 C.B. 246.

to all electoral candidates in compliance with federal communications law was ruled to not be in violation of the proscription against partisan political activities.[16]

Inasmuch as organizations function only through individuals, who have the personal freedom to engage in political campaign activities, the law distinguishes between activities that are undertaken in conjunction with "official" responsibilities and those that are "personal"; only the former activities are relevant in assessing an organization's qualification for tax exemption in the face of political campaign efforts.[17] Political activities of individuals (particularly directors and officers), however, will be imputed to the organization if it has, directly or indirectly, authorized or ratified the acts.[18]

(c) Requirement of a *Candidate*

The Internal Revenue Code does not define the term *candidate*. The tax regulations provide a definition of the term in the context of defining the phrase *candidate for public office*, which is an "individual who offers himself [or herself], or is proposed by others, as a contestant for an elective public office, whether such office be national, State, or local."[19]

An analysis of the political campaign intervention rules by the staff of the Joint Committee on Taxation, U.S. Congress, stated that "[c]lear standards do not exist for determining precisely at what point an individual becomes a candidate for purposes of the rule."[20] This analysis added: "On the one hand, once an individual declares his [or her] candidacy for a particular office, his [or her] status as a candidate is clear." That, of course, is obvious. This analysis continued: "On the other hand, the fact that an individual is a prominent political figure does not automatically make him

---

[16] Rev. Rul. 74-574, 1974-2 C.B. 160.

[17] Gen. Couns. Mem. 34631.

[18] Gen. Couns. Mem. 33912.

[19] Reg. § 1.501(c)(3)-1(c)(3)(iii).

[20] Joint Committee on Taxation, "Lobbying and Political Activities of Tax-Exempt Organizations" 14 (JCS-5-87, Mar. 11, 1987).

[or her] a candidate, even if there is speculation regarding his [or her] possible future candidacy for particular offices." Thus, the matter of determining who is a candidate, and when, often is a facts-and-circumstances exercise.

There is little law on this point. Despite the second of the foregoing observations, the IRS has been known to conclude that an individual is a candidate solely on the basis of mention in the popular media—even if the individual is not already a prominent political figure. This determination may be made in hindsight, perhaps many months after media coverage. Consequently, a charitable organization may be considered, at a subsequent point in time, to have provided assistance or other support to a *candidate*, even though his or her status as a candidate was unclear or even nonexistent at the time the assistance or other support was provided.

(d) Requirement of a *Campaign*

The term *campaign* is not defined, with any precision, in the federal tax law. This definition, too, is embedded in a facts-and-circumstances test.

A federal court of appeals observed that a "campaign for a public office in a public election merely and simply means running for office, or candidacy for office, as the word is used in common parlance and as it is understood by the man in the street."[21] This phraseology was subsequently adopted by another court.[22]

(e) Requirement of a *Public Office*

Neither the Internal Revenue Code nor the tax regulations define the term *public office* for purposes of the political campaign activity prohibition applicable to charitable organizations. Nonetheless, the private foundation rules defining *disqualified persons* make reference to the phrase *elective public*

---

[21] *Norris* v. *United States*, 86 F.2d 379, 382 (8th Cir. 1936), *rev'd on other grounds*, 300 U.S. 564 (1937).

[22] *Association of the Bar of the City of New York* v. *Commissioner*, 858 F.2d 876, 880 (2d Cir. 1988), *cert. den.*, 490 U.S. 1030 (1989).

office.[23] While the statute does not define that term, the tax regulations state:

> In defining the term "public office" . . . , such term must be distinguished from mere public employment. Although holding a public office is one form of public employment, not every position in the employ of a State or other governmental subdivision . . . constitutes a "public office." Although a determination whether a public employee holds a public office depends on the facts and circumstances of the case, the essential element is whether a significant part of the activities of a public employee is the independent performance of policymaking functions. . . . [S]everal factors may be considered as indications that a position in the executive, legislative, or judicial branch of the government of a State, possession of the United States, or political subdivision or other area of any of the foregoing, or of the District of Columbia, constitutes a "public office." Among such factors to be considered, in addition to that set forth above, are that the office is created by the Congress, a State constitution, or the State legislature, or by a municipality or other governmental body pursuant to authority conferred by the Congress, State constitution, or State legislature, and the powers conferred on the office and the duties to be discharged by such office are defined either directly or indirectly by the Congress, State constitution, or State legislature, or through legislative authority.[24]

The only other instance, in the law of tax-exempt organizations, where the tax regulations make reference to the term *public office* is in the context of the rules concerning political organizations, where the term *public office* is used in the definition of an exempt function for a political organization.[25] The accompanying regulations use the same definition of the term *public office* as is used in the setting of the private foundation rules defining disqualified persons.[26]

---

[23] IRC § 4946(c)(1), (5).

[24] Reg. § 53.4946-1(g)(2)(i).

[25] IRC § 527(e)(2).

[26] Reg. § 1.527-2(d).

The IRS Chief Counsel's office took the position that precinct committee persons in a state were holders of a public office.[27] This position was based on the content of the state's law, which accorded these officeholders the following six characteristics:

1. The position was created by statute
2. Holders of the position swear an oath to uphold the state and U.S. constitutions in the performance of their duties
3. They assist in the selection of election officers [28]
4. They participate in the party's county central committee and state committee [29]
5. There is a fixed term of office
6. The positions are "not occasional or contractual"

The IRS conceded that, if the above-quoted regulation was applied to these facts, the precinct committee persons "would not be considered as holding public office because their duties entail no independent policy-making functions." Nonetheless, this IRS pronouncement continued: "However, the additional factors to be considered as indicative of a public office and which are listed in the latter part of that regulation would support the Service's position." Thus, the IRS chief counsel's office advised that the tax exemption of the organization involved should be revoked because it encouraged its members to seek election to precinct committees and to support these candidacies.

A state court of appeals held that an individual who was a candidate for delegate to a county political convention was a candidate for state law purposes but was not a candidate for public office.[30] The court pointed out that the state's election law did not define the word *candidate*. Thus, the court concluded, applying a "general rule of statutory construction . . . that words and phrases should be construed according to their common meaning," "[l]ogically, most people would believe that if an individual's

---

[27] Gen. Couns. Mem. 39811.

[28] The IRS characterized this as an "essential function in the State's regulation of elections."

[29] The IRS characterized this as "essential to the electoral process."

[30] *Templin v. Oakland City Clerk*, 387 N.W.2d 156 (Mich. Ct. App. 1986).

name is listed on an election ballot, that individual is a candidate for something."[31] In the court's opinion, the "common meaning" of the word *candidate* includes state precinct delegates,[32] although, as noted, these individuals are not pursuing election to a *public office*.

A federal appellate court held that the phrase *candidate for office* is "used in common parlance and as it is understood by the man in the street."[33] Relying on this observation, the above IRS pronouncement stated that, to the "average person, the appearance of precinct candidates on the general election ballot indicates that the position is a public office."[34]

§ 6.2 GENERAL RULES

(a) Introduction

One of the fundamental criteria for qualification as a tax-exempt charitable organization[35] is that it must "not participate in, or intervene in (including the publishing or distributing of statements), any political campaign on behalf of (or in opposition to) any candidate for public office."[36] A charitable organization that violates this rule is termed an *action organization*,[37] and thus may be disqualified as to tax-exempt status. As one court stated (before the political campaign activities tax[38] was enacted): "It should be noted that exemption [of a charitable organization] is lost . . . by participation in any political campaign on behalf of *any* candidate for public office."[39]

---

[31] *Id.* at 159.

[32] *Id.*

[33] *Association of the Bar of the City of New York v. Commissioner, supra* note 22, 858 F.2d at 880.

[34] Gen. Couns. Mem. 39811.

[35] That is, an organization that is tax-exempt pursuant to IRC § 501(a) as an organization described in IRC § 501(c)(3).

[36] IRC § 501(c)(3).

[37] Reg. § 1.501(c)(3)–1(c)(3)(iii).

[38] See *infra* § 4(a).

[39] *United States v. Dykema*, 666 F.2d 1096, 1101 (7th Cir. 1981), *cert. den.*, 456 U.S. 983 (1982) (emphasis in original).

The political campaign activities prohibition applicable to charitable organizations embodies four elements, all of which must be present for the limitation to be operative. These elements are that

1. A charitable organization may not *participate* or *intervene* in a political campaign[40]

2. The campaign must be with respect to an individual who is a *candidate*[41]

3. The political activity that must be involved is a political *campaign*[42]

4. The individual must be a candidate for a *public office*[43]

(b) Scope of the Proscription on Charitable Organizations

The prohibition on involvement by a tax-exempt charitable organization in a political campaign is generally considered by the IRS to be absolute, although neither the legislative history of the provision nor the regulations provide any clarification.[44] Certainly, on the face of the statute, there is no insubstantiality threshold, as there is in the law pertaining to lobbying activities by charitable organizations.[45]

The view of the IRS is that "this is an absolute prohibition," with the agency adding that "[t]here is no requirement that political campaigning be substantial."[46] Thus, the chief counsel of the IRS opined that a charitable organization is "precluded from engaging in *any* political campaign activities."[47]

Nonetheless, although a court has never ruled directly on the point, courts often resist absolutes in statutes, engrafting some form of de minimis exception when appropriate. For example, a comparable statute was

---

[40] See *supra* § 1(b).

[41] See *supra* § 1(c).

[42] See *supra* § 1(d).

[43] See *supra* § 1(e).

[44] Reg. §§ 1.501(c)(3)–1(b)(3)(ii), 1.501(c)(3)–1(c)(iii).

[45] See § 5.2(b), (c).

[46] IRS Exempt Organizations Handbook (IRM 7751) § 370(2).

[47] Gen. Couns. Mem. 39694 (emphasis supplied).

also facially absolute: the Federal Corrupt Practices Act (repealed), which made "[i]t . . . unlawful for . . . any corporation whatever . . . to make a contribution or expenditure in connection with" various federal elections. Yet courts read a substantiality test into this law.[48] Further, it was stated that a "slight and comparatively unimportant deviation from the narrow furrow of tax approved activity is not fatal."[49] It was also observed that "courts recognize that a nonexempt purpose, even 'somewhat beyond a de minimis level,' may be permitted without loss of exemption."[50] Indeed, the Commissioner of Internal Revenue stated, in congressional testimony describing the political campaign limitation: "If political intervention is involved, the prohibition is absolute; however, some consideration may be given to whether, qualitatively or quantitatively, the organization is in the circumstance where the activity is so trivial it is without legal significance and, therefore, de minimis."[51]

Thus, there is somewhat of an anomaly in this aspect of the federal tax law. This prohibition on political campaign activities is generally considered to be absolute, yet there is little law and guidance as to this aspect of the prohibition.

(c) Rules for Social Welfare Organizations

Tax-exempt social welfare organizations[52] generally are forbidden from participating or intervening in any political campaign on behalf of or in opposition to any candidate for public office.[53] Traditionally, the IRS has been strict in applying this restriction, as illustrated by the denial of classification

---

[48] E.g., *United States* v. *Construction Local 264*, 101 F. Supp. 873 (W.D. Mo. 1951); *United States* v. *Painters Local 481*, 172 F.2d 854 (2d Cir. 1949).

[49] *St. Louis Union Trust Co.* v. *United States*, 374 F.2d 427, 431–432 (8th Cir. 1967).

[50] *Living Faith, Inc.* v. *Commissioner*, 950 F.2d 365, 370 (7th Cir. 1991).

[51] Statement of Lawrence B. Gibbs, in "Lobbying and Political Activities of Tax-Exempt Organizations," Hearing before the Subcommittee on Oversight, Committee on Ways and Means, House of Representatives, Serial 100-5, 100th Cong., 1st Sess. 96–97 (1987).

[52] That is, organizations that are tax-exempt pursuant to IRC § 501(a) because they are described in IRC § 501(c)(4).

[53] Reg. § 1.501(c)(4)–1(a)(2)(ii).

as a tax-exempt social welfare organization to a group that rated candidates for public office on a nonpartisan basis and disseminated its ratings to the general public, on the theory that its rating process was intervention or participation on behalf of those candidates favorably rated and in opposition to those less favorably rated.[54]

Objectivity will not necessarily ward off an unfavorable IRS determination, as evidenced by the nonprofit group that selected slates of candidates for school board elections and engaged in campaigns on their behalf and that was accordingly denied tax exemption as a charitable organization (and thus presumably as a social welfare organization) because of these political activities, "even though its process of selection may have been completely objective and unbiased and was intended primarily to educate and inform the public about the candidates."[55]

This does not mean, however, that tax-exempt social welfare organizations are—like charitable organizations—completely foreclosed from involvement in political campaign activities. An organization the activities of which were primarily directed, on a nonprofit and nonpartisan basis, toward encouraging individuals in business to become more active in politics and government, and toward promoting business, social, or civic action was held to qualify for tax exemption as a social welfare organization.[56]

Determinations in this context that organizations are charitable and educational in nature otherwise illustrate the activities that social welfare organizations may engage in, on the supposition that if the former can undertake the programs so too may the latter. A group that engaged in nonpartisan analysis, study, and research, made the results available to the public, and publicized the need for a code of fair campaign practices, was ruled to be a tax-exempt educational organization.[57] An organization that recruited college students for an internship program providing employment with municipal agencies qualified as a tax-exempt charitable and educational organization.[58]

---

[54] Rev. Rul. 67-368, 1967-2 C.B. 194.

[55] Rev. Rul. 67–71, *supra* note 5.

[56] Rev. Rul. 60-193, 1960-1 C.B. 145.

[57] Rev. Rul. 66-258, 1966-2 C.B. 213.

[58] Rev. Rul. 70-584, 1970-2 C.B. 114.

The IRS, therefore, in determining an organization's tax-exempt status in light of the requirements for a social welfare entity, adheres to the distinction between organizations that actively participate or intervene in a political campaign for or against candidates for public office and those that more passively seek to stimulate public interest in improved government, better campaign practices, and the like.

The prohibition on political campaign activities by tax-exempt social welfare organizations, however, is not absolute, in that the requirement is that these organizations must be *primarily* engaged in activities that promote social welfare. Thus, a tax-exempt organization primarily engaged in social welfare functions may also carry on activities, such as financial assistance and in-kind services, involving participation and intervention in political campaigns on behalf of or in opposition to candidates for nomination or election to public office.[59] Thus, social welfare organizations have an insubstantiality threshold in this context, much the same as the threshold for charitable organizations as to permissible lobbying activities.[60]

(d) Rules for Associations

There is no specific federal tax law prohibition on political campaign activities by associations and other business leagues.[61] Like all types of tax-exempt organizations, however, these entities are required to engage in their exempt functions at least to a substantial (or primary) extent. Thus, within that constraint, the federal tax law permits some political campaign activity by these organizations.[62]

---

[59] Rev. Rul. 81-95, 1981-1 C.B. 332.

[60] Although the federal tax law may permit an exempt social welfare organization to engage in some political campaign activity, federal and/or state campaign financing law may prohibit the practice. Also, political campaign activity by a social welfare organization will cause the organization to be subject to the tax imposed by IRC § 527(f) with respect to the expenditures for political activities that are within the meaning of IRC § 527(e)(2) (see *infra* § 2(e)).

[61] These are organizations that are tax-exempt pursuant to IRC § 501(a) by reason of description in IRC § 501(c)(6).

[62] Again, however (see *supra* note 60), other law may prohibit political campaign activities by these organizations and/or such activities will give rise to a tax.

A business expense deduction generally is denied for an amount paid or incurred in connection with participation in, or intervention in, a political campaign on behalf of or in opposition to any candidate for public office or for any attempt to influence the general public, or segments of it, with respect to elections.[63] This denial of a business expense deduction is applicable to all or a portion of dues paid to a business league that engages in political campaign activity.[64]

Many business leagues elect to maintain affiliated political organizations (usually political action committees) for the purpose of conducting political campaign activities. With this approach, associations can avoid the tax imposed with respect to political activities and be in compliance with federal and state campaign regulation laws.

(e) Rules for Political Organizations

Tax exemption is available for the *political organization*.[65] This is an entity that is organized and operated primarily for the purpose of directly or indirectly accepting contributions or making expenditures for an exempt function. In this setting, an *exempt function* is the activity of influencing or attempting to influence the selection, nomination, election, or appointment of any individual to any federal, state, or local public office or office in a political organization, or the election of presidential or vice-presidential electors, whether or not these individuals or electors are selected, nominated, elected, or appointed.[66] Thus, the concept of *political activity* is broader than the concept of *political campaign activity*.

Although political organizations are generally tax-exempt, they are subject to the highest rate of corporate tax on their *political organization taxable income*.[67] A political organization's taxable income is its gross income, less exempt function income and allowable deductions directly connected with the production of gross income (other than exempt function

---

[63] IRC § 162(e)(1)(B), (C).

[64] IRC § 162(e)(3).

[65] IRC § 527.

[66] IRC § 527(e)(2).

[67] IRC § 527(b).

income).[68] *Exempt function income* includes amounts received as contributions of money or other property, membership dues or assessments, proceeds from a fundraising event, and proceeds from the sale of political campaign materials.[69]

Although a political organization is exempt from taxation on amounts expended for an exempt function, if another type of tax-exempt organization[70] expends any amount during a tax year, either directly or through another organization, for what would be a political organization exempt function, it must include in its gross income for the year involved an amount equal to the lesser of its net investment income for the year or the aggregate amount expended during the year for the exempt function.[71] Generally, this amount is taxed at the highest corporate tax rate.[72]

(f) Rules for Other Tax-Exempt Organizations

There are no specific federal tax law prohibitions on political campaign activities by other categories of tax-exempt entities, including labor organizations,[73] veterans' organizations,[74] and social clubs.[75] All types of tax-exempt organizations, however, are required to engage in their exempt functions at least to a substantial (or primary) extent. Thus, within that constraint, the federal tax law permits some political activity by these organizations.[76]

---

[68] IRC § 527(c).

[69] IRC § 527(c)(3).

[70] That is, an organization that is tax-exempt pursuant to IRC § 501(a) as an organization described in IRC § 501(c).

[71] IRC § 527(f).

[72] IRC § 527(b).

[73] That is, organizations that are tax-exempt pursuant to IRC § 501(a) as organizations described in IRC § 501(c)(5).

[74] That is, organizations that are tax-exempt pursuant to IRC § 501(a) as organizations described in IRC § 501(c)(4) or (19).

[75] That is, organizations that are tax-exempt pursuant to IRC § 501(a) as organizations described in IRC § 501(c)(7).

[76] Once again, however (see *supra* notes 60 and 62), other law may prohibit political campaign activities by these organizations and/or such activities will give rise to a tax.

Some of these types of organizations may elect to maintain affiliated political organizations (usually political action committees) for the purpose of conducting political campaign activities. With this approach, associations can avoid the tax imposed with respect to political activities and be in compliance with federal and state campaign regulation laws.

§ 6.3 OTHER RULES

(a) Educational Activities in General

A charitable organization may instruct the public on matters useful to the individual and beneficial to the community.[77] In carrying out this form of an educational purpose, a charitable organization may cautiously enter the political milieu. Thus, for example, a charitable organization was permitted to assemble and contribute to libraries the campaign speeches, interviews, and other materials of an individual who was a candidate for a "historically important elective office."[78] (By contrast, a charitable organization will imperil its tax exemption if it solicits the signing or endorsing of a fair campaign practices code by political candidates.[79])

In undertaking activities in this setting that are to be considered educational, however, a charitable organization must present a sufficiently full and fair exposition of pertinent facts to permit members of the public to form their own opinion or conclusion independent of that presented by the organization, although the organization may also advocate a particular position or viewpoint.[80] Thus, while a charitable organization may seek to educate the public on patriotic, political, and civic matters, and alert the citizenry to the dangers of an extreme political doctrine, it may not do so by the use of disparaging terms, insinuations, innuendoes, and/or suggested implications drawn from incomplete facts.[81]

Consequently, whether a charitable (or other tax-exempt) organization is participating or intervening, directly or indirectly, in a political campaign on

---

[77] Reg. § 1.501(c)(3)-1(d)(3).

[78] Rev. Rul. 70-321, 1970-1 C.B. 129.

[79] Rev. Rul. 76-456, 1976-2 C.B. 151.

[80] Reg. § 1.501(c)(3)-1(d)(3).

[81] Rev. Rul. 68-263, 1968-1 C.B. 256.

behalf of or in opposition to a candidate for public office "depends upon all of the facts and circumstances of each case."[82]

(b) Voter Guides

There is, therefore, a tension between the concepts of impermissible political campaign activities and permissible voter education activities. Certain voter education activities conducted in a nonpartisan manner do not constitute prohibited political activities, while other so-called voter education activities are prohibited by the federal tax law.

For example, a charitable organization may annually prepare and make generally available to the public a compilation of voting records of all members of Congress on major legislative issues involving a wide range of subjects. This is permissible voter education activity as long as the publication does not contain any editorial opinion and its contents and structure do not imply approval or disapproval of any member or any member's voting record.[83]

Likewise, a charitable organization may, as one of its activities in election years, send a questionnaire to all candidates running for governor in a state. The questionnaire solicits a brief statement of each candidate's position on a wide variety of issues. All responses are published in a voters' guide that the organization makes generally available to the public. The issues covered are selected by the organization solely on the basis of their importance and interest to the electorate as a whole. This is allowable voter education activity where neither the questionnaire nor the voters' guide, in content or structure, evidences a bias or preference with respect to the views of any candidate or group of candidates.[84]

By contrast, another charitable organization undertakes a "voter education" activity patterned after the foregoing approach. It, too, sends a questionnaire to candidates for major public offices and uses the responses to prepare a voters' guide that is distributed during an election campaign. In

---

[82] Rev. Rul. 78–248, 1978-1 C.B. 154.

[83] *Id.*, Situation 1.

[84] *Id.*, Situation 2.

this instance, however, some questions evidence a bias on certain issues. By using a questionnaire structured in this manner, the organization is considered by the IRS to be participating in a political campaign.[85]

In another instance, a charitable organization, primarily concerned with land conservation matters, publishes a voters' guide for its members and others concerned with these matters. The guide is intended as a compilation of incumbents' voting records on selected land conservation issues of importance to the organization and is factual in nature. It does not contain any express statements in support of or in opposition to any candidate. The guide is widely distributed among the electorate during an election campaign. The IRS wrote that, while this guide may provide the voting public with "useful information," its "emphasis on one area of concern" indicates that its purpose is not nonpartisan voter education. Thus, because this organization concentrated on a "narrow range of issues" in its voters' guide and widely distributed it while a political campaign was under way, the organization was found to have participated in a political campaign.[86]

Notwithstanding these latter two illustrations, the IRS subsequently ruled that a charitable organization may publish a newsletter containing the voting records of congressional incumbents on selected issues without engaging in prohibited involvement in political campaigns.[87] The IRS indicated that the format and content of the publication need not be neutral, in that each incumbent's votes and the organization's views on selected legislative issues can be reported, and the publication may indicate whether the incumbent supported or opposed the organization's views. Nonetheless, the IRS considered the following factors as demonstrating the absence of political campaign activity:

- The voting records of all incumbents will be presented

- Candidates for reelection will not be identified

- Comment will not be made on an individual's overall qualifications for public office

---

[85] *Id.*, Situation 3.

[86] *Id.*, Situation 4.

[87] Rev. Rul. 80-282, 1980–2 C.B. 178.

- Statements expressly or impliedly endorsing or rejecting any incumbent as a candidate for public office will not be offered
- A comparison of incumbents with other candidates will not be made
- The organization will point out the inherent limitations of judging the qualifications of an incumbent on the basis of certain selected votes by stating the need to also consider matters such as performance on subcommittees and constituent service
- The organization will not widely distribute its compilation of incumbent's voting records
- The publication will be distributed to the organization's usual readership (a few thousand nationwide)
- There will not be an attempt to target the publication toward particular areas in which elections are occurring or to time the date of publication to coincide with an election campaign

The position of the IRS on this issue in general is that, "in the absence of any expression of endorsement of or opposition to candidates for public office, an [charitable] organization may publish a newsletter containing voting records and its opinions on issues of interest to it provided that the voting records are not widely distributed to the general public during an election campaign or aimed, in view of all the facts and circumstances, towards affecting any particular elections."[88]

A case involved the practice of a bar association (qualified as a charitable organization) of rating candidates for public office in the judiciary of a state. The candidates were rated as "approved," "not approved," or "approved as highly qualified"; more than one candidate for the same office may receive the same rating. The ratings were disseminated to the public in press releases and by means of the association's publications. A court held that this rating process did not constitute prohibited participation or intervention in political campaigns on behalf of or in opposition to candidates; the court found that the "ratings do not support or oppose the candidacy of any particular individual or recommend that the public vote for or

---

[88] Gen. Couns. Mem. 38444.

against a specific candidate."[89] This court added that "we do not believe that the mere practice of rating candidates for elective office without more is, per se, a prohibited political activity" for a charitable organization.[90] On appeal, this holding was reversed, however, with the appellate court concluding that the rating activity constituted participation or intervention in the political campaigns for the judgeships.[91] The court of appeals characterized the ratings as "[p]ublished expressions of . . . opinion, made with an eye toward imminent elections."[92]

A traditional distinction between political campaign activity and voter education activity has been that the latter can be *nonpartisan*. This bar association case focused on this aspect of the law as well, with the appellate court finding that the prohibition on political campaign activity for charitable organizations embraces nonpartisan activity; the court wrote that the "statute and pertinent regulations thereunder are not limited in their application to the partisan campaigns of candidates representing recognized political parties."[93] Writing of the rating process, the court of appeals noted that a "candidate who receives a 'not qualified' rating will derive little comfort from the fact that the rating may have been made in a nonpartisan manner."[94] By contrast, the lower court took the position that the rating effort was not campaign activity because the association engaged in the "totally passive, not active" function of merely reporting its ratings (which were not, according to that court, based on partisan or political preferences) and did "not actively seek to influence the outcome of elections."[95]

The IRS concluded that the use by a charitable organization of panels of citizens to review and rate political candidates was a form of intervention or

---

[89] *Association of the Bar of the City of New York v. Commissioner,* 89 T.C. 599, 609–610 (1987).

[90] *Id.* at 610.

[91] *Association of the Bar of the City of New York v. Commissioner, supra* note 22.

[92] *Id.* 858 F.2d at 880.

[93] *Id.*

[94] *Id.*

[95] *Association of the Bar of the City of New York v. Commissioner, supra* note 89, at 611.

participation in their campaigns.[96] These groups of individuals questioned expert witnesses and candidates, analyzed the information and views presented, and prepared reports for public dissemination. Most of these reports included a rating of the candidates by members of the panels, including an analysis of their stands on several major issues, in a box score style. The organization viewed these processes as forms of issue education and means to stimulate public dialog, but the IRS determined that the candidates' ratings provided "political editorial opinions to the general public and went beyond the neutral forums" that are permissible.

A charitable organization was found to have engaged in prohibited political campaign activity because of language in, and the timing of mailing of, fundraising letters.[97] This organization had a variety of programs, all focused on a certain position on the political spectrum; its direct-mail fundraising letters were mailed mostly to individuals of this political persuasion. These letters, sent contemporaneously with election periods, implied—in the view of the IRS—that a contribution to the organization would help candidates for public office who share this political view. The IRS wrote that the letters were biased against candidates of opposing political aims or in favor of the candidates supporting its view of political issues. One letter was found by the IRS to entail not "voter education" but rather "voter direction."

An activity undertaken by a charitable organization can have a *dual character*, in that it can be both lobbying and political campaign activity. This is particularly the case where the lobbying is grassroots lobbying.[98]

(c) Candidate Debates

Another permissible, for charitable organizations, aspect of voter education in the context of political campaign activities is the conduct of public forums at which debates and lectures on social, political, and international questions are considered.[99]

---

[96] Tech. Adv. Mem. 9635003.

[97] Tech. Adv. Mem. 9609007.

[98] See § 5.1(e). E.g., Priv. Ltr. Rul. 9652026.

[99] Rev. Rul. 66-256, 1966-2 C.B. 210.

In one instance, a charitable membership organization had as one of its programs the monitoring and reporting on legislative, judicial, administrative, and other governmental activities and developments considered to be of important interest to its members. This organization proposed to conduct a series of public forums. The forums were to be conducted in congressional districts during congressional election campaigns. All legally qualified candidates for the House of Representatives from the congressional districts involved were invited to participate in a forum. The agenda at each of the forums covered a broad range of issues, including issues considered to be of important educational interest to the organization's members. Questions to forum participants were prepared and presented by a nonpartisan, independent panel of knowledgeable persons composed of representatives of the media, educational organizations, community leaders, and other interested persons. Each candidate was allowed an equal opportunity to present his or her views on each of the issues discussed. The organization selected a moderator for each forum, whose sole function was limited to ensuring that the general ground rules were followed. At both the beginning and end of each forum, the moderator stated that the views expressed are those of the candidates and not those of the organization and that the sponsorship of the forum is not intended as an endorsement of any candidate.

In this case, the IRS observed that the provision of a forum for candidates is not, in and of itself, prohibited political activity.[100] Nonetheless, the agency noted that a forum for candidates could be operated in a manner that would show a bias or preference for or against a particular candidate. This could be done, wrote the IRS, through "biased questioning procedures." Conversely, the IRS said, a forum held for the purpose of educating and informing the voters, which provides "fair and impartial treatment" of candidates, and which does not "promote or advance" one candidate over another, would not constitute participation or intervention in any political campaign on behalf of or in opposition to any candidate

---

[100] For this proposition, the IRS cited Rev. Rul. 74–574, *supra* note 16, which allowed organizations that operate broadcast stations to provide equal air time to political candidates. The import of this ruling as a matter of tax policy, however, is uncertain, in that these organizations were required by the federal communications law to provide free air time to political candidates.

for public office. The IRS ruled that the facts and circumstances of this case established that both the format and content of the proposed forums will be presented in a "neutral manner." Thus, the agency ruled that the organization will not be considered to be engaged in prohibited political activity.[101]

§ 6.4 SANCTIONS

(a) Public Charitable Organizations

The principal sanction that may be imposed on public charities for engaging in political campaign activity is revocation or denial of tax-exempt status.[102] This type of activity does not have to be manifested in terms of *expenditures*, as is the case with respect to the expenditure test in the lobbying setting.[103]

Another sanction is the levy of taxes in situations where a charitable organization makes a political expenditure.[104] Generally, a *political expenditure* is any amount paid or incurred by a charitable organization in any participation in, or intervention in (including the publication or distribution of statements), any political campaign on behalf of or in opposition to any candidate for public office.[105]

In an effort to discourage the use of ostensibly educational organizations operating in tandem with political campaigns, the concept of a political expenditure applies with respect to an "organization which is formed primarily for purposes of promoting the candidacy (or prospective candidacy) of an individual for public office (or which is effectively controlled by a candidate or prospective candidate and which is availed of primarily for

---

[101] Rev. Rul. 86-95, 1986-2 C.B. 73. In this ruling, the IRS emphasized that the "presence or absence of a particular fact here in other similar situations is not determinative of other cases but would have to be considered in light of all the surrounding factors in that case."

[102] See the text accompanied by *supra* note 4.

[103] See § 5.2(c).

[104] IRC § 4955.

[105] Reg. § 53.4955-1(c)(1).

such purposes."[106] In these circumstances, the term *political expenditure* includes any of the following amounts paid or incurred by the organization:

- Amounts paid to or incurred by the individual for speeches or other services
- Travel expenses of the individual
- Expenses of conducting polls, surveys, or other studies, or the preparation of papers or other materials, for use by the individual
- Expenses of advertising, publicity, and fundraising for the individual
- Any other expense "which has the primary effect of promoting public recognition or otherwise primarily accruing to the benefit of" the individual[107]

A political expenditure triggers an *initial tax*, payable by the organization, of 10 percent of the amount of the expenditure.[108] An initial tax of 2½ percent of the expenditure is imposed on each of the organization's managers (such as directors and officers), where he or she knew it was a political expenditure, unless the agreement to make the expenditure was not willful and was due to reasonable cause.[109] The IRS has the authority to abate these initial taxes where the organization can establish that the violation was due to reasonable cause and not to willful neglect, and timely corrects the violation.[110]

An additional tax is imposed on a charitable organization, at a rate of 100 percent of the political expenditure.[111] This tax is levied where the initial tax was imposed and the expenditure was not timely corrected. An additional tax is imposed on the organization's manager, at a rate of 50 percent of the expenditure.[112] This tax is levied where the additional tax

---

[106] Reg. § 53.4955-1(c)(2)(i), (ii).

[107] Reg. § 53.4955-1(c)(iii).

[108] IRC § 4955(a)(1).

[109] IRC § 4955(a)(2); Reg. § 53.4955-1(b).

[110] IRC § 4962; Reg. § 53.4955-1(d).

[111] IRC § 4955(b)(1).

[112] IRC § 4955(b)(2).

was imposed on the organization and where the manager refused to agree to part or all of the correction.

As to management and as to any one political expenditure, the maximum initial tax is $5,000 and the maximum additional tax is $10,000.[113]

In this context, *correction* means "recovering part or all of the expenditure to the extent recovery is possible, establishment of safeguards to prevent future political expenditures, and where full recovery is not possible, such additional corrective action" as may be prescribed by federal tax regulations.[114]

The IRS, upon finding political campaign activity by a charitable organization, has the discretion to impose these taxes and/or revoke tax-exempt status. Thus, the agency can levy the tax and not disturb the organization's exemption.[115] Likewise, the IRS can cause an organization to forfeit its tax exemption for the years involved but not impose the taxes.[116]

Under certain circumstances, the IRS is empowered to commence an action in federal district court to enjoin a charitable organization from the further making of political expenditures and for other relief to ensure that the actions of the organization are preserved for tax-exempt purposes.[117] These circumstances are the following:

- The IRS has notified the organization of its intention to seek this injunction if the making of the political expenditures does not immediately cease; and

- The Commissioner of Internal Revenue has determined that the organization has flagrantly participated or intervened in a political campaign on behalf of or in opposition to a candidate for public office and that injunctive relief is appropriate to prevent future political expenditures.

---

[113] IRC § 4955(c)(2).

[114] IRC § 4955(f)(3); Reg. § 53.4955-1(e).

[115] E.g., Tech. Adv. Mem. 9635003.

[116] E.g., *Branch Ministries, Inc.* v. *Rossotti, supra* note 4.

[117] IRC § 7409; Reg. § 301.7409-1.

If the federal district court finds, on the basis of clear and convincing evidence, the same facts as the commissioner found, the court is authorized to enjoin the expenditures and grant other appropriate relief.

If the IRS finds that a charitable organization has flagrantly violated the prohibition against the making of political expenditures, the IRS is required to determine and assess any income and/or excise tax(es) due immediately, by terminating the organization's tax year.[118]

(b) Private Foundations

The prohibition on political campaign activity is applicable to private foundations, inasmuch as they are charitable entities.[119] Also, a private foundation generally is not permitted to influence the outcome of any specific public election or carry on any voter registration drive,[120] although certain types of voter registration drives are allowed.[121]

If a private foundation violates the political campaign activities constraint, it can have its tax-exempt status revoked. Also, an attempt to influence the outcome of a specific public election is a *taxable expenditure*, which would subject the foundation to a tax of 10 percent of the expenditure[122] and perhaps trigger a companion tax on those managing the foundation.[123]

(c) Other Tax-Exempt Organizations

The law as to other types of tax-exempt organizations, like that regarding political campaign activities, is, as noted, unclear. An exempt social welfare organization can lose its tax-exempt status if it engages in political campaign activities that are more than insubstantial.[124] While, from a federal

---

[118] IRC § 6852; Reg. § 301.6852-1.

[119] See § 7.7.

[120] IRC § 4945(d)(2).

[121] IRC § 4945(f).

[122] IRC § 4945(a)(1).

[123] IRC § 4945(a)(2).

[124] See *supra* § 2(c).

tax standpoint, a business league can engage in political campaign activities without limitation, activities of this nature will have an adverse impact on the deductibility of dues paid to it.[125] The law as to other categories of exempt organizations is, from a tax standpoint, nonexistent.

Political campaign activity by tax-exempt organizations is likely, however, to lead to violations of federal and/or state campaign financing and regulation laws. For this reason, and also to avoid tax law difficulties, many types of exempt organizations conduct their political campaign activities through related political organizations,[126] predominately political action committees.

§ 6.5 INTERNET COMMUNICATIONS

(a) Internet Political Campaign Activity in General

Political campaign activity can involve forms of communication, such as the solicitation of campaign contributions and the conduct of a political campaign. The Internet is a medium of communication. Thus, political campaign activities by tax-exempt organizations (and other persons) can be undertaken by means of the Internet. As is the case in other contexts, however, the federal tax law does not provide any unique treatment to transactions or activities of tax-exempt organizations involving political campaign activity simply because the Internet is the medium of communication. Thus, the rules regarding political campaign activity by tax-exempt organizations embrace this type of activity by means of the Internet.[127]

There are four forms of Internet communications in this setting:

---

[125] See *supra* § 2(d).

[126] See *supra* § 2(e).

[127] In one instance, the IRS proposed denial of tax-exempt status to an organization seeking IRC § 501(c)(3) classification on the thought that it would be intervening in political campaigns; the organization, however was able to convince the IRS that it qualified for exemption, after promising not to engage in political campaign activity (determination letter issued to Adversity.Net, Inc., on January 31, 2002 (*Daily Tax Report*, Feb. 5, 2002, p. K–1)).

1. A communication published on a publicly accessible Web page
2. A communication posted on a password-protected portion of a Web site
3. A communication on a listserv (or by means of other methods such as a newsgroup, chat room, and/or forum)
4. A communication by means of e-mail

The IRS recognized, in the Announcement, that, "[b]y publishing a webpage on the Internet, an exempt organization can provide the general public with information about the organization, its activities, and issues of concern to the organization, as well as immediate access to websites of other organizations." The agency added: "An exempt organization can provide information to subscribers about issues of concern to the organization as well as enable people with common interests to share information via the Internet through a variety of methods," referencing mailing lists and the methods referred to above in the third category of Internet communication.

An e-mail communication from a tax-exempt organization clearly can constitute a participation or intervention in a political campaign. An exempt organization may post a political campaign message on the portion of its Web site that is publicly accessible or on a protected portion of its Web site. A tax-exempt organization can communicate a political message in the context of a listserv, news group, chat room, or forum it maintains.

Because the amount of the tax sanction for political campaign activity[128] is based on expenditures and because Web-based expenditures can be so low, the IRS may, in a situation where a tax-exempt charitable entity engages in political campaign activity, be inclined to revoke exempt status rather than simply impose a tax.

Private foundations have unique worries in this setting. Certainly, as is the case with any tax-exempt charitable organization, a private foundation should not place material on its Web site that constitutes a political campaign message. A private foundation can, however, post material in conjunction with a permissible voter registration drive.[129]

---

[128] See *supra* § 4(a).

[129] See *supra* § 4(b).

A private foundation may make a grant to an organization—most likely only a charitable one—that subsequently violates the constraint on political campaign activities. Indeed, the foundation may have made the grant for the specific purpose of funding development and/or maintenance of a Web site, and it was the site that contained the political campaign material. Nonetheless, the foundation should not be penalized for transgressions of this nature by the grantee unless the grant was earmarked for the forbidden purposes. A private foundation grant is *earmarked* for political campaign activity purposes if it is made "pursuant to an agreement, oral or written, that the grant will be used for specific purposes."[130]

If a private foundation violates the political campaign prohibition rules, it could have its tax-exempt status revoked. Also, if funds were involved, it would have made a taxable expenditure and thus be liable for the 10 percent excise tax.[131]

(b) Questions Posed by IRS Announcement

The IRS wrote, with considerable understatement, that "[w]hen a charitable organization engages in advocacy on the Internet, questions arise as to whether it is conducting political . . . activity, and if so, to what extent." The agency added: "This situation is further complicated by the affiliation of charitable organizations with other organizations engaging in political . . . activities on the Internet. The ease with which different websites may be linked electronically (through a 'hyperlink') raises a concern about whether the message of a linked website is attributable to the charitable organization."

(i) General Issues. The Announcement posed six general questions that have relevance with respect to the conduct of political campaign activities, with the IRS reiterating that tax-exempt organizations "use the Internet to carry on activities that otherwise can be conducted through other media, such as radio or television broadcasts, print publications, or direct mailings." Political campaign activities are conducted using these

---

[130] Reg. § 53.4945-3(a)(1). Also, in general, Reg. § 53.4945-2(a)(5)(i).

[131] See *supra* § 4(b), text accompanied by note 122.

four forms of communication, of course, and are conducted by means of the Internet as well.

These six questions are stated and discussed in the context of lobbying communications.[132] There it is noted that, while a Web site maintained by a tax-exempt organization may be considered a single *publication*, it is not likely to constitute a single *communication*. In the political campaign activities setting, for example, even if a tax-exempt organization posted a message on its Web site in an effort to support or oppose a candidate, presumably it would also have messages about its purposes and exempt programs and perhaps also fundraising and unrelated business activity. (Certainly it would prove inadvisable for a charitable organization to maintain a Web site devoted solely to political campaign messages.) The second question, suggesting the answer to the first question, was how a Web site should be separated into distinct publications or communications.

Other questions pertain to the matter of allocation of expenses for a Web site, which obviously is important when attempting to assign costs to political campaign activities. This matter of cost allocation is made the more complex in situations where a Web site is modified frequently, perhaps on a daily basis.

The last of these general questions, which is highly significant in connection with political campaign activity, was: "To what extent are statements made by subscribers to a forum, such as a listserv or newsgroup, attributable to an exempt organization that maintains the forum?" Existing law[133] indicates that the general answer to this question must be that attribution is not appropriate (or fair). At least, attribution should not be the case in the political campaign activities context, where the tax-exempt organization cannot (or should not) be held responsible for the speech of others. For an organization to be denied or lose tax-exempt status because of political campaign activity, the activity must be undertaken as an act of the organization itself.

This question had a follow-up component: "Does attribution vary depending on the level of participation of the exempt organization is

---

[132] See § 5.5(b)(i).

[133] See § 1(b), text accompanied by notes 17–18.

maintaining the forum (e.g., if the organization moderates discussion, acts as editor, etc.)?" Generally, the answer to this question should continue to be that there is no attribution. For example, if a tax-exempt organization maintains a chat room and, in the midst of an election campaign, initiates a discussion of a pending issue, and an individual sends a message in support of or in opposition to a political candidate's position on that issue, that message should not be attributed to the organization. An organization may wish to garner some protection in this area by posting a statement requesting chat room participants to refrain from sending political messages.

At some point, of course, the answer to this question would have to be that attribution is appropriate. As an illustration, if a tax-exempt organization, in the waning days of an election campaign, announced its support of a candidate for public office and requested those who participate in a forum to send messages in support of this candidate, so that the organization could compile them and send them to the candidate, that aspect of maintenance of the forum would constitute political campaign activity. (This practice may violate political campaign regulation law(s) and certainly would be an inadvisable one for a charitable organization.)

(ii) Specific Questions. The Announcement posed three questions specifically pertaining to political campaign activities by tax-exempt organizations by means of the Internet.

The first of these questions was: "What facts and circumstances are relevant in determining whether information on a charitable organization's website about candidates for public office constitutes intervention in a political campaign by the charitable organization or is permissible charitable activity consistent with the principles set forth in" IRS revenue rulings concerning voter guides and candidate debates?[134] This pertains to the matter of voter education activity, which in some settings is an exempt function rather than impermissible political campaign activity.[135] The niceties of these distinctions depend on the facts and circumstances of each case.

---

[134] Rev. Rul. 78-248, *supra* note 82; Rev. Rul. 86-95, *supra* note 101.

[135] See *supra* § 3.

One of the key concepts in this context is *objectivity*. For example, a compilation of voting records of all members of Congress on major legislative issues involving a wide range of subjects is an exempt educational publication, as long as there is no editorial opinion and no signaling of approval or disapproval of voting records. Likewise, a voters' guide containing statements of candidates' positions on a wide variety of issues is permissible, where there is no evidence of bias or preference with respect to the views of any candidate or group of candidates. If there is a bias shown or if a voters' guide concentrates on a narrow range of issues and is widely distributed during an election campaign, the organization is considered to be participating in a political campaign.

A related element is *neutrality*—what the IRS termed "fair and impartial treatment" of candidates.[136] Publications containing voting records and the like are allowable where there is no endorsement of or opposition to candidates for public office. This is particularly the case where the timing of the date of publication does not coincide with an election campaign. The ultimate test is whether the publication would help or hurt candidates in their political campaigns. The IRS examines communications in these contexts looking for a "bias or preference for or against a particular candidate."[137] Communications are permissible where they do not "promote or advance" one candidate over another.[138]

Thus, the facts and circumstances to be used in assessing information on the Web site of a charitable organization, to determine if there is or is not political campaign participation or intervention, are the same as those in connection with other types of communications:

- The communication may contain analyses of voting records of legislators, as long as there is no editorial opinion, there is no bias as to approval or disapproval of the records, and a wide range of subjects is covered

- The communication is likely to be impermissible where there is bias shown or concentration on a narrow range of issues

---

[136] See the text accompanied by *supra* note 100.

[137] See the text accompanied by *supra* note 101.

[138] *Id.*

- Obviously, the communication may not amount to an endorsement of or expression of opposition to a candidate

- A key factor will be the timing of placement of the communication on the Web site; if it is posted in the heat of an election campaign, there will be a greater likelihood that the communication will be regarded by the IRS as a political one, for it certainly will be *widely distributed*

Another question of considerable import has been alluded to: "Does providing a hyperlink on a charitable organization's website to another organization that engages in political campaign intervention result in *per se* prohibited political intervention?" Truly, the implications of this question are enormous, as discussed in the larger context.[139]

Surely, as long as the link itself is all that is involved, the answer to this question must be no. This is the case as a matter of law and as an inherent characteristic of a link. As discussed in the context of the lobbying rules,[140] a link from one organization to another does not generally, by itself, cause any activity of the linked organization to be attributed to the linking organization. An answer to the contrary would be impractical, not to say unfair. The consequences would be stupendous if the mere existence automatically gave rise to such widespread attribution of words and deeds.

This no answer is reflected in existing law. Generally, for an organization to be denied or lose tax-exempt status because of political campaign activity, the political activity must be undertaken as an act of the organization itself; there generally is no attribution rule.

Years ago, the IRS issued a revenue ruling stating that a university did not intervene in a political campaign by conducting a political science course that required the students' participation in political campaigns of their choice. As part of the course, each student participated in several weeks of classroom work to learn about political campaign methods and then was excused from classes for two weeks to participate in a political campaign. The university was reimbursed or paid for any facilities provided to the students for use in connection with the campaigns. The IRS reasoned that, under the circumstances, the university was not a party to

---

[139] See § 1.8(b).

[140] See § 5.5(b)(ii), text accompanied by notes 164–166.

the expression or dissemination of the political views of the individual students in the course of their actual campaign activities.[141]

At that same time, the IRS took the position, in another revenue ruling, that a university did not intervene in a political campaign by providing faculty advisors and facilities for a campus newspaper that published the students' editorial opinions on political matters. Neither the university administration nor the advisors exercised any control or direction over the newspaper's editorial policy. A statement on the editorial pages made it clear that the views expressed were those of the student editors and not of the university. The IRS was of the view that, under the circumstances, the university's provision of assistance to the student newspaper did not make the expression of political views by the students in the publishing of the newspaper the acts of the university.[142]

A recent private letter ruling bears directly on this question. Citing both of these revenue rulings as authority, the IRS ruled that a charitable organization may administer a payroll deduction plan under a collective bargaining agreement to collect and remit its employees' voluntary contributions earmarked for political action committees established by the employees' unions.[143] The IRS emphasized that the charity has no "control or influence" over the beneficiary political action committees; indeed, the charity did not even select them. The political action committees are sponsored by the unions, not the charity.

This private letter ruling stressed the fact that this matter of political campaign participation or intervention by charitable organizations often depends on the facts and circumstances. In that context, the IRS concluded that there was no "identity of interests" between the charitable organization and the political action committees. That is a standard to use in the Internet setting as well: Is there an identity of interests between the charitable organization involved and the organization to which it is linked? There may be other reasons for the link. The ruling illustrates the point that there can be circumstances where the political campaign activity of another organization is not attributable to a charity.

---

[141] Rev. Rul. 72-512, *supra* note 14.

[142] Rev. Rul. 72–513, *supra* note 15.

[143] Priv. Ltr. Rul. 200151060.

This second revenue ruling is of particular consequence in the Internet communications context. If the content of a newspaper published by its students on its campus is not attributable to a university for political campaign intervention purposes, then how can the content of a Web site of another organization be attributable to a charitable organization for these purposes merely because of a link to the charity's Web site?

In furtherance of this question, the IRS also asked: "What facts and circumstances are relevant in determining whether the hyperlink constitutes a political campaign intervention by the charitable organization?" This aspect of the question not-so-subtlely answers the first part of the question. It must be hoped that the IRS asked the first part of the question to generate a no answer to it and then to set the stage for consideration of the second part of the question, so that while the sheer existence of a link should not automatically cause attribution of any political campaign activity, attribution can arise under certain sets of circumstances.

Certainly, for example, if a charitable organization was supportive of a particular political candidate and were to expressly request visitors to its Web site to link with another organization's site for the purpose of viewing an explanation as to why that individual should be elected to the public office involved, the provision of the link would constitute political campaign activity by the charitable organization. Also, if the charitable organization controlled the organization to which it provided the link, that would be a major factor indicating political campaign intervention by the charitable organization.

Another argument has been advanced in this setting, this one based on the thought that links "function entirely at the user's discretion."[144] The example is given of an individual reading educational material on the Web site of a charitable organization who thereafter uses a link in that material to move to educational material on a Web site created by a noncharitable entity and then links to a third site that contains a political campaign message. The thought presumably is that the charitable organization created the first link but not the second, so that the political message should not be attributed to it. The observation was that the charitable organization

---

[144] Livingston at 426.

"did not connect that series of events even though it invited the reader to take the first step." To the extent that that is all the argument advances, the conclusion is correct. But there is danger in assigning too much neutrality in links; the argument can border on disengenuity. If, in this example, the charity knew that the second link would be created, once it initiated the first link, the outcome would be different. In these circumstances, it will not do to blandly assert that the political message should not be attributable to the charity because the user exercised "discretion" in getting to it. If the charity builds it, the charity has responsibility when they come. Again, the matter boils down to intent, not some inherent characteristic of a hyperlink or user discretion.

Another factor to be taken into account was referenced above: the matter of *identity of interests*. In determining whether the content of an organization's Web site should be attributed to a charitable organization because of a hyperlink connecting the two entities, the IRS should explore whether there is an identity of interest between them. In the private letter ruling, the IRS noted that the political action committees are sponsored by the unions, which, on labor issues, may have political interests differing from those of the charity. This fact was relied on in the IRS's conclusion that there was no identity of interest between the charity and the political action committees. Thus, if there is no identity of interest between two organizations with linked sites, that fact should go a long way—perhaps give rise to a presumption—in showing that the political activity of an organization is not to be attributable to a charity. (At the same time, just because there is an identity of interest, that should not mean that attribution of views because of a link is automatic.)

The above ruling that the editorial content of a student newspaper is not to be attributed to a university for political campaign purposes[145] contains an element that should resolve this issue in many instances. There the newspaper contained a statement that the views expressed in it were those of the student editors and not the university. If a charitable organization is linked to the Web site of an organization that contains or reflects political

---

[145] Rev. Rul. 72-513, *supra* note 15.

campaign activity and has a valid reason for doing so, other than adoption or endorsement of the political views, a disclaimer on the charity's site should suffice to eliminate the problem (assuming, of course, that the disclaimer is credible).

These analyses concern situations where an organization forges a link with another organization. It is another matter entirely when an organization links to the Web site of a tax-exempt organization, where the exempt organization did not participate in the linkage and may not even be aware of it. Certainly there ought not be attribution in that setting.

Suppose, however, the exempt organization subsequently learns of the link. More specifically, suppose a charitable organization learns that an entity, which has a Web site bearing a political campaign message, has linked to the charity. That link alone should not result in attribution of the message to the charity. Nonetheless, once the charity learns of such a link, does it have a responsibility to seek to have the link removed? If the charity does not pursue delinkage, does that mean that, as this observer noted, this state of affairs could be seen as meaning that the charity is "tacitly reciprocating in the association of views"? The answer to this question should be no, although some extreme set of facts and circumstances may suggest otherwise. There is room in this setting for abuse. Thus, a charity in this circumstance should make some effort to have the link deleted or, if there is a good reason for preserving the link, should disclaim the message.

The IRS did not ask any questions about political campaign activities by any other category of tax-exempt organization. The question about attribution in instances of a hyperlink is applicable, of course, to categories of exempt organizations other than charitable ones. Also, the analysis of the law as to the use of voter guides and candidate debates is of some applicability to other tax-exempt organizations, particularly social welfare organizations.

§ 6.6 PENDING LEGISLATION

The House Subcommittee on Oversight, a subcommittee of the House Committee on Ways and Means, held a hearing, on May 14, 2002, to review the federal tax law exemption requirements for religious organizations, and to consider legislation to change the law in this area by allowing churches and certain other religious organizations to engage in political campaign activity. In essence, the proposals would import the insubstantiality standard used in the lobbying context,[146] and apply it in the political campaign activities setting.

(a) Proposed Legislation

Two bills were the focus of this hearing. One is the Houses of Worship Political Speech Protection Act.[147] The other is the Bright-Line Act of 2001.[148]

The Houses of Worship legislation basically would engraft the substantiality test, in the present-day lobbying rules, onto the rules concerning participation or intervention in political campaigns. This loosening of the standard, however, would only apply with respect to churches, their integrated auxiliaries, and conventions or associations of churches.[149]

The Bright-Line Act would place a 20 percent cap on allowable lobbying and a 5 percent cap on political campaign activity. These caps would be a percentage of an organization's gross revenues. Expenditures in excess of these caps would lead to denial or revocation of tax-exempt status. The outer limits standard, however, would be available only for churches, integrated auxiliaries of churches, conventions or associations of churches, and members of an affiliated group of such organization.[150]

---

[146] See § 5.2.

[147] H.R. 2357, 107th Cong., 1st Sess. (2001).

[148] H.R. 2931, 107th Cong., 1st Sess. (2001).

[149] The organizations benefited by this legislation would be those described in IRC § 508(c)(1)(A). This is the federal tax law provision that exempts these organizations from the requirement of filing applications for recognition of tax exemption (see § 7.2, note 17).

[150] The organizations benefited by this limitation would be those described in IRC § 501(h)(5). These are the organizations that are prohibited from electing the expenditure test (see § 5.3(c), text accompanied by note 105).

(b) Commentary

Congress undoubtedly has the authority, under the Constitution, to permit political campaign activity by churches and other religious organizations.[151] This is the case as a matter of *classifications* for *income* tax exemption.[152] Put another way, if this proposal is unconstitutional, then so too must be the other tax law benefits that Congress has accorded these religious organizations.[153]

The Houses of Worship bill, by introducing the standard of substantiality in the political area, would import into this area all of the uncertainties as to what this word means. Pressure would mount for the equivalent of a

---

[151] Tax exemption for a variety of nonprofit organizations is constitutional (*Walz v. Tax Commission*, 397 U.S. 664 (1970)). A tax exemption solely for religious organizations, however, violates the establishment clause of the First Amendment (*Texas Monthly, Inc. v. Bullock*, 489 U.S. 1 (1989)). Relying on the latter decision, a federal district court held that a state's sales and use tax exemptions, available only to religious organizations, violated the establishment clause and thus are unconstitutional (*American Civil Liberties Union Foundation of Louisiana v. Crawford*, 2002 WL 461649 (E.D. La. 2002) (Civil Action No. 00-1614, filed March 21, 2002). Moreover, the U.S. Court of Appeals for the Ninth Circuit, on March 5, 2002, requested briefs from parties in a case concerning an interpretation of the parsonage allowance (IRC § 107) (*Warren v. Commissioner*, No. 00-71217); this appellate court may question the constitutionality of the parsonage allowance in light of the opinion in *Texas Monthly*. Congress, however, has attempted to moot the *Warren* case by enactment of the Clergy Housing Allowance Clarification Act of 2002 (Pub. L. No. 107–181).

[152] The Supreme Court held that Congress has an "especially broad latitude in creating classifications and distinctions in tax statutes" and has "broad power in this area" (*Regan v. Taxation With Representation of Washington*, 461 U.S. 540, 547 (1983)).

[153] For example, churches and certain other religious organizations are not required to file applications for recognition of exemption with the IRS (see *supra* note 149), churches and certain other religious organizations are not required to file annual information returns with the IRS (see § 7.1(a)), and churches are protected by special audit rules (see § 7.10, note 136), making the audit of them by the IRS more difficult than is the case with respect to other tax-exempt organizations.

safe-harbor election[154] in the realm of participation and intervention in political campaigns.

Your author testified at this hearing. This testimony emphasized the point that, as these proposals highlight, another approach to defining *substantiality* is required. Traditional definitions in terms of *expenditures* and *time* are no longer always working. How does one place a monetary value (for percentage cap purposes) on a clergyperson's endorsement of a candidate from the pulpit? Or, in the context of this analysis, what is the similar value of a church Web site communication? There will have to be a new definition, some sort of facts-and-circumstances test, to capture the factor of *importance* or *influence*.[155]

The Bright-Line Act likewise does not resolve this problem, inasmuch as it focuses only on *expenditures*. An expenditure for a political act may be miniscule but exert enormous influence in the context of a political campaign. Also, political activities conducted by volunteers would be disregarded.

These two bills address the matter of *income* tax exemption but not other taxes. For example, while the Bright-Line Act would preserve a church's tax exemption if its political expenditures were within the 5 percent limitation, these expenditures would still be taxed.[156] The political activities tax[157] may also be involved. Presumably, the drafters of these bills did not intend this result.

This legislation highlights another point directly pertinent to the matter of political campaign activities by tax-exempt organizations by means of the Internet. That is, because the cost of these communications is relatively small, the task of ferreting out that cost (including allocations) may be too daunting and the resulting amount so little, the IRS may have no interest in computing an amount that would be subject to the political expenditures tax and may thus be inclined toward only revocation of tax-exempt status instead.

---

[154] That is, an election comparable to that in IRC § 501(h) (see § 5.3(c)).

[155] See § 1.8(a).

[156] IRC § 4955(a), (b).

[157] IRC § 527(f).

CHAPTER 7

Still Other Aspects of the Law

Regrettably, for nonprofit organizations, the law unique to Internet communications by and for these organizations is not confined to the topics reviewed in the foregoing chapters. That is, in addition to the federal and state law concerning related and unrelated business endeavors, administration of charitable giving programs, fundraising regulation, lobbying activities, and political campaign activities, the following aspects of federal law should be considered by nonprofit entities:

- Annual reporting requirements
- Application for recognition of tax-exempt status
- Disclosure requirements
- Private inurement doctrine
- Private benefit doctrine
- Intermediate sanctions
- Public charities and private foundations
- Tax exemption rules
- Charitable giving rules
- IRS audits
- Electronic Signatures Act
- Penalties

§ 7.1 ANNUAL REPORTING REQUIREMENTS

(a) Existing Law

Nearly all nonprofit organizations that are tax-exempt are required to file an annual information return with the IRS.[1] For most exempt organizations, the return is Form 990.[2] Churches, small organizations, and certain other entities are not required to file.

This return requires filing organizations to report a considerable amount of information, including gross revenues and expenses,[3] assets and liabilities,[4] expenses on a functional accounting basis,[5] program service accomplishments,[6] expenditures for political purposes,[7] income-producing activities,[8] and relationships with certain other organizations.[9] Charitable organizations must also report information about compensation paid and any expenditures for lobbying.[10]

Thus, Internet activities are, as discussed in previous chapters, implicated here. For example, amounts expended for business, lobbying, and/or political activities conducted by means of the Internet must be calculated and reported. One of the principal difficulties is the assigning of amounts of expenses to, or allocating expenses among, these activities.[11]

---

[1] IRC § 6033.

[2] Organizations with annual gross receipts that are normally in excess of $25,000 but less than $100,000, and that have end-of-year assets with a value below $250,000, may file a considerably shorter annual information return (Form 990-EZ). Private foundations file Form 990-PF. Political organizations (IRC § 527 entities) file Form 990-POL. Unrelated business activity is reported on Form 990-T (which is a tax, rather than an information, return).

[3] Form 990, Part I.

[4] *Id.*, Part IV.

[5] *Id.*, Part II.

[6] *Id.*, Part III.

[7] *Id.*, Part VI, line 81.

[8] *Id.*, Part VI, line 78; Part VII.

[9] *Id.*, Part VI, lines 80, 88; Part IX.

[10] *Id.*, Schedule A.

[11] See § 1.8(a).

(b) Electronic Filing

The IRS is in the process of determining whether there is sufficient interest in the nonprofit community in an electronic filing system (*e-filing*) for the annual information returns of tax-exempt organizations. Public comment on this subject has been sought.[12]

The IRS observed that the information available to it suggests that the ability to file exempt organization returns electronically would reduce the filing burden of these organizations as well as provide easier and quicker access to information for users of return data. Studies show that 80 percent of these returns[13] filed are prepared using software. The IRS manually inputs a large amount of return data that it and others use.

The IRS noted that the returns filed by tax-exempt organizations are unique in several respects. They are filed by diverse organizations, ranging from volunteer membership organizations to complex hospital systems. In addition, they are primarily information returns rather than tax returns. As such, they typically include a significant amount of narrative text in addition to financial data. Another unique aspect of these returns is that most exempt organization information returns are subject to public disclosure.[14] Finally, the returns assist with federal tax administration, state regulation, and public oversight of exempt organizations.

The agency stated that the success of an e-filing system for tax-exempt organizations will depend on the extent to which these organizations can use it to fulfill reporting requirements and the extent to which various stakeholders can use it to satisfy their information needs. Accordingly, the IRS has requested comments from exempt organizations and all interested stakeholders on factors to be considered in developing an e-filing system. The following questions were posed:

- Which Form 990 series returns should be introduced first, and why?
- What factors or concerns would encourage exempt organizations to file electronically?

---

[12] Announcement 2002-27, 2002-11 I.R.B. 629.

[13] Form 990 and Form 990-EZ (see *supra* note 2).

[14] See *infra* § 3(a).

- What factors or concerns would discourage exempt organizations from filing electronically?
- What could be done to address concerns that would discourage exempt organizations from filing electronically?
- How will your experience with any other IRS e-file program affect your decision to file your exempt organization returns electronically?
- Should the system be designed so organizations can use it to satisfy multiple filing or reporting requirements (such as state reporting requirements or grant reports)?
- What specific changes to the current Form 990 series of returns would facilitate e-filing of these forms?

Tax-exempt organizations and individuals authorized to submit comments on behalf of a specific organization were encouraged to include the following information to help ensure that the needs of various types of exempt organizations were met:

- The organization's gross receipts and net assets
- Who (lawyer, accountant, employee, volunteer) prepares the organization's returns
- Form filed (such as 990, 990-EZ, or 990-PF)
- How the returns are prepared (tax return software, forms software, spreadsheets, and the like)

Practitioners were encouraged to provide the following information:

- Size of their organization (such as law firm, accounting firm, or sole practitioner)
- Reports prepared (such as Form 990, charitable solicitation, or grant request)
- Volume of reports prepared on an annual basis

All other interested parties were encouraged to provide a statement explaining their interest in an e-filing system for exempt organization returns and any other information that would be useful in the development of such a system.

At a briefing on this development on March 13, 2002, the IRS said that, in the short term, the only alterations to be made to the Form 990 will be those necessary to convert the returns to an electronic format. Yet it was also noted that market research and analysis of the information currently requested on the returns may lead to substantive changes. As the IRS Director of Exempt Organizations exclaimed, the "information we're gathering may be fabulously useful for revising the form down the road."[15]

§ 7.2 APPLICATION FOR RECOGNITION OF TAX-EXEMPT STATUS

Whether a nonprofit organization is entitled to federal income tax exemption, on an initial or continuing basis, is a matter of law. Federal tax law defines the categories of organizations that are eligible for tax exemption. The function of the IRS in this regard is to recognize tax-exempt status where it is warranted.

For many nonprofit organizations that are eligible for tax exemption, there is no requirement that the IRS be called upon to recognize the exemption. Charitable organizations,[16] however, to be tax-exempt and be charitable donees, must file an application for recognition of tax exemption with the IRS and have the exemption recognized.[17] Thus, entities such as social welfare organizations,[18] labor organizations,[19] trade and professional associations,[20] social clubs,[21] and veterans' organizations[22] need not—but may—file an application for recognition of tax-exempt status. Charitable organizations file Form 1023; most other organizations file Form 1024.

---

[15] Bureau of National Affairs, *Daily Tax Report*, March 14, 2002, at G-5.

[16] That is, tax-exempt entities described in IRC § 501(c)(3).

[17] IRC § 508(a). Churches and certain other religious organizations, however, are excused from this requirement (IRC § 508(c)(1)(A)). Certain employee benefit organizations must also file for recognition of exemption (IRC § 505(c)(1)). Political organizations, to be exempt, must file a notice with the IRS (IRC § 527(i)); these are the only tax-exempt entities that are *required* to file with the IRS *electronically* (IRC § 527(i)(1)(A)).

[18] IRC § 501(c)(4) entities.

[19] IRC § 501(c)(5) entities.

[20] IRC § 501(c)(6) entities.

[21] IRC § 501(c)(7) entities.

[22] IRC § 501(c)(19) entities.

The application filed by charitable organizations requires submission of a volume of information, such as the organization's purposes and activities,[23] sources of financial support,[24] fundraising program,[25] composition of its board of directors,[26] any planned legislative and/or political campaign activities,[27] the nature of its products or services,[28] and any relationship with other organizations.[29]

The application for recognition of tax exemption requires the applicant organization to report its Web site address.[30] The IRS may visit the site, to compare statements there with what is stated in the application. This address also enables representatives of the IRS to surf the Net, looking to see what exempt organizations are saying about their program and fundraising activities, and ferreting out lobbying, political, and unrelated business undertakings. Web site content may result in a telephone call or letter from the IRS.[31]

§ 7.3 DISCLOSURE REQUIREMENTS

Five sets of disclosure requirements are imposed on tax-exempt organizations. Internet communications can be implicated in these requirements.

(a) Annual Information Returns

As a general rule, a tax-exempt organization must provide a copy, without charge, other than a reasonable fee for reproduction and actual postage

---

[23] Form 1023, Part II, question 1.

[24] *Id.*, Part II, question 2.

[25] *Id.*, Part II, question 3.

[26] *Id.*, Part II, question 4.

[27] *Id.*, Part II, questions 13, 14.

[28] *Id.*, Part II, question 12.

[29] *Id.*, Part II, questions 5-7, 10.

[30] *Id.*, Part I, question 1e.

[31] Calls of this nature may also be made by individuals on the staff of a member or a committee of Congress.

costs, of all or any part of an annual information return to any individual who makes a request for the copy in person (during business hours) or in writing (including e-mail requests).[32] Certain information can be withheld from public disclosure, such as trade secrets, patents, and donors.[33] This requirement applies to the three most recent returns.

A tax-exempt organization, however, is not required to comply with these requests for copies of the returns if the organization has made the documents widely available. An exempt organization can make a return *widely available* by posting it on a Web site that the organization has established and maintains. It can also satisfy this exception if the return is posted as part of a database of returns of other exempt organizations on a Web site established and maintained by another organization.[34]

The implications of this disclosure are just now becoming known. The returns are being reviewed by the media, government officials, prospective donors, and others. Thus, for example, fundraising by charitable organizations must be undertaken in an entirely new environment, where open access to information is the rule and decisions are made, based on disclosures, as to whether to contribute, without the charity's involvement or even knowledge. Among other aspects of all this, posting of these returns on the Internet makes it even more important that the documents be accurate and complete, and tell the organization's full story.[35]

(b) Applications for Recognition of Exemption

Tax-exempt organizations are required to make a copy of their application for recognition of tax exemption available to those who request it (assuming the exemption is recognized), subject to the same rules and exceptions that apply with respect to annual information returns.[36]

---

[32] IRC § 6104(d)(1)(B).

[33] IRC § 6104(d)(3)(B), (a)(1)(D).

[34] Reg. § 301.6104(d)-4(b)(2)(i).

[35] Statements can be attached to these returns to more fully explain programs, fundraising programs, and the like.

[36] IRC § 6104(d)(1)(A)(ii).

(c) Fundraising Disclosure by Noncharitable Organizations

The federal tax law imposes certain disclosure requirements on tax-exempt organizations other than charitable ones. The focus in this context is on social welfare organizations. These rules are designed to prevent noncharitable organizations from engaging in fundraising activities under circumstances in which donors assume that the contributions are tax-deductible, when in fact they are not.

(i) Rules in General. Under these rules, each fundraising solicitation by or on behalf of a tax-exempt organization must contain an express statement, in a "conspicuous and easily recognizable format," that gifts to it are not deductible as charitable contributions for federal income tax purposes.[37] A *fundraising solicitation* is any solicitation of gifts made in written or printed form, by television, radio, or telephone (although there is an exclusion for letters or calls not part of a coordinated fundraising campaign soliciting no more than 10 persons during a calendar year).[38] The IRS promulgated rules in amplification of this law.[39]

These rules are not applicable, however, to organizations that have annual gross receipts that are normally no more than $100,000.[40] Also, where all of the parties being solicited are tax-exempt organizations, the solicitation need not include the disclosure statement.

IRS rules contain a safe harbor guideline for *print media*.[41] This guideline requires that the statement be in at least the same type size as the primary message stated in the body of the document, the statement be included on the message side of any card or tear-off section that the contributor returns with the contribution, and the statement be either the first sentence in a paragraph or itself constitute a paragraph.

If an organization makes a solicitation to which these rules apply and the solicitation does not comport with the safe harbor guideline, the IRS

---

[37] IRC § 6113(a).

[38] IRC § 6613(c).

[39] Notice 88-120, 1988-2 C.B. 454.

[40] IRC § 6113(b)(2)(A).

[41] Notice 88-120, *supra* note 39.

is authorized to evaluate all of the facts and circumstances to determine whether the solicitation meets the disclosure rule. A "good-faith effort" to comply with these requirements is an important factor in the evaluation of the facts and circumstances. In any event, disclosure statements made in "fine print" do not conform to the statutory requirement. In one instance, a political organization that conducted fundraising by means of telemarketing and direct mail was found by the IRS to be in violation of these rules; a notice of nondeductibility of contributions was not included in its telephone solicitations or pledge statements, and the print used in some of its written notices was considered to be too small.[42]

(ii) Internet Communications. In the Announcement, the IRS raised the question as to whether solicitations for contributions made on the Internet (either on an organization's Web site or by e-mail) are in "written or printed form" for purposes of this body of law. This is the same issue raised by the IRS in the context of the substantiation requirements and the quid pro quo contributions rules, which require "written" acknowledgments and disclosures. The analysis of the word *written* in those settings[43] is equally applicable here. That is, the IRS has the authority to treat a printed confirmation from a Web site or a copy of an e-mail message as a written document for purposes of these disclosure rules. In any event, the Electronic Signatures Act compels this result.[44]

Oddly, however, the IRS overlooked a much larger issue. The statute provides that a *fundraising solicitation* is a solicitation of contributions made by television, radio, or telephone.[45] The Internet obviously is not any of these three media. The IRS lacks the authority to extend these disclosure rules to Internet communications. Such an expansion must be accomplished by an amendment to the statute. These rules, then, cannot apply to fundraising efforts conducted by noncharitable organizations by means of the Internet.

In the Announcement, the IRS also inquired as to what facts and circumstances are relevant in determining whether a disclosure, regarding

---

[42] Priv. Ltr. Rul. 9315001.

[43] See § 3.7(a), (b).

[44] See *infra* § 8.

[45] IRC § 6113(c)(B), (C).

these Internet transactions, is in a "conspicuous and easily recognizable format." The answer is that the facts and circumstances are the same as those utilized when the disclosure is made by means of any other medium.

(d) Fundraising Disclosure by Charitable Organizations

As discussed, fundraising disclosure rules are applicable to charitable organizations. Most notable are the gift substantiation requirements[46] and the quid pro quo contribution rules.[47]

§ 7.4 PRIVATE INUREMENT DOCTRINE

Nearly all tax-exempt organizations are subject to the federal tax law rule that the net earnings of the organization may not be allowed to inure to persons who are insiders with respect to the organization.[48] Read literally, this means that the profits of an exempt organization may not be passed along to individuals in their private capacity, in the way that dividend payments are made to shareholders of for-profit corporations. In fact, the private inurement rule, as expanded and amplified by the IRS and the courts, today means much more.

(a) Rules in General

The contemporary concept of private inurement is broad and wide-ranging. On one occasion, lawyers for the IRS advised that private "[i]nurement is likely to arise where the financial benefit represents a transfer of the organization's financial resources to an individual solely by virtue of the individual's relationship with the organization, and without regard to accomplishing exempt purposes."[49] More recently, the IRS stated that the

---

[46] See § 3.2.

[47] See § 3.3.

[48] E.g., IRC § 501(c)(3). Reg. § 1.501(c)(3)-1(c)(2).

[49] General Counsel Memorandum 38459.

"prohibition of inurement, in its simplest terms, means that a private shareholder or individual [that is, an insider] cannot misappropriate the organization's funds to himself [or herself] except as reasonable payment for goods or services."[50] Another of these observations, this one more bluntly expressed, stated that the "inurement prohibition serves to prevent anyone in a position to do so from siphoning off any of a charity's [or other tax-exempt organization subject to the doctrine] income or assets for personal use."[51] These descriptions are correct for a contemporaneous reading of the private inurement doctrine, but they are a substantial embellishment of the statutory rule as originally stated.

The essence of the private inurement concept, as applied to charitable organizations, is to ensure that a tax-exempt organization is serving public interests, not private interests. To be or remain exempt, an organization must establish that it is not organized and operated for the benefit of private interests—designated individuals, the creator of the entity or his or her family, persons controlled (directly or indirectly) by private interests, or any persons having a personal and private interest in the activities of the organization.

As noted, to entail private inurement, a transaction must involve an insider.[52] Generally, an insider includes the members of an organization's board of directors or board of trustees and its officers and key employees. The members of the family of insiders are themselves insiders, as are controlled entities (such as corporations, partnerships, trusts, and estates). One of the hot issues of the day is whether a vendor of services can be an insider (because of the extent of control over the organization) and the circumstances under which this occurs.[53]

There are several ways to have a private inurement transaction. The most common way is the payment of excessive compensation to an

---

[50] IRS CPE FY 2000 Text, Topic T.

[51] General Counsel Memorandum 39862.

[52] In the intermediate sanctions context (see *infra* § 6) and the private foundation context (IRC Chapter 42, particularly IRC § 4946), an insider is referred to as a *disqualified person*.

[53] See, e.g., *United Cancer Council, Inc. v. Commissioner*, 165 F.3d 1173 (7th Cir. 1999).

insider.[54] The doctrine requires that compensation arrangements of this nature be reasonable, using criteria such as amounts paid to persons in comparable circumstances, the education and experience of the person compensated, and the size of the organization (based on assets, income, and/or number of employees). Other ways to violate the private inurement doctrine include loans, rental arrangements, and sales of assets.[55] Retained interests in an organization's assets may be a form of private inurement, such as where the officers of a school leased property to the school and caused it to make expensive improvements that would benefit them individually following expiration of the lease.[56]

The private inurement doctrine does not prohibit transactions between tax-exempt organizations and persons who are insiders with respect to them. Rather, it requires that the terms and conditions of the transactions be reasonable, based on the facts and circumstances.

If the private inurement doctrine is violated, the tax-exempt status of the organization involved can be denied or revoked.

(b) Internet Communications

As in the offline world, a charitable or other tax-exempt organization should make every reasonable effort to identify those persons who are insiders with respect to it. Insiders can include the person who designs a Web site, an Internet service provider, a person to whom a link is made, a vendor of services in connection with an online fundraising program, or a consultant. Trustees, directors, officers, and/or key employees (themselves insiders) may have a relationship with or other involvement in a Web-based operation that could give rise to a private inurement transaction.

Some exempt organizations have adopted conflict-of-interest policies, which can be useful in identifying potential dealings with insiders— online and off. Again, the private inurement doctrine does not ban these

---

[54] E.g., *Birmingham Business College, Inc.* v. *Commissioner,* 276 F.2d 476 (5th Cir. 1960).

[55] E.g., *Anclote Psychiatric Center, Inc.* v. *Commissioner,* 76 T.C.M. 175 (1998).

[56] *Texas Trade School* v. *Commissioner,* 30 T.C. 642 (1968), *aff'd,* 272 F.2d 168 (5th Cir. 1969).

transactions; rather, the test is whether the terms and conditions of them are reasonable.

§ 7.5 PRIVATE BENEFIT DOCTRINE

The body of law that concerns *private benefit* is considerably different from the law encompassed by the private inurement doctrine. The relatively new private benefit doctrine, created and advanced largely by the courts, is more sweeping, in that it covers a wider range of activities. This is because the doctrine of private benefit does not require an insider; a charity can be involved in a private benefit transaction with anyone. At the same time, unlike the private inurement doctrine, the law tolerates *insubstantial* private benefit.

(a) Rules in General

A benefit that amounts to private inurement is also private benefit, yet the private benefit doctrine encompasses transactions that go beyond the reach of private inurement. It has been held that a charitable organization can, because of the nature of its operations, confer inappropriate *primary* private benefit; it can, conversely, operate primarily for exempt ends, yet confer unwarranted *secondary* private benefit.[57]

Historically, private benefit has been found where a charitable organization conferred undue benefit on individuals. Impermissible private benefit, however, can be provided to organizations, both for-profit and tax-exempt. As to the former, for example, a nonprofit organization was formed to generate community interest in retaining classical music programming on a commercial radio station, by seeking sponsors for the programs, urging listeners to patronize the sponsors, and soliciting listener subscription to promote the programs; the IRS ruled that the organization was ineligible for tax-exempt status because these activities increased the station's revenues and thus benefited it in more than an incidental manner.[58] Two for-profit organizations that coordinated the functions of a

---

[57] *American Campaign Academy* v. *Commissioner*, 92 T.C. 1053 (1989).

[58] Rev. Rul. 76-206, 1976-1 C.B. 154.

number of exempt educational organizations were held to be the recipients of private benefit; the court concluded that the nonprofit organizations were part of a "franchise system" that made them "simply the instrument to subsidize the for-profit corporations."[59]

Perhaps the most significant of the private benefit cases is the one involving a once-exempt hospital that became a co-general partner with a for-profit organization in a partnership that owned and operated a surgery center. The hospital thought it was engaging in an exempt activity (promotion of health) but the IRS[60] and the courts[61] concluded that it ceded control over its operations to the for-profit entity by entering into the joint venture. These decisions stand as a warning to public charities to examine their relationships with for-profit entities to see if they have, or can be perceived as having, lost control of their resources to one or more for-profit organizations. Examples are relationships reflected in management agreements, leases, fundraising contracts, and, of course, partnership or other joint venture agreements. The law can characterize a relationship between two organizations as a *joint venture* even though neither organization has an intent or desire to be in the venture.

Instances of private benefit involving only tax-exempt organizations seem to be on the increase. A court held that a nonprofit organization that audited structural steel fabricating companies in conjunction with a quality certification program conducted by a related trade association[62] did not constitute a charitable organization, in part because it yielded inappropriate private benefit to the association.[63] The IRS is considering revoking the tax-exempt status of, or denying it to, organizations that believe they are charitable because they make grants for scholarships, on the ground that the grant recipients are contestants in beauty pageants; the pageants

---

[59] *est of Hawaii* v. *Commissioner*, 71 T.C. 1067, 1080, 1082 (1979), *aff'd*, 647 F.2d 170 (9th Cir. 1981).

[60] Rev. Rul. 98-15, 1998-1 C.B. 718.

[61] *Redlands Surgical Services* v. *Commissioner*, 113 T.C. 47 (1999), *aff'd*, 242 F.3d 904 (9th Cir. 2001).

[62] An IRC § 501(c)(6) organization.

[63] *Quality Auditing Company* v. *Commissioner*, 114 T.C. 498 (2000).

are conducted by social welfare organizations,[64] and the IRS believes that at least some of the scholarship-granting foundations are bestowing undue private benefit on the pageant-sponsoring organizations.[65]

The private benefit doctrine is becoming so pervasive that it is sneaking up on the unsuspecting. As an example, a private foundation sought a ruling from the IRS that a proposed transaction would not be an act of self-dealing on the ground that the individual involved was not a disqualified person; the IRS obliged with the ruling but then pointed out to the foundation that it would lose its tax-exempt status because the transaction would confer improper private benefit on the individual.[66] Indeed, in another case, private benefit was conferred on an individual and the IRS (and apparently the court) did not detect the issue, being focused instead on whether the transactions involved amounted to acts of self-dealing.[67]

If the private benefit doctrine is violated, the tax-exempt status of the organization involved can be denied or revoked. The private benefit doctrine is applicable only with respect to charitable organizations.

(b) Internet Communications

The same comments made in the private inurement doctrine context apply equally here. That is, as in the offline world, a charitable organization should make every reasonable effort to be certain that it is not, as part of a relationship or transaction, conferring inappropriate private benefit on one or more persons. This includes the person who designs a Web site, an Internet service provider, a person to whom a link is made, a vendor of services in connection with an online fundraising program, or a consultant. Again, it is not necessary, for the doctrine to apply, that these persons be insiders with respect to the charitable organization. Trustees, directors,

---

[64] IRC § 501(c)(4) organizations.

[65] "Beauty Pageants: Private Benefit Worth Watching," IRS Exempt Organizations Continuing Professional Education Technical Instruction Program book for Fiscal Year 2002.

[66] Priv. Ltr. Rul. 200114040.

[67] *Graham v. Commissioner*, 83 T.C.M. 334 (2002).

officers, and/or key employees (themselves insiders) may have a relationship with or other involvement in a Web-based operation that could give rise to a private benefit arrangement.

As an example, caution should be exercised in particular with respect to this matter of links. Until the law sorts out the essence of hyperlinks—what the presence of them means and what the tax consequences of them are[68]—charitable organizations should fret about the private benefit doctrine. (If the other linked person is an insider, the exempt organization should worry about the private inurement doctrine.) Today, where there is a tax law focus on links, the tendency is to assess the relationship in terms of whether the unrelated business rules are implicated: Does the arrangement destroy the corporate sponsorship exclusion? Are the payments royalties? and the like.[69] Some say these rules are of no concern, inasmuch as the tax-exempt organization is providing the link without compensation. (The ultimate in exempt organization tax planning: If there is no income, there is no unrelated business income.) But if the linkage has more than an insubstantial value to the other party, private benefit may be lurking. (Those who thought they were doing good deeds by preserving classical music programming in a community inadvertently conferred private benefit on a radio station.[70])

§ 7.6 INTERMEDIATE SANCTIONS

The intermediate sanctions rules[71] are designed to curb abuses in the cases of private inurement, using a mechanism other than revocation of the tax exemption of the organization involved. These rules are applicable with respect to all tax-exempt public charities and exempt social welfare organizations. These two categories of organizations are termed *applicable tax-exempt organizations.*[72]

---

[68] See § 1.8(a).

[69] See Chapter 2.

[70] See the text accompanied by *supra* note 58.

[71] IRC § 4958.

[72] IRC § 4958(e)(1).

(a) Rules in General

The heart of this body of law is the *excess benefit transaction* (essentially the same as a private inurement transaction). A transaction is considered an excess benefit transaction if an economic benefit is provided by an applicable tax-exempt organization directly or indirectly to, or for the use of, a disqualified person, if the value of the economic benefit provided exceeds the value of the consideration received by the exempt organization for providing the benefit.[73] The principal focus of the intermediate sanctions is compensation—where a person's level of compensation is deemed to be in excess of the value of the economic benefit derived by the organization from the person's services. An economic benefit may not be treated as compensation for the performance of services unless the organization clearly indicated its intent to so treat the benefit.[74] The rules can also apply, however, to any type of private inurement transaction, such as rental and borrowing arrangements, sales of assets, and involvement in partnerships or other joint ventures.

The concept of the excess benefit transaction includes any transaction in which the amount of any economic benefit provided to, or for the use of, a disqualified person is determined in whole or in part by the revenues of one or more activities of the organization, where the transaction is reflected in tax regulations (not issued) and it results in private inurement.[75] These are known as *revenue-sharing arrangements*.

A *disqualified person* is any person, member of the family of such an individual, or certain controlled entities who were, at any time during the five-year period ending on the date of the transaction, in a position to exercise substantial influence over the affairs of the organization.[76] This designation is comparable to that of an *insider* in the private inurement setting.[77]

---

[73] IRC § 4958(c)(1)(A).

[74] *Id.*

[75] IRC § 4958(c)(2).

[76] IRC § 4958(f)(1)(A).

[77] See *supra* § 4(i).

The intermediate sanctions rules do not apply to a fixed payment made to a person pursuant to an initial contract.[78] A *fixed payment* is an amount of money or other property specified in the contract, or determined by a fixed formula specified in the contract, which is to be paid or transferred in exchange for the provision of specified services or property. An *initial*

---

[78] This *initial contract exception* is informally known as the *first-bite rule*. This exception has a contorted history (filled, some believe, with errors). When the intermediate sanctions regulations were proposed, the initial contract exception was not in them. During the period the IRS was working on what would become the temporary regulations, the U.S. Court of Appeals for the Seventh Circuit issued its opinion in *United Cancer Council, Inc. v. Commissioner, supra* note 53. That appellate court decision, which reversed the Tax Court, held that the entity involved with a charity (a fundraising company) was not an insider with the charity and sort of concluded that, in any event, private inurement never took place. The words *initial contract* are not to be found in the opinion, nor was there a finding that the lack of any prior relationship between the parties had anything to do with the case.

Nonetheless, the IRS seized on the Seventh Circuit's decision as the rationale for inclusion of the exception in the regulations (both in the temporary and final ones). In the IRS's preamble to the final intermediate sanctions regulations, the agency said: "The Seventh Circuit concluded that prohibited inurement under section 501(c)(3) cannot result from a contractual relationship negotiated at arm's length with a party having no prior relationship with the organization, regardless of the relative bargaining strength of the parties or resultant control over the tax-exempt organization created by the terms of the contract."

Three comments. This decision (which was wrong) is arguably one of the worst court opinions ever, whether assessed in terms of writing style (as in the organization's tax-exempt status was "yanked" rather than revoked), tone, accuracy, reasoning, and/or conclusions. It is, without peer, the most atrocious federal appellate court opinion in the law of tax-exempt organizations. The conclusions ostensibly reached by the Seventh Circuit as articulated by the IRS are simply not in the opinion (although some elements of the initial contract exception can be gleaned from the facts of the case, it is a stretch of some elongation to assert that the court reached the *conclusions* formulated by the IRS).

contract is a binding written contract between an applicable tax-exempt organization and a person who was not a disqualified person immediately before entering into the contract.[79]

A disqualified person who benefited from an excess benefit transaction is subject to an *initial tax* equal to 25 percent of the excess benefit. Moreover, this person is required to *correct* the transaction by returning the excess benefit amount (usually in money), plus appropriate interest, to the tax-exempt organization. An *organization manager* (most likely a director or officer) who participated in an excess benefit transaction, knowing that it was such a transaction, is subject to a tax of 10 percent of the excess benefit. An *additional tax*, at the rate of 200 percent of the excess benefit, may be imposed on a disqualified person where the initial tax was levied and the requisite correction of the excess benefit transaction did not occur.[80] These taxes are excise taxes.

If a transaction creating a benefit was approved by an independent board, or an independent committee of the board, and if appropriate data were used in approving the transaction and it was adequately documented, a presumption arises that the terms of the transaction are reasonable.[81] The burden of proof in these instances shifts to the IRS, which would then have to overcome (rebut) the presumption to prevail.

Disqualified persons and organization managers liable for payment of excise taxes as the result of excess benefit transactions are required to file Form 4720 as the return by which these taxes are paid. An excess benefit transaction must also be reported on the appropriate annual information return[82] of the applicable tax-exempt organization.

The intermediate sanctions may be imposed by the IRS in lieu of or in addition to revocation of an organization's tax-exempt status. It is significant that, in the first two of the sets of cases filed in court, the IRS imposed the

---

[79] Reg. § 53.4958-4(3).

[80] IRC § 4958(a), (b).

[81] Reg. § 53.4958-6.

[82] See *supra* § 1.

sanctions *and* proposed revocation of exemption.[83] The sanctions are, in general, to be the sole penalty imposed in these cases in which the excess benefit does not rise to such a level as to call into question whether, on the whole, the organization functions as an exempt charitable or social welfare organization.

(b) Internet Communications

As was noted in the private inurement and private benefit contexts,[84] just as in the offline world, a charitable or social welfare organization should make every reasonable effort to identify those persons who are disqualified persons with respect to it. Disqualified persons can include the person who designs a Web site, an Internet service provider, a person to whom a link is made, a vendor of services in connection with an online fundraising program, or a consultant. If the benefits to these or other disqualified persons are excessive (unreasonable), the transaction would be an excess benefit one. Trustees, directors, officers, and/or key employees (themselves disqualified persons) may have a relationship with or other involvement in a Web-based operation that could give rise to an excess benefit transaction.

If there is an excess benefit transaction, it is the disqualified person who becomes liable for the penalty (one or more taxes, plus the responsibility of correction). The charitable or social welfare organization involved, however, does not escape completely unscathed. For one thing, the caper is likely to prove embarrassing, even if the exempt organization acted innocently. Also, the taxes and an explanation of the transaction must be

---

[83] *Caracci* v. *Commissioner*, 118 T.C. No. 25 (2002); *Peters* v. *Commissioner* (U.S. Tax Court Docket No. 8446-00 (settled)). The *Caracci* case involved the reasonableness of the value of properties transferred by charitable organizations to disqualified persons. The *Peters* case involved the reasonableness of compensation paid by a charitable organization to a disqualified person. In the *Caracci* case, however, the court refused to approve revocation of the tax-exempt status of the charities involved on the grounds that the excess benefits transactions were not sufficiently egregious and that their exemption should be preserved to allow the prospect of correction of the transactions by transfer of the properties back to the charities.

[84] See *supra* §§ 5, 6.

reported on the organization's annual information return,[85] which is a public document.[86]

Further, there is a trap here. Suppose, for example, that a transaction is shielded from penalty as being an excess benefit transaction because of availability of the initial contract exception.[87] That does not mean that an excess benefit was not a component of the transaction. Thus, the transaction could be regarded as a private benefit transaction, endangering the tax-exempt status of the charitable organization involved. Thus, a charitable organization, engaging in an Internet-based transaction (or, for that matter, an offline one), should not relax its vigilance in avoiding private benefit arrangements just because the other party to the transaction is protected by the initial contract exception.

§ 7.7 PUBLIC CHARITY AND PRIVATE FOUNDATION RULES

Under the federal tax law, every charitable organization[88]—including every church, university, school, hospital, or local community group—is presumed to be a private foundation.[89] Each charitable organization (with few exceptions) must either rebut that presumption and thus become public (if it can) or exist as a private foundation.

(a) Definition of *Private Foundation*

Three types of charitable organizations are not private foundations and thus are *public charities*:

1. The *institutions* of the charitable world
2. *Publicly supported charities*
3. *Supporting organizations*

---

[85] Form 990, Part VI, line 89.

[86] See *supra* § 3(a).

[87] See the text accompanied by *supra* notes 78–79.

[88] That is, an entity described in IRC § 501(c)(3).

[89] IRC § 508(b).

The law does not define what a private foundation is; the law defines what a private foundation is not (namely, a public charity).

The institutions in the philanthropic sector that are exempted from the private foundation rules include:

1. Churches, and conventions or associations of churches
2. Universities, colleges, and schools
3. Healthcare providers and certain medical research organizations
4. Governmental units[90]

A way for a charitable organization to be a public charity is to draw its funding from many sources (the public). There are two basic types of publicly supported organizations. The *donative* charity is one that normally receives a substantial part of its support from direct or indirect contributions from the general public and/or government grants.[91] A *service-provider* charity normally receives more than one-third of its support from gifts and grants, membership fees, and/or gross receipts form the performance of exempt functions.[92]

A *supporting organization* is an entity that is related, structurally or operationally, to one or more institutions or publicly supported organizations. A supporting organization must be organized and operated in an active relationship with one or more public charities.[93]

(b) Private Foundation Rules

If a charitable organization fails to become classified as a public charity, it is a private foundation. With that status, it becomes subject to a battery of stringent requirements that are not applicable to any other type of tax-exempt organization, charitable or otherwise.

---

[90] IRC §§ 170(b)(1)(A)(i)–(v), 509(a)(1).

[91] IRC §§ 170(b)(1)(A)(vi), 509(a)(1).

[92] IRC § 509(a)(2).

[93] IRC § 509(a)(3).

These requirements concern transactions that amount to self-dealing,[94] force a minimum payout (grant-making) amount,[95] limit the extent of holdings in businesses,[96] pertain to the nature of permissible investments,[97] concern the nature and scope of programs,[98] impose a tax on net investment income,[99] make it unlikely that a private foundation will make a grant to another private foundation,[100] force more detailed annual reporting to the IRS,[101] and make charitable giving to private foundations less attractive.[102]

(c) Internet Communications

Because of the stringency of the private foundation rules, these charitable entities need to be even more cautious than public charities when it comes to Internet communications. The more limiting rules for private foundations, for example, as to legislative and political campaign activities have been discussed.[103]

The self-dealing rules applicable with respect to private foundations[104] are tougher than the intermediate sanctions rules[105] in that self-dealing essentially is prohibited. That is, it is not tested against a standard of reasonableness. Thus, private foundations should be far more concerned

---

[94] IRC § 4941.

[95] IRC § 4942.

[96] IRC § 4943.

[97] IRC § 4944.

[98] IRC § 4945.

[99] IRC § 4940.

[100] IRC §§ 4942, 4945.

[101] IRC § 6033(c).

[102] See *infra* § 8.

[103] See §§ 5.4(c), 6.4(b).

[104] IRC § 4941.

[105] See *supra* § 6.

about dealings with disqualified persons in the Internet applications context (as well as others). Also, private foundations, notwithstanding the self-dealing rules, are subject to the doctrines of private inurement and private benefit.[106]

§ 7.8 CHARITABLE GIVING RULES

(a) Rules in General

The federal tax law provides for income, gift, and estate tax deductions for contributions of money and property to charitable organizations.[107] Many issues infuse and confuse this aspect of the law, not the least of which include the meaning of the words *contribution* and *charitable organization*, the timing of a charitable gift in relation to its deductibility, valuation of charitable gift property,[108] and the world of planned giving or, more technically, partial interest gifts.[109]

Most contributions made today by means of the Internet are gifts of money. For most of these donors, the principal aspect of the federal tax law that may be of interest or concern are the *percentage limitations* on allowable deductions for income tax purposes. The extent of charitable contributions that can be deducted for a particular tax year is limited to a certain amount, which for *individuals* is a function of the donor's *contribution base*—essentially, the individual's adjusted gross income.[110] This level of annual deductibility is determined by five percentage limitations. They are dependent on several factors, principally the nature of the charitable recipient and the nature of the property donated.

The first three limitations apply to gifts to public charities and private operating foundations.[111]

---

[106] See *supra* §§ 4, 5.

[107] IRC §§ 170, 2055, 2522.

[108] See § 3.5.

[109] In general, see Hopkins, *The Tax Law of Charitable Giving, Second Edition* (John Wiley & Sons 2000, annually supplemented).

[110] IRC § 170(b)(1)(F).

[111] See *supra* § 7.

First, there is a percentage limitation of 50 percent of the donor's contribution base for contributions of money and ordinary income property.[112] If an individual makes contributions that exceed the 50 percent limitation, the excess generally may be carried forward and deducted over the subsequent years, up to five.[113]

The second percentage limitation is 30 percent of the donor's contribution base for gifts of capital gain property.[114] Any excess (more than the 30 percent limitation amount) is subject to a like carryforward rule.[115]

A donor who makes gifts of cash and capital gain property to public charities and/or private operating foundations in any one year generally must use a blend of these percentage limitations.

The third percentage limitation allows a donor of capital gain property to use the 50 percent limitation, instead of the 30 percent limitation, where the amount of the contribution is reduced by all of the unrealized appreciation in the value of the property.[116] This election is usually made by donors who want a larger deduction in the year of the gift for a property that has not appreciated in value to a great extent.

The fourth and fifth percentage limitations apply to gifts to private foundations and certain other charitable donees (other than public charities and private operating foundations). These donees are generally veterans' and fraternal organizations.

Under the fourth percentage limitation, contributions of cash and ordinary income property to private foundations and other entities may not exceed 30 percent of the individual donor's contribution base.[117] The carryover rules apply to this type of gift.[118]

The fifth percentage limitation is 20 percent of the contribution base for gifts of capital gain property to private foundations and certain other

---

[112] IRC § 170(b)(1)(A).

[113] IRC § 170(d)(1).

[114] IRC § 170(b)(1)(B).

[115] IRC § 170(b)(1)(C)(ii).

[116] IRC § 170(b)(1)(C).

[117] IRC § 170(b)(1)(B)(i).

[118] IRC § 170(b)(1)(B), last sentence.

charitable donees.[119] There is a carryforward for any excess deductible amount.[120]

Deductible charitable contributions by corporations in any tax year may not exceed 10 percent of pretax net income.[121] Excess amounts may be carried forward and deducted in subsequent years (up to 5 years).[122] As to gifts by corporations, the federal tax laws do not differentiate between gifts to public charities and gifts to private foundations.

A business organization that is a *flow-through entity* generates a different tax result when it comes to charitable deductions. These organizations are partnerships, other joint ventures, small business (S) corporations, and limited liability companies. These organizations, even though they may make charitable gifts, do not claim charitable contribution deductions. Instead, the deduction is passed through to the members or other owners on an allocable basis, and these persons claim their share of the deductions on their tax returns.

(b) Internet Communications

For the most part, the rules as to the deductibility of charitable contributions are the same irrespective of whether the gifts are made online or offline. There are, however, some nuances.

For example, the IRS ruled that an individual who purchases an item online, receives a "rebate" from the vendor, and elects to contribute the rebate to a charitable organization has made a deductible charitable gift.[123] In this situation, a for-profit company owns the Web site, which is an e-commerce Internet shopping Web page through which a customer may purchase products from specialty boutiques and companies selling general consumer products. For each purchase, the company receives a commission from the vendor and, as agent for the customer, receives from the

---

[119] IRC § 170(b)(1)(D)(i).

[120] IRC § 170(b)(1)(D)(ii).

[121] IRC § 170(b)(2).

[122] IRC § 170(d)(2).

[123] Priv. Ltr. Rul. 200142019.

vendor a rebate equal to a percentage of the purchase price. The customer elects to either receive the rebate in cash or donate it to a charity.

The IRS observed that a charitable contribution, to be deductible, must be made voluntarily and with donative intent. In this instance, the element of choice makes the transaction a deductible gift. The IRS wrote that the "opportunity to decide whether payments will be made to a charity or received in cash renders the payments voluntary." As long as the requisite donative intent is present, the contribution of these rebates to charitable organizations gives rise to a deduction.[124]

§ 7.9 TAX-EXEMPT ORGANIZATION RULES

As discussed, tax-exempt, nonprofit organizations can make great use of the Internet in advancement of their programs.[125] This includes Web page program communications, conference and membership online registration, and document storage and retrieval.

There is, moreover, a little law about computer use by nonprofit organizations as their primary program undertakings and the impact of such activities on their tax-exempt status.[126]

As discussed, nonprofit organizations—specifically, universities and research institutions—were involved at the outset in the creation of the Internet.[127] It did not take long for this involvement in Internet communications to be reflected in the tax law. What seems to be the first of the

---

[124] Almost always, a charitable gift of money is made with after-tax income. In this circumstance pertaining to gift of rebates, however, the rebate is considered a reduction in the purchase price and thus is not income to the customer. This position is based on Rev. Rul. 76-96, 1976-1 C.B. 23 (holding that rebates paid by a manufacturer of automobiles to qualifying retail customers who purchase or lease new automobiles are not includible in the customers' gross incomes) and Rev. Rul. 84-41, 1984-1 C.B. 130 (holding that a manufacturer's rebate received by an automobile dealer represents a trade discount and thus must be treated as a reduction in the cost of the automobile in the year of its purchase).

[125] See § 1.6.

[126] In general, see Hopkins, *The Law of Tax-Exempt Organizations, Seventh Edition* (John Wiley & Sons 1998, annually supplemented).

[127] See § 1.3(d).

few IRS rulings in this area appeared in 1974. The matter concerned an organization that operated a regional computer network to collect and disseminate scientific and educational information among member educational institutions. The organization did not own any computers. Rather, it acted as an information clearinghouse to inform members of resources available at member institutions. The IRS concluded that, by providing a coordinated program that enabled the member institutions to benefit from the research and scientific projects developed by other members, the organization was eligible for tax-exempt status in that it was operating in a charitable manner because it was advancing education.[128]

In 1981 the IRS considered an organization that developed a computer network to provide bibliographic information to member libraries. Once again the IRS concluded that, by making useful bibliographic information available to researchers, the organization qualified as an exempt charitable entity because its services constituted the advancement of education.[129]

These two rulings constitute the totality of the "formal" law on this point. This will, of course, soon change. In the meantime, lawyers and others endeavoring to discern the "law" in this area are required to extrapolate from existing rulings and cases, such as they are. Sometimes this exercise requires some acrobatics.

Here is an example. The IRS ruled that an organization cannot be tax-exempt as a charitable entity simply because it functions as an Internet service provider (ISP) for members of the public, although it can be exempt if it serves members of a charitable class on a highly subsidized basis and provides services to others by means of a for-profit subsidiary.[130]

The IRS, in 1993, recognized this nonprofit organization as a tax-exempt public charity. The agency based its determination for tax exemption on the organization's representation that it intended to provide and operate an educational and charitable "community telecommunication network." The organization's articles of incorporation stated that its purpose is to "establish and operate an online, community-based, public access information and communications service."

---

[128] Rev. Rul. 74-614, 1974-2 C.B. 164.

[129] Rev. Rul. 81-29, 1981-1 C.B. 329.

[130] Tech. Adv. Mem. 200203069.

It turned out that this organization was, as noted, an ISP. Visiting its Web site, the IRS read that it maintained a site for "all members of the public regardless of their income or other factors." The organization's service fees varied depending on the type of membership. Low-income individuals, disadvantaged businesses, schools, libraries, and the like were charged a lower fee.

The organization's services were provided primarily by volunteers, and it was controlled by an all-volunteer large "Governing Council" that represented a broad cross-section of the general public. This Council elected a volunteer board of directors, which managed its corporate and financial affairs. An executive director oversaw the entity's daily operations, including the performance of the volunteers and small staff.

Over 75 percent of the organization's financial support was derived from user fees for Internet services. The balance came from gifts and grants.

At a conference with the IRS in 1998, the organization conceded that its primary activity of providing Internet services for fees was an unrelated business. In early 1999 the organization created a for-profit subsidiary and transferred to it all of the activities that the IRS determined to be neither charitable nor educational. Five of its board members will serve on the nine-member board of the subsidiary. The organization will lease equipment to its subsidiary. The subsidiary will contribute its profits to the nonprofit organization.

The organization will confine its ISP program to serve only low-income individuals and charitable organizations at a charge substantially below cost. The organization's articles of incorporation were amended accordingly. Contributions and grants will continue to constitute the balance of the organization's financial support. The organization sought to retain its tax-exempt status.

The IRS began its analysis of this case with the observation that "it is a clearly established principle of the law of charity that a purpose is not charitable unless it is directed to the public benefit." The IRS went on to say that "providing services of an ordinary commercial nature in a community, even though the undertaking is conducted on a nonprofit basis, is not regarded as conferring a charitable benefit on the community unless the service directly accomplishes one of the established categories of charitable purposes."

The agency concluded that the organization's Internet services did not directly accomplish any of the categories of charitable purposes. By providing services to disadvantaged businesses, individuals, and communities, the organization was seen as going beyond the provision of services exclusively for the relief of the poor, distressed, or underprivileged.[131] In particular, the IRS was troubled that the organization served as an ISP for individuals. This function was likened to a nonprofit lawyer referral service, which has been ruled to be a nonexempt activity.[132]

The IRS observed that the organization received support primarily from fees for providing these nonexempt Internet services. It explored case law, citing opinions where the courts have denied tax exemption to organizations that conducted nonexempt activities which generated income in excess of 22, 25, 30, and 45 percent of the organization's total annual income. The agency concluded, therefore, that the organization's tax-exempt status should be revoked.

As noted, the organization restructured itself, by establishing the for-profit subsidiary. The IRS used its authority to approve relief[133] to preserve the entity's tax-exempt status for the period during which it conducted disqualifying activities.

The final issue was whether the organization will be providing its Internet services to the charitable class in a manner that is *substantially below cost*. On this point, the IRS analogized to a ruling concerning an organization that provided assistance in the management of participating colleges' and universities' endowment or investment funds for a charge substantially below cost (more than 85 percent of outside funding).[134] The IRS did not say so in so many words, but apparently grants from the subsidiary, which will defray the cost of operating the Internet services, were within the 85 percent range. The IRS ruled that the organization's operations were distinguishable from those described in an IRS ruling,[135] which concerned an organization providing managerial and consulting

---

[131] Reg. § 1.501(c)(3)–1(d)(2).

[132] Rev. Rul. 80-287, 1980-2 C.B. 185.

[133] IRC § 7805(b).

[134] Rev. Rul. 71-529, 1971-2 C.B. 234.

[135] Rev. Rul. 72-369, 1972-2 C.B. 245.

services for nonprofit organizations on a cost basis; that type of entity was held to be ineligible for tax-exempt status.

It is obvious that an ISP cannot, as such, qualify as a tax-exempt charitable organization. This is true even if only nonprofit organizations are being served and the fees are set to only cover costs. There has to be a charitable class and outside subsidization of these types of services. Extrapolation from the law pertaining to referral services and fund management services is nonetheless quite the leap.

This is the type of ruling that can be expected from the IRS on many occasions over the coming months and years, extrapolating from the law of tax-exempt organizations in general to begin creating exemption law directly pertaining to Internet activities.

§ 7.10 IRS Audits And Litigation

The IRS, of course, audits tax-exempt organizations and sometimes proposes revocation of their tax-exempt status.[136] On occasion, the issue is litigated. Often this litigation is conducted pursuant to a special declaratory judgment procedure.[137] These cases are frequently tried before the United States Tax Court.

These Tax Court cases are based on a set of facts contained in an *administrative record*.[138] One of these cases concerned an organization that uses the Internet to conduct seminars. In this case, the review by the Tax Court of the administrative record included information found on the organization's Web site. (This is, thus, one of the first cases where the administrative record entailed information that was distributed by means of the Internet.)

The court in this case[139] referenced the organization's Web site and cited, by title, several articles posted there.[140] The court observed, however, that the organization refused to place these articles in the administrative record.

---

[136] Special rules make the audit of churches by the IRS more difficult (IRC § 7611).

[137] IRC § 7428.

[138] Tax Court Rule 217(b)(1).

[139] *The Nationalist Foundation* v. *Commissioner*, 80 T.C.M. 507 (2000).

[140] *Id.* at 508.

The court also noted that the organization produced only one transcript of a seminar conducted from its Web site.

The implication of this opinion (pursuant to which the organization was denied tax-exempt status) is that material on an organization's Web site is not part of the Tax Court's administrative record in a declaratory judgment proceeding until and unless it is printed out and made part of the record along with other hard copy documents.

§ 7.11 ELECTRONIC SIGNATURES ACT

The body of law created by the enactment of the Electronic Signatures in Global and National Commerce Act[141] provides for the acceptance, or validation, of electronic signatures, electronic contracts, and other electronic records in interstate commerce. This law is written in the negative, in that these signatures, contracts, and other records are not to be denied validity simply because they are in electronic form. With exceptions,[142] this law preempts state law.

More formally, this legislation provides that, "[n]otwithstanding any statute, regulation, or other rule of law," other than provisions of the legislation, "with respect to any transaction in or affecting interstate or foreign commerce (1) a signature, contract, or other record relating to such transaction may not be denied legal effect, validity, or enforceability solely because it is in electronic form; and (2) a contract relating to such transaction may not be denied legal effect, validity, or enforceability solely because an electronic signature or electronic record was used in its formation."[143]

---

[141] P. L. No. 106-229 (2000) (for purposes of this section, "Act").

[142] Act § 102. A principal exception is where state law is in the form of the Uniform Electronic Transactions Act, which is in effect in several states. Nearly every state has some type of legislation that establishes the validity of electronic signatures; the federal law "provides a way to harmonize the different state regulations and a framework for interstate commerce" (Zoellick, "Commentary on the Electronic Signatures in Global and National Commerce Act," available in the Fastwater Library at e-think.com ("Zoellick")).

[143] Act § 101(a).

For this purpose, a *transaction* is an "action or set of actions relating to the conduct of business, consumer, or commercial affairs between two or more persons," including the following "types of conduct":

1. The "sale, lease, exchange, licensing, or other disposition of (i) personal property, including goods and intangibles, (ii) services, and (iii) any combination thereof"
2. The "sale, lease, exchange, or other disposition of any interest in real property, or any combination thereof"[144]

Presumably, this term includes contributions to charitable organizations, except those made by means of a will, codicil, or testamentary trust.[145]

The term *electronic* means "relating to technology having electrical, digital, magnetic, wireless, optical, electromagnetic, or similar capabilities."[146] The term *electronic record* means a "contract or other record created, generated, sent, communicated, received, or stored by electronic means."[147] The term *electronic signature* means an "electronic sound, symbol, or process attached to or logically associated with a contract or other record and executed or adopted by a person with the intent to sign the record."[148]

There are certain limitations on the use of electronic contracts involving consumers. If a statute, regulation, or rule of law requires information to be provided in writing, the use of an electronic record will suffice only if the consumer has:

- Affirmatively consented to the use
- Been provided with notice regarding rights to receive a written record and to withdraw consent
- Confirmed that he or she has the hardware and software necessary to read and save the electronic record[149]

---

[144] Act § 106(13).

[145] See the text accompanied by *infra* note 154.

[146] Act § 106(2).

[147] *Id.* § 106(4).

[148] *Id.* § 106(5).

[149] *Id.* § 101(c).

The term *consumer* means an "individual who obtains, through a transaction, products or services which are used primarily for personal, family, or household purposes, and also means the legal representative of such an individual."[150]

If a statute, regulation, or other rule of law requires that a contract or other record relating to a transaction in or affecting interstate commerce be retained, the requirement can be met by retaining an electronic record of the information in the contract that accurately reflects the information in the contract and that is accessible to all persons who are entitled to access to it.[151]

If a statute, regulation, or other rule of law requires that a contract or other record relating to a transaction in or affecting interstate commerce be in writing, the legal effect, validity, or enforceability of an electronic record of such contract or other record "may be denied" if the record "is not in a form that is capable of being retained and accurately reproduced for later reference by all parties or persons who are entitled to retain the contract or other record."[152]

This law does not limit or supersede any requirement by a federal regulatory agency, self-regulatory organization, or state regulatory agency that records be filed with the agency or organization in accordance with specified standards or formats.[153]

There are some exceptions to this law. For example, it does not apply to the creation and execution of wills, codicils, and testamentary trusts. Likewise, it is inapplicable with respect to court orders or notices and other official court notices.[154]

Of particular relevance is the matter of the *electronic signature*, which, as noted, is generally defined. To place this in context, the law merely provides that an electronic signature may be used in instances where otherwise there would have been a more conventional type of signature (such as by use of a pen). The law "does not speak to the technical merits of different signature

---

[150] *Id.* § 106(1).

[151] *Id.* § 101(d).

[152] *Id.* § 101(e).

[153] *Id.* § 104.

[154] *Id.* § 103.

technologies, much less to the requirements for certification."[155] The reference to "requirements for certification" is to the manner in which the signature is authenticated, so that the recipient of a document signed in this fashion has a reasonable basis for believing that the document was sent by the individual who is the signatory. Thus, this law "does not augment the existing authentication infrastructure with a new one that is appropriate for e-commerce."[156] One commentator asserted that, "[b]efore electronic signatures are used in new ways, supporting new kinds of paperless commerce, we need to establish mechanisms for authenticating electronic signatures."[157] For the immediate future, it appears, safe use of electronic signatures requires a preexisting positive relationship between the parties. That is, at the present, "there is very little in the way of legislation, accepted practice, or widely used infrastructure that makes use of electronic signature safe for use between parties that do not already have a basis for trusting each other."[158]

As to this matter of the electronic signature itself, one observer summed up the options: "An electronic signature could be my name, spelled in ASCII characters, at the bottom of a document. It could be a digitized image of my handwritten signature. It could be a digital signature using a public key architecture and a certification authority. It could be a biometric signature such as an electronically recorded thumbprint or a retina scan. It could be a voiceprint of me saying my name or it could be the digital encoding of the biometric factors (pressure, speed, direction) that I use in creating my handwritten signature as detected on a digital pad." It was noted that "attorneys and legislators, however, prefer to reserve the term 'digital signature' for applications that use public encryption keys and matching private encryption keys to transmit documents securely and to 'sign' them."[159]

---

[155] Zoellick, *supra* note 142.

[156] *Id.*

[157] *Id.*

[158] *Id.*

[159] *Id.*

302 CHAPTER 7 STILL OTHER ASPECTS OF THE LAW

This observer added: "Clearly, some of these signature technologies will be more secure or easier to authenticate than others." The Electronic Signatures Act "lets the market sort out the winners from the losers."[160]

§ 7.12 PENALTIES

The federal tax law involving nonprofit organizations and use by them of the Internet is strewn with penalties. Here is a summary of them.

(a) Annual Reporting Requirements

As noted, nearly all nonprofit organizations that are tax-exempt are required to file an annual information return with the IRS.[161] There are penalties for failure of a tax-exempt organization to file the appropriate annual information return.

In general, a penalty of $20 a day, not to exceed the lesser of $10,000 or 5 percent of the gross receipts of the organization for the year, may be imposed where a return is filed late, unless the organization can show that the late filing was due to reasonable cause.[162] In the case of an organization having gross receipts in excess of $1 million for a year, however, the penalty can be $100 per day, with the maximum penalty set at $50,000. These penalties may also be imposed if an incomplete return is filed or incorrect information is submitted.

Further, if a complete return is not filed or correct information is not furnished, and a period of correction has expired, the individual failing to comply will be charged a penalty of $10 per day, not to exceed $5,000, unless he or she is able to show that the noncompliance was due to reasonable cause.[163] If more than one individual is responsible for noncompliance, these persons are jointly and individually liable for the penalty.[164]

---

[160] *Id.*

[161] See *supra* § 1.

[162] IRC § 6652(c)(1)(A), (3).

[163] IRC § 6652(c)(1)(B)(ii), (3).

[164] IRC § 6652(c)(4)(B).

(b) Disclosure Requirements

As noted, there are disclosure requirements imposed on tax-exempt organizations, accompanied by penalties.

(i) Annual Information Returns. In connection with the requirement that copies of annual information returns be made available to the public,[165] there are penalties for noncompliance.

In connection with a failure to comply with these disclosure requirements, with respect to an annual information return, a penalty of $20 per day, with a maximum penalty of $10,000, must be paid by the person failing to meet the requirements.[166] This penalty will not be imposed in an instance of reasonable cause.[167] A person who willfully fails to comply with this requirement is subject to an additional penalty of $5,000.[168]

(ii) Applications for Recognition of Exemption. In connection with the requirement that copies of applications for recognition of tax exemption be made available to the public,[169] there are penalties for noncompliance.

In connection with a failure to comply with this disclosure requirement, a penalty of $20 per day, with a maximum penalty of $10,000, must be paid by the person failing to meet the requirement.[170] This penalty will not be imposed in an instance of reasonable cause.[171] A person who willfully fails to comply with this requirement is subject to an additional penalty of $5,000.[172]

(c) Fundraising Disclosure by Noncharitable Organizations

Failure to satisfy the disclosure requirements applicable in an instance of fundraising by noncharitable organizations[173] can result in imposition of

---

[165] See *supra* § 3(a).

[166] IRC § 6652(c)(1)(C).

[167] IRC § 6652(c)(3).

[168] IRC § 6685.

[169] See *supra* § 3(b).

[170] IRC § 6652(c)(1)(D).

[171] IRC § 6652(c)(3).

[172] IRC § 6685.

[173] See *supra* § 3(c).

penalties.[174] The penalty is $1,000 per day (maximum of $10,000 per year), albeit with an exception for instances of reasonable cause.

In an instance of an intentional disregard of these rules, however, the penalty for the day on which the offense occurred is the greater of $1,000 or 50 percent of the aggregate cost of the solicitations that took place on that day, and the $10,000 limitation is inapplicable. For these purposes, the days involved are those on which the solicitation was telecast, broadcast, mailed, otherwise distributed, or telephoned.[175]

(d) Fundraising Disclosure by Charitable Organizations

As discussed, there are fundraising disclosure rules that are applicable to charitable organizations.[176] These consist of the gift substantiation requirements and the quid pro quo contribution rules.

The sanction for violation of the substantiation requirement is that the donor is not entitled to the charitable contribution deduction that would otherwise be available.[177] The sanction for violation of the quid pro quo contribution rules is imposition of a penalty.[178]

(e) Other Penalties

The penalties for violation of the private inurement doctrine[179] and the private benefit doctrine[180] are denial or revocation of tax-exempt status of the nonprofit organization involved. The penalties for violation of the intermediate sanctions rules consist of one or more taxes that can be

---

[174] IRC § 6710.

[175] The phrase *otherwise distributed* would seem to apply to solicitations made by means of the Internet. As discussed, however (see *supra* § 3(c)), these disclosure rules are inapplicable to Internet solicitations by reason of the statutory limitation (see *supra* note 45).

[176] See *supra* § 3(d).

[177] See § 3.2.

[178] See § 3.3, text accompanied by notes 39–40.

[179] See *supra* § 4.

[180] See *supra* § 5.

imposed on disqualified persons and/or organization managers.[181] Some charitable giving promotions can be considered abusive tax shelters, and their promoters can be penalized under the tax law for the promotion[182] and become subject to a court injunction.[183]

---

[181] See *supra* § 6.

[182] IRC § 6700.

[183] E.g., *United States* v. *Estate Preservation Services et al.*, 38 F. Supp. 2d 846 (E.D. Cal. 1998), *aff'd* 202 F.3d 1093 (9th Cir. 2000).

Table of Cases

Reno v. American Civil Liberties Union, § 1.1(b)

Rensselaer Polytechnic Institute v. Commissioner, § 2.5(b)

Rio Properties, Inc. v. Rio International Interlink, § 3.7(a)

San Antonio District Dental Society v. United States, § 2.1(b)(vi)

Seasongood v. Commissioner, §§ 5.2(b), 5.2(e)

Sierra Club, Inc. v. Commissioner, § 2.3(a)(iii)

Sklar v. Commissioner, § 3.1

St. Joseph Farms of Indiana Brothers of the Congregation of Holy Cross, Southwest Province, Inc. v. Commissioner, § 2.3(b)(i)

St. Louis Union Trust Co. v. United States, § 6.2(b)

State v. Blakney, § 4.2(b)

State Police Association of Massachusetts v. Commissioner, § 2.2(a)(i)

Steamship Trade Association of Baltimore, Inc. v. Commissioner, §§ 2.1(b)(ii), 2.1(b)(vi)

Suffock County Patrolmen's Benevolent Association, Inc. v. Commissioner, §§ 2.1(c)(iii), 2.1(c)(iv), 2.2(c)(ii)

Templin v. Oakland City Clerk, § 6.1(e)

Texas Farm Bureau, Inc. v. United States, § 2.3(a)(iii)

Texas Monthly, Inc. v. Bullock, § 6.6(b)

Texas Trade School v. Commissioner, § 7.4(a)

Todd v. Commissioner, § 3.4

United Cancer Council, Inc. v. Commissioner, §§ 3.7(a), 7.4(a), 7.6(a)

United States v. American Bar Endowment, §§ 2.1(b)(ii), 4.1

United States v. American College of Physicians, §§ 2.2(a)(iii), 2.5(a)(iv)

United States v. Auxiliary to the Knights of St. Peter Claver, Charities of the Ladies Court No. 97, § 2.2(c)(i)

United States v. CB Radio Association, No. 1, Inc. v. Commissioner, § 2.2(c)(i)

United States v. Construction Local 264, § 6.2(b)

United States v. Dykema, § 6.2(a)

United States v. Estate Preservation Services et al., § 7.12(e)

United States v. Painters Local 481, § 6.2(b)

United States v. Thomas, § 4.3

Table of IRS Revenue Rulings

79-46, § 2.2(c)

79-222, § 2.4(a)

79-370, § 2.2(a)(iii)

80-69, § 3.5

80-233, § 3.5

80-282, § 6.3(b)

80-287, §§ 1.9, 7.9

81-29, § 7.9

81-95, § 6.2(c)

84-41, § 7.8(b)

85-124, § 3.6(f)

86-95, §§ 6.3(b), 6.5(b)(2)

98-15, § 7.5(a)

Table of IRS
Technical Advice Memoranda

Table of IRS
Private Letter Rulings

7823062, § 2.1(d)(v)

7905129, § 2.1(c)(i)

7946001, § 2.2(c)(i)

7948113, § 2.2(a)(iii)

8203134, §§ 2.1(c)(ii), 2.2(c)(i)

8232011, § 2.2(c)(i)

8725056, § 2.2(c)(i)

8832003, § 3.1

9137002, § 2.1(c)(iv)

9302023, § 2.3(b)(i)

9315001, § 7.1(c)(i)

9316032, § 2.1(b)(vi)

9320042, § 2.1(d)(ii)

9425030, § 2.1(c)(i)

9535023, §§ 2.1(d)(ii), 2.3(b)(ii)

9641011, § 2.2(e)

9651047, § 2.2(e)

9652026, § 5.1(e)

9723046, §§ 2.5(a)(iv), 2.5(b)(ii)

9839039, § 2.2(e)

9841049, § 2.3(b)(ii)

9849027, § 2.2(e)

199910060, § 2.2(e)

200022056, § 2.2(e)

200033049, § 2.1(b)(v)

200051049, § 2.1(a)

200108045, § 2.2(e)

200108048, § 2.2(e)

200114040, § 7.5(a)

200119061, § 2.1(b)(v)

200128059, §§ 2.1(c)(iv), 2.2(c)(ii)

200131034, § 2.1(b)(vi)

200142019, § 7.8(b)

200151060, §§ 1.9, 6.5(b)(ii)

200218008, § 3.7(f)

Table of IRS Announcements

2000-84, §§ 1.9, 2.5(b), 3.7(a),
    3.7(b), 5.5(b), 6.5(b), 7.1(c)(ii)

2002-27, § 7.1(b)

Glossary

Here are the principal terms to know in connection with nonprofit organization operations (as well as others) on the Internet:

Archive A collection of stored material available for retrieval.

ASCII A computer code for text characters, with the acronym standing for "American Standard Code for Information Interchange."

Banner advertisement A graphic advertisement, usually a moving image, measured in pixels.

Bookmarks A feature of the *browser* that stores the name and location of *Web sites* for easy return.

Browser Software that interprets *HTML* and presents it to the viewer as a *World Wide Web* page; most browsers are either Netscape Navigator or Microsoft Explorer.

Chat Live online conversations, usually occurring in chat rooms, conducted over the Internet or through an online *Internet service provider.*

Click A click of a mouse on a *hyperlink,* graphic, or *banner advertisement* that transports the *Web site* visitor to another Web site or location within the site.

Cyberfundraising Fundraising that is accomplished by utilizing online methods; in many cases, this type of fundraising involves use of an electronic commerce provider; in other cases, the Internet is used to solicit the funds and another method (such as telephone or mail) is used to complete the transaction.

Cyberspace The community of Internet users.

Download The copying of *files* from the Internet or any remote source to a user's personal computer.

E-mail Mail sent *online* over a *network* from one computer to another.

FAQ An acronym for "frequently asked questions"; a listing of commonly asked questions and their respective answers.

File Information grouped together and stored.

Gateway A computer or server that moves data between *networks.*

Hit A term referring to the number of visitors to a *Web site* or the number of *files downloaded* from a site.

Hardware Computer equipment such as a monitor, printer, modem, and scanner.

Home page The first and introductory page to a *Web site*; users who travel to a Web site most often begin at the home page, which offers explanations, instructions, and *links* to the rest of the site. (See *hyperlink.*)

Host A computer directly connected to the Internet or to a *network.*

Hyperlink, hypertext link, link A connection between two *hypertext* documents, which allows users to travel freely in any direction throughout an *HTML* document series or *Web site.*

Hypertext Markup Language A computer language used on the *World Wide Web* that formats text *files* through the use of special commands; *browsers* interpret HTML for viewing by the user.

Hypertext Transfer Protocol (http) The commonly accepted *protocol* for transporting *hypertext* documents on the *World Wide Web.*

Information superhighway An all-encompassing title for *online* information access; in general terms, it is the Internet itself.

Internet service provider (ISP) An organization that provides a *gateway* to the Internet; many ISPs are commercial ventures.

Keyword The use of specific words as references to perform a search; use of keywords allows for expansive searches for information in numerous resources.

Netiquette The Internet community's informal code of conduct for proper Internet use and behavior.

Netizen A citizen of the Internet.

Netruism The willingness to give to charitable causes using the Internet; philanthropy that is linked to nonprofit Web sites, as the result of donors' demonstrated preference for online convenience.[1]

Network A series of computers that have been electronically *linked* or are *online.*

Newbie An individual who is new to the Internet, especially to discussion groups.

Online A computer that is connected to a *network* is online, similar to a printer being online through its connection to a computer; computers that are connected to the Internet are online, as are individuals who are connected through their computers.

Protocol An understanding on how to communicate between different computers.

Search engine A device that searches a database of *Web sites*, documents, and other information available through the Internet; the search usually is done on the basis of *keywords.*

Signature Text that an *e-mail* program will add at the bottom of each outgoing e-mail message to identify the sender; details can include company name, address, and telephone and fax number.

---

[1] This is not (yet) a word, but rather a clever invention by the company GivingCapital and used in its advertisements.

SMTP An acronym for Simple Mail Transfer Protocol; the standard *protocol* used on the Internet for moving *e-mail* between computers.

Software A computer program or application that is run on a computer; it operates the computer and allows it to perform tasks assigned to it by the user.

Uniform resource locator (URL) The name of a *World Wide Web* or other address that is inputted into a *browser* or other *software* to retrieve files from that location.

Web site A location on the *World Wide Web* dedicated to a specific purpose; the Web is composed of thousands of sites, all *hyperlinked* together (hence the name Web).

World Wide Web (designated www) An Internet service that has grown to dominate information distribution on the Internet because of its combined text, graphics, and audio and video capabilities as well as its ease of use; it is composed of thousands of *Web sites* connected to one another via *hyperlinks*.

Bibliography

Berners-Lee, *Weaving the Web* (HarperBusiness 2000).

Biersdorfer, "When Worship Gets Wired," CLI *The New York Times* E1 (May 16, 2002).

Blau, "Internet Giving: Not the Perfect Revolution," XIV *Chronicle of Philanthropy* (No. 2) 85 (Nov. 1, 2001).

Castells, *The Internet Galaxy* (Oxford University Press 2001).

Chasin, Ruth, and Harper, "Tax Exempt Organizations and World Wide Web Fundraising and Advertising on the Internet," *IRS Exempt Organization Continuing Professional Education Text for Fiscal Year 2000* (1999).

Chronicle of Philanthropy, "2002 Technology Guide for Nonprofits," XIV *Chronicle of Philanthropy* (No. 6) T-1 (Jan. 10, 2002).

Chronicle of Philanthropy, "Astride the Digital Divide," XIII *Chronicle of Philanthropy* (No. 6) 1 (Jan. 11, 2001).

Chronicle of Philanthropy, "High-Tech Hopes Meet Reality," XIII (No. 17) 1 (June 14, 2001).

Cockfield, "Designing tax policy for the digital biosphere: how the Internet is changing tax laws," 34 Conn. L. Rev. 333 (2002).

Comer, *The Internet Book, Third Edition* (Prentice-Hall, 2000).

Cooper, Milner, and Worsley, *Essential Internet Guide* (DK Publishing, Inc., 2000).

Curtis and Quick, *how to get your e-Book published* (Writer's Digest Books, 2002).

Fastread, *Internet: Understand how to get online and surf the Web!* (Adams Media Corp., 2001).

Ferrera et al., *Cyberlaw: Your Rights in Cyberspace* (Thomson Learning, 2001).

Gillies and Cailliau, *how the web was born* (Oxford University Press, 2000).

Gralla, *How the Internet Works, Sixth Edition* (QUE, 2002).

Hafner, "The Internet's Invisible Hand," CLI *The New York Times* D1 (Jan. 19, 2002).

Hall, "A Brave New World of Giving," XII *Chronicle of Philanthropy* (No. 17) 1 (June 15, 2000).

Hafner and Lyon, *where wizards stay up late: the origins of the internet* (Touchstone, 1996).

Independent Sector, "Wired, Willing and Ready: Nonprofit Human Service Organizations' Adoption of Information Technology" (2001).

Johnston, *The Nonprofit Guide to the Internet, Second Edition* (John Wiley & Sons, 1999).

Kaplan, "A Libel Suit May Establish E-Jurisdiction," CLI *The New York Times* C1 (May 27, 2002).

Lewis, "You've Got a Charity Solicitation," XIII *Chronicle of Philanthropy* (No. 4) 25 (Nov. 30, 2000).

Livingston, "Tax-Exempt Organizations and the Internet: Tax and Other Legal Issues," 31 *Exempt Organization Tax Review* (No. 3) 419 (March 2001).

Lubka and Holden, *KISS Guide to the Internet* (Dorling Kindersley Publishing, Inc., 2001).

Mayo, *Internet in an Hour: 101 Things You Need to Know* (DDC Publishing, Inc., 1998).

McDonnell, *The Everything Internet Book* (Adams Media Corp., 1999).

Nielsen, *The Internet All in One Desk Reference for Dummies* (Hungry Minds, Inc., 2000).

Reaves and Bennett, "UBIT.COM? Can the Old Laws Apply in the New Cyber Frontier?," 27 *Exempt Organization Tax Review* (No. 2) 251 (Feb. 2000).

Rheingold, *The Virtual Community, Revised Edition* (MIT Press, 2000).

Schweiter, "Virtual Values," 54 *Association Management* (No. 3) 32 (Mar. 2002).

Schwinn, "How Charities Give Thanks," XIV *Chronicle of Philanthropy* (No. 4) 21 (Nov. 29, 2001).

Schwinn, "New Fund Exposes Charities to the Outer Limits of Technology," XIII *Chronicle of Philanthropy* (No. 6) 8 (Jan. 11, 2001).

Segaller, *Nerds 2.0.1: A Brief History of the Internet* (Oregon Public Broadcasting, 1999).

Smedinghoff (ed.), *Online Law: The SPA's* [Software Publishers Association] *Legal Guide to Doing Business on the Internet* (Addison-Wesley, 1996).

TERANA and Netskills, *Internet Users' Reference, 2002 Edition* (Addison-Wesley, 2002).

Wallace, "Charities Use Internet to Educate Voters," XIII *Chronicle of Philanthropy* (No. 1) 36 (Oct. 19, 2000).

Wallace, "High-Tech Tooling Around," XIV *Chronicle of Philanthropy* (No. 10) 33 (Mar. 7, 2002).

Wertheim, *the pearly gates of cyberspace* (W.W. Norton & Co., 1999).

Wilhelm, "Most Americans Oppose Charity Disclosure of Information on Donors, Study Finds," XIV *Chronicle of Philanthropy* (No. 2) 18 (Nov. 1, 2001).

Zoellick, "Commentary on the Electronic Signatures in Global and National Commerce Act," available in the Fastwater Library at e-think.com.

Index